Documentary Time

VISIBLE EVIDENCE

Edited by Michael Renov, Faye Ginsburg, and Jane Gaines

VISIBLE EVIDENCE, VOLUME 21

Documentary Time

Film and Phenomenology

Malin Wahlberg

University of Minnesota Press

Minneapolis

London

Portions of an early version of chapter 4 were previously published as "Wonders of Cinematic Abstraction: J. C. Mol and the Aesthetic Experience of Science Film," *Screen* 47, no. 3 (2006): 273–90; reprinted with permission from *Screen*. Portions of chapter 7 are based on the article "Inscription and Re-framing: At the Editing Table of Harun Farocki," *Journal of Art History/Konsthistorisk tidskrift* 73, no. 1 (2004): 15–26; reprinted with permission from Taylor and Francis Group.

Published by the University of Minnesota Press
111 Third Avenue South, Suite 290
Minneapolis, MN 55401-2520
http://www.upress.umn.edu

Library of Congress Cataloging-in-Publication Data
Wahlberg, Malin.
    Documentary time : film and phenomenology / Malin Wahlberg.
        p. cm.
    Includes bibliographical references and index.
    ISBN: 978-0-8166-4968-6 (hc : alk. paper)
    ISBN-10: 0-8166-4968-5 (hc : alk. paper)
    ISBN: 978-0-8166-4969-3 (pb : alk. paper)
    ISBN-10: 0-8166-4969-3 (pb : alk. paper)
    1. Documentary films—History and criticism. 2. Time in motion pictures.
I. Title
    PN1995-9.D6W24 2008
    070.1′8—dc22
                                    2007019083

Printed in the United States of America on acid-free paper
The University of Minnesota is an equal-opportunity educator and employer.

15 14 13 12 11 10 09 08   10 9 8 7 6 5 4 3 2 1

Contents

Acknowledgments

This book is the outcome of a long-standing theoretical and philosophical interest. The methodological reflection on film aesthetics and existential phenomenology grew out of my earlier work, but thanks to the inspiration and input of several Visible Evidence conferences, it gradually moved toward the problems and concerns of documentary theory. Many of the discussions in this text were presented at various conferences and were inspired by panels dedicated to the aesthetic and affective aspects of documentary film and video. The annual event of Visible Evidence has deepened my interest in the theory and practice of documentary cinema and provided a global network of research colleagues and friends.

First, I am grateful to the editors of the Visible Evidence series and especially to Michael Renov, who supported the theoretical aims of the manuscript and whose belief in this project was of great importance. This book would never have appeared without his encouragement and commitment. I am grateful for the insightful critiques and suggestions provided by the anonymous reviewer. Many thanks also to the staff at the University of Minnesota Press, in particular to Jason Weidemann, Adam Brunner, and Mike Stoffel, for their help and support throughout the production of this book. I also want to thank Douglas Korb who assisted in editing the text.

I am grateful to my colleagues at the Department of Cinema Studies at Stockholm University, who offered important critiques, pointers, and stimulating debates at various stages in this project. Astrid Söderbergh Widding and Trond Lundemo deserve thanks for their sincere and lucid readings of earlier drafts. Jan Olsson and John Fullerton helped me extend this work by encouraging related conference papers and essays, which propelled my theoretical interests in other research areas.

I am equally indebted to the generous support of benevolent filmmakers who granted the use of images and who took time to discuss aspects of their work. I am especially grateful to Yo Ota, Péter Forgács, and Harun Farocki, whose feedback, along with their thought-provoking achievements in film and video, inspired the writing of this book.

During the past two years I benefited from two longer periods of study abroad that allowed me to complete the manuscript. Consequently, many people outside Stockholm directly and indirectly contributed to this book. I am grateful for the scholarship provided by The Swedish Foundation for International Cooperation in Research and Higher Education (STINT), which made it possible to spend three months as a visiting research fellow at Instituut voor Media & Re/presentatie, Theater-, Film- en Televisiewetenschap at Universiteit Utrecht. It was a great pleasure to work in Utrecht and at the Amsterdam Film Museum, and I express my gratitude to Frank Kessler at Utrecht University for his generous invitation and for his research seminar, where I had the opportunity to present a section of this book. Thanks also to the very helpful and efficient staff at the archive in Amsterdam.

Because of the kind invitation of Dudley Andrew in the Department of Comparative Literature and the Film Studies Program and a much appreciated grant from The American-Scandinavian Foundation (ASF), I spent a rewarding time as a visiting research fellow at Yale University between 2005 and 2006. I am greatly indebted to Dudley Andrew, who facilitated my visit, showed generosity in introducing me to many interesting people, encouraged an invited speech, and provided new insights into classical film theory.

Last but not least, I thank family and friends for support and for providing welcome, beneficial distractions. Jens Rydgren followed the development of this project with unswerving interest. Aside from his love and consideration, Jens provided intellectual response as well as immeasurable inspiration and comfort throughout the writing process. I dedicate this book to Jens and our daughter Vera, who was born only a few days after I had finished the manuscript in September 2006.

Introduction

Jacques Aumont once suggested that any approach to cinema and temporality should involve an initial choice between two possible perspectives: (a) the created space-time of the image or (b) the time of film viewing. The latter corresponds to the fact that images are viewed during a certain period of time and that, to be appreciated, they require the spectator's gaze. The temporal status of an image depends on a viewer's attention and, therefore, on the duration of contemplation. Aumont argues that we have to distinguish between these two axes of image-time and experienced time.[1] The *ocular time* spent watching a picture would therefore be separated from the *pragmatic time* of the image.[2]

Whether we look at a painting, a photograph, or a moving picture, the image requires the time of our perception. But in film and audiovisual media the image takes time; it unfolds and scrolls by. The border between the *time of viewing* and the *time of the image* becomes in itself an issue that may be explored conceptually.

Different from a painting or a photograph the viewer may look at for as long as she wishes, a film is offered to our gaze for a fixed duration of projection, which significantly delimits the screen-time. The moving image challenges the classical contemplative mode of watching an image during an elective moment. In this case our eye meets with the time of artificial views, not forgetting the time of edited sounds.

Aumont's suggestion is biased toward the iconographic, plastic, and symbolic aspects of visual representation. He overlooks the temporal contingency of photographic representation and the inherent quality of film as a *technology of memory*.[3] Still, Aumont's perspective has merit in that it recognizes the creative possibilities of film and video to transform and play with time and space. The temporal aspects of film narration, such as the order, duration, and frequency of story events, are subordinate here to the formal expression and sensory impact of film as screen event.

This book aims at a reassessment of image and time from the perspective of documentary film. The aesthetic and affective dimensions of documentary film were once highly disregarded in a scholarly field traditionally dominated by discourses on social representation and the rhetoric incentive of nonfiction cinema. Hopefully, the discussions that follow will add to recent work on film and media, which has convincingly shown that aesthetic and psychological aspects of cinema are indeed issues relevant for studying documentary film. Documentary aesthetics has been the subject of several panels at the Visible Evidence conference, which in many ways inspired the writing of this book.

In classical film theory the varied expressions of documentary film have often been marginalized or overlooked. If the aesthetic and formal experimentation of documentary film calls for further research, aspects of temporality in these nonfictitious genres represent an even more significant lacuna. Not even Gilles Deleuze recognized the complex relation between the time of the image, allegories of time, and time experience in documentary.[4] This is remarkable given that his idea of cinema as the mnemonic machine par excellence has much in common with the sublime representations of time, history, and memory offered by documentary. Although documentary examples have been rare in the classical context of film aesthetics, important reflections have been made regarding the material and existential signification of cinema and temporality. Looking back at this long-standing debate and the related issues of television, video, and digital culture, it is striking to note how the problem of image and time has always oscillated between ontological claims about the specific medium and the experience of moving images.

The phenomenological tradition in film theory demands recognition in this respect. A critical mapping of this philosophical inheritance may be helpful in contextualizing some persistent themes on time experience in film that remain salient in the contemporary culture of moving images. Aside from a contextualization of the phenomenology of image and time, the discussion in this book aims at a deepened account of the promises and pitfalls of a phenomenological perspective in film studies and, more specifically, aims to reconsider some phenomenological issues that may advance our current understanding of documentary film and video. I cannot aspire to exhaustive answers to the overall methodological problems addressed or touched upon here, although it has been my ambition to grapple with these concerns on both a metatheoretical and a practical level. The title of this book demands clarification, and I will begin by demarcating the French context of existential phenomenology, the philosophical tradition of primary interest for the following discussion.

The last three decades of semiotics and poststructuralism have taught us to reject the fallacies of transcendental idealism and the solipsism that clings to the subject of classical phenomenology. Pierre Bourdieu's uncompromising opinion of phenomenology and aesthetic theory attests to this critique as he dryly questions the intellectual situation in France in 1965, commenting on the "seductions of intuitionism [which conjures up] the blinding evidence of false familiarity [and] transfigure everyday banalities about temporality, eroticism and death into false essentialist analyses."[5] Poststructuralist and deconstructivist projects that questioned classical thought and enclosed models of structuralism gained importance during the following decades. In the international scope of film and media studies, the influence of, for example, Michel Foucault, Gilles Deleuze, and Jacques Derrida is not less important today than in the late 1980s. Yet the same era also witnessed a renewed interest in issues of subjectivity, otherness, and ethics, which in turn propelled constructive interrelations between poststructuralism and psychoanalysis as well as between phenomenology and poststructuralism.[6]

The theoretical framework of this book is firmly rooted in the latter group of attempts to reassess phenomenological themes in an interdisciplinary field of philosophy, aesthetic theory, narrative theory, and social psychology. *Semiotic phenomenology* is the generic term for these projects within and beyond French philosophy that address phenomenological problems of subjectivity, time, perception, and ethics from the horizon of the intellectual conquests of both semiotics and post-structuralism. Paul Ricœur, one of the initiators of existential phenomenology in France, is a crucial reference in this context. Throughout his career, Ricœur provided an ongoing hermeneutic approach to the problems of phenomenology, while continuously reflecting on, or questioning, the premises of his earlier work in relation to other, often opposing, methodological perspectives. His lifework includes the initial introduction and translation of Husserl's *Ideas* into French, and he made numerous attempts to map the methodologically parallel, yet historically converging, directions of phenomenology and poststructuralism.[7]

The expression *semiotic phenomenology* stands out as a provoking oxymoron. To put it bluntly, phenomenology offers a metaphysical inquiry into (time) experience, whereas semiotics radically opposes the totalizing project of metaphysics, while rejecting the incontestable notion of the experiencing "I." The former opts for a transcendental method to reveal sensory data through a precise system of description, whereas the latter draws upon the intersubjective realm of language and a systematic analysis of structural patterns that are primordial to specific meanings. The direction of existential phenomenology in France became a discourse of mixed influences in which interpretations of Husserl and Heidegger fused with existentialism and philosophy of religion and also with important influences from Freud and Marx. Still, the very opposition between phenomenology and semiotics was at the core of the 1960s structuralist movement.[8] The 1970s witnessed a growing mistrust for the enclosed models of structuralism, and from the 1980s on a renewed interest in issues of subjectivity, otherness, and ethics resulted in intersections between phenomenology and poststructuralism. What I find interesting are the ways in which this encounter between semiotic theory and phenomenology points to problems and shortfalls in both fields, while also highlighting some issues that the structuralist movement consciously bracketed and excluded. My impression is that the poststructuralist urge for open-ended systems of thought, for mapping philosophical themes rather than constructing philosophical doctrines, paradoxically offers an intellectual ambience that seems particularly apt for a renewed interest in phenomenology. Rejecting the totalizing perspective of a metaphysical agenda does not necessarily mean that the intricate problems of time experience, perception, and imagination are outdated subjects for a contemporary perspective. Semiotic phenomenology designates a project to re-posit the enigmas (Husserl, *Rätsel*) formulated by phenomenology but to do so with respect to the achievements of French structuralism, poststructuralism, and American pragmatism.[9] In recent years this debate reverberated in discussions on time, image, representation, historiography, and memory. I refer to many of these discussions throughout this book.

I acknowledge semiotic phenomenology as a continuous, mind-opening, and nontotalizing discourse where the problems and shortfalls of both classical philosophy and contemporary theory meet with insights into existential, psychological, and aesthetic issues that were consciously bracketed and excluded after the structuralist turn. This post-Husserlian context of film theory, philosophy, and social psychology provides for the reassessment of image and time in this book.

The discussions that follow represent a critique of film and phenomenology in the sense of a nondogmatic reflection on the important influence of existential phenomenology in classical film theory and its persistence in more recent approaches to time and memory. Hence, I have intended a *critique* in Kant's sense of an unbiased study on phenomenology and documentary theory, which means that neither do I reject existential phenomenology, nor do I suggest a new phenomenology of film experience.

The aims of this book are less missionary or polemic than hermeneutic and case oriented. I have attempted to illuminate the phenomenological inheritance of classical film theory and to discuss some of the ideas of theory from a documentary perspective. The chapters in this book provide a context- and problem-oriented discussion on the aesthetics and experience of image and time. The preferred theoretical framework of this book draws on classical film theory—primarily the French context of aesthetic theory and film criticism—and the interdisciplinary perspective of semiotic phenomenology. Film examples will furthermore challenge the assertions of phenomenology, while also affirming the persistence of phenomenological themes in film and visual culture.

The temporal contingency of film has been subject to a variety of theoretical and historical approaches, and scholars have addressed related issues without any reference to the philosophical tradition of phenomenology. Among the recent publications on cinema and temporality, Mary Ann Doane's *the Emergence of Cinematic Time: Modernity, Contingency, the Archive* is an outstanding contribution in its extensive picturing of time-based images and sociocultural aspects of temporality in the late nineteenth and early twentieth centuries.[10] Still, in the history of ideas there are important intersections between aesthetic theory, existential phenomenology, and the conception of cinema and temporality, which deserve a thorough consideration from a film studies perspective. In the contemporary discussion on documentary film we tend recurrently to make observations about aspects of image-affect and imagination, often overlooking the related themes of film and phenomenology. I hope this book offers a correction to this situation. Moreover, this book also considers the different directions and methodological assertions that characterize the contemporary field of film and phenomenology.

The following discussions center on two basic problems of cinema and temporality. The first problem corresponds with the time-space malleability of moving images and the creative possibilities of film to manipulate rhythm, duration, and repetition and to take advantage of the chance element of photographic representation in order to both stress and curb the accidental element of the represented event. I will refer to this formal and expressive quality in terms of the *time-image,* which denotes the various ontological claims that have defined film as a time-based medium and a temporal art.[11] As to the creative modes in film and video to experiment with the time-image, I will account for meanings of *time measurement* in documentary. Aside from the formal aspects of space-time manipulation and attempts to frame the unfolding of an event, this notion refers to the sensory and affective aspects of the moving image, that is, the viewer's qualitative judgment of a temporal dimension.

The second problem deals with the implied archive memory of film, that is, the mnemonic quality of recorded images and sounds that add to the cultural meanings and expressive potential of film as a time-based medium. In the context of film theory and photography the notion of *the trace* denotes the material and existential meaning of the image as imprint. This notion is at the core of the recurrent index argument and the analysis of film and photography, which has often involved a consideration of the image as a presence of absence. In the contemporary debate on film and media it is now customary to question the image-imprint from the perspective of nonanalog representation and digital technology. Yet, as Thomas Elsaesser argued in 1998, "our culture is evidently more than little reluctant to leave the episteme of the trace and the imprint, that is to say, give up the concept of record and evidence, of truth and authenticity."[12] Moreover, in filmmakers' and video artists' approaches to historical experience the trace may be less about the ontology of film and the photographic per se than a reflection on the testimonial function and historical value of the moving picture as archive memory. Discussions in this book relate these ideas to the trace as a crucial theme of existential phenomenology. As a philosophical discourse the trace goes beyond the materiality of the imprint. Indissociable from affect, the trace is more "contingent than the image and richer than the index."[13] The trace opens up to time experience and recollection; it designates the transcendental impact of an image-memory, the aporia of memory and imagination, the now of reminiscence, and the then and there of the historical referent. In the context of film and historiography, documentary cinema, and historical experience, the creative staging of the trace in moving images demands recognition. With reference to Paul Ricœur, I will consider the historical and philosophical meaning of the trace as a persistent theme in classical film theory and in Western culture write large. Despite Ricœur's bias toward narrative time and the written word, I argue that his phenomenology of time and memory may provide for the reflection on historical representation and the production of cultural memory in film and visual culture.

Documentary time may suggest that in documentary film, the problem of cinema and temporality would be essentially different from that of fiction film. Although I will look at some aspects of filmic representation that I believe are of special importance for the expectations and experiences of documentary film, a major assertion of this book is that the sensory and affective implications of temporalization in moving images are crucial to the attraction and pleasures of film viewing as a whole. In some respects the affective dimension of cinema counterbalances the evident difference between documentary and fiction filmmaking with regard to production, exhibition, and audience expectation. Still, the traditional exclusion of nonfiction cinema in the scholarly context of film aesthetics justifies the focus on documentary time in this book.

The book consists of two parts. Part I—"Framing Change, Invoking the Moment"—demarcates the object of study and the current approach to film and phenomenology. Part II—"Experimental Figures of Time"—consists of four case-oriented discussions where the theoretical premises of Part I will be reconsidered in relation to specific examples of documentary representation in film, video, and digital media.

Part I accounts for the classical problem of image and time in film theory and in the practice of filmmaking. I argue that the ephemeral and concrete work in cinema of mediated rhythm, stasis, and the existential impact of the film image as a trace of the past represent two overlapping concerns of image and time that have always appealed to filmmakers and film critics and that illuminate the phenomenological inheritance of existential phenomenology in classical film theory. Two related analogies have been predominant in the attempts to define the ontology of film: the analogy between film and music and the analogy between the photograph and the film image. I will consider these classical perspectives, while relating the assertions of film and ontology to the context of phenomenology and contemporary theory.

A closer look at the philosophy of time experience and the mutual interest in duration and change further recognizes the important continuities between classical and more recent approaches to image and time, legitimatizing the fruitful exchange between film theory and phenomenology. André Bazin, Gilles Deleuze, and Paul Ricœur are crucial references in this context, and I argue that, together with their shared grounding in existential phenomenology, the problem of cinema and temporality justifies a consideration of their divergent perspectives.

An overall objective of Part I is to initiate a methodological reflection on phenomenology. Special attention will be paid to Vivian Sobchack and her pioneering approach to film and phenomenology in *The Address of the Eye*.[14] Aside from a broader charting of this and other attempts in film studies to promote phenomenology as a method and theoretical perspective, I will look more closely at a recurrent theme, with specific implications for documentary theory: the phenomenology of image and death. With reference to theoretical and cinematic approaches to this theme of visible excess and motifs beyond representation, I will suggest an alternative perspective on film and image-affect. In search for appropriate tools for dealing with concepts such as the viewer, experience, and expectation, I will turn to Erving Goffman's phenomenology of everyday life and, more specifically, to his analysis of frame-breaking events.[15]

Part II consists of a series of case studies where I develop the major themes of previous chapters in relation to individual films. Although some film examples are referred to in Part I, in Part II, I will offer more extensive analyses on the time-image and the trace. I also acknowledge the creative experimentation with interval and rhythm in moving images and the affective and sensory impact of images blurred by speed or extended into frame-breaking figures of duration. An important question regarding temporalization in documentary film deals with the expressive and symbolic function of space-time abstraction and how the formal elaboration of the represented realm may have an impact on our experience of the documentary film.

Chapters 6 and 7 aim at a deepened consideration of the material and existential significations of the trace. I will develop my reading of Ricœur and the phenomenology of memory, in order to illuminate strategies in film and media to realize an enactment of historical time and to animate (in Jean-Paul Sartre's sense) the film image as a mnemonic sign. Examples will show that the phenomenology of the trace is both affirmed and radically questioned in the process of staging cinematographically the imprint of the past. There will also be reason to challenge Ricœur's assumptions about memorizing and forgetting, by taking a closer account of the culture of preservation, reproduction, and oblivion, which in various ways affects the documentary representation of past events.

The case studies of Part II exemplify and celebrate the expressive possibilities of documentary film as a poetics of social representation and historical experience. The preference for experimental film and video—and the historically important interrelations between experimental filmmaking and documentary cinema—is in tune with the aesthetic perspective of this book. I turn to films where representation itself, the formal and narrative process of mediation, becomes subject to reflection. I think of these examples as "meta-cinematographic gestures," to quote Roger Odin.[16] The reflexive approach to film and media representation offered by experimental cinema is often illuminating in the ways it questions any simplified assumption of what cinema normally is and usually offers.

The classical discourse of image and time involves an outspoken interest in the materiality of the image-object. The predominant reflection on cinematic temporality is inseparable from the film image, and accordingly ontological ideas have always been primordial to discussions on the *temporal status* of cinema. Although this book offers a discussion that hopefully opens up beyond such a narrow perspective, some of these classical discussions are still relevant for a consideration of time-based media and the representation of time in film. My aim throughout the book has been to recognize the coexistence of different media technologies in contemporary film production, which contradicts any ontological notion of the cinematic. A conscious strategy to balance the bias toward the film image has been to relate the notions of classical film theory to a wider conception of the moving image. I will also refer to examples that transgress the border of different media technologies and screening contexts, such as the work by Chantal Akerman, Péter Forgács, and Harun Farocki, which have been shown outside the movie theater, in television and art galleries. Moreover, despite the actual mode of production, a figure of time in video may, for example, relate to a 1920s discourse on visual rhythm, and yet the mosaic outline of a digital editing may exemplify a layering texture that requires a special consideration of nonanalog representation. I have chosen to acknowledge this ambivalence as a creative possibility and a pragmatic issue beyond the enclosed problem of ontology.

As meta-cinematographic gestures, the examples accounted for in this book provide theoretical references that force us "to reflect on the definition of the cinematic object such as it functions in social space."[17] The reference to individual films and experimental approaches to image and time will both affirm and question the premises of a phenomenological perspective. The examples illuminate the phenomenology of time and the persistence of related motifs in cinema, while also bringing attention to the limits of philosophical abstractions in the sociocultural and political realm of media culture.

Part I. Framing Change, Invoking the Moment

[1] *The Phenomenology of Image and Time*

In documentary theory the phenomenology of the image as imprint and record fuses with the classical index argument, which has commonly been associated with the ascribed veracity of documentary representation. Hence, the trace status of photography and film represents a crucial problem in the ongoing discussion on film and historical representation. More recently, various approaches to the aesthetics and experience of documentary film have dealt with classical issues of image and time, including an important recognition of the affective and psychological impact of documentary representation in film and media. In this context the phenomenology of image and time corresponds with theoretical perspectives that aim beyond any a priori account of the documentary truth claim. These approaches address aspects of desire and imagination, which shed light on problems of image-affect and the specific expectations and experiences that belong to documentary cinema.

▶

Unfolding Moments and Representations of Lived Time

Ontology has been crucial to film theory where critics and filmmakers have defined the film image in relation to other images and arts. For an overview of time experience in film, I recall two analogies of particular importance for the conception of cinematic temporality in theory and practice: the analogy between film and music and the analogy between film and photography. In retrospect, these analogies stand out as competing models of importance for attempts in film history to theorize the physical medium of cinema and the existential impact of time in moving images.

The comparison between music and film originates from the theory and practice of avant-garde cinema in the 1910s and 1920s. The filmic production of rhythmic entities and the organization of sequences within the overall montage motivated the musical analogy. Filmmaking was compared to both composing and mathematics, and film was first recognized as a time-based medium, dependent on the artistic elaboration of rhythm and tempo. Chapter 4 will exemplify the creative elaboration of filmic inscription and space-time abstraction, which characterizes the cinematic experiments of both avant-garde filmmakers and scientists and which continues to revitalize documentary practice. In this context the belief in the ideal matching of sound-image rhythm with the pulse of the viewer, who engages both intellectually and physically in film viewing, is important.

During the 1920s critics based the kinship between music and film on the idea of a visual rhythm. A similar focus on measured views and the unfolding of a flow of images and sounds resulted in describing film as *Zeitobjekt*. The notion of the *Zeitobjekt*, or "temporal object," was ascribed to the melody by Edmund Husserl, who used the melody as a conceptual model for his analysis of time experience. The melody permitted him to grasp time within its transit as flux. In the famous seventh paragraph on the temporal objects in *On the Phenomenology of the Consciousness of Internal Time (1893–1917)* Husserl writes, "By temporal objects in the specific sense we understand objects that are not only united in time but that also contain temporal extension in themselves."[1] Although the notion of the *Zeitobjekt* may affirm the analogy between music and film, the analogy between film and the flux of perception has been subject to critique and modification. In Bernard Stiegler's opinion Husserl overlooked the possibility that the melody can be recorded.[2] From this perspective the model of flux contradicts the recorded sequence, which may be preserved and repeated beyond the memory of the subject. The legitimacy of the musical metaphor in moving images, however, resides in the rhythmic and sensory aspect of unfolding movement and changes in tempo.

The inherent time of the image combines with the filmmaker's skills to stress the sculptural and existential dimension of time in film. Different from music, of course, transformation and tempo materialize in the audiovisual and imaginative space of the film image. A recognition of this kinetic impact of metamorphosis is implied in André Bazin's emphasis on photographic inscription and filmic duration as the ontological and psychological kernel of cinema: "Now, for the first time, the image of things is likewise the image of their duration, change mummified as it were."[3]

Related to, although different from, the pure rhythm and transcendence suggested by the musical analogy, this recognition of film as a phenomenology of sound-image transformation is more akin to Ovid's sense of metamorphosis: "water constantly gives and receives new figures."[4] The metamorphic quality of cinema is, of course, taken for granted and therefore usually transparent to film experience. In trick film devices, however, this metamorphic quality has been the very locus of attraction, in order to produce disappearances or uncanny substitutions of one space by another. Metamorphosis is also akin to the abstraction of photographic detail provided by the poetics of cinema. Hence, films as different as those made by Georges Méliès—staging of imaginary realms— and Joris Ivens—contemplating events, things, and gestures—focus attention to the creative representations of time within and beyond the mimetic attempt of filmic representation.

This space-time malleability is not restricted to the film image. Electronic and digital media also demonstrate this plastic quality. Bill Viola's video *The Reflecting Pole* (1977–1979) offers an illustrative example beyond any narrow, ontological sense of the film image. *The Reflecting Pole* stands out as a striking parallel to Ovid's metamorphosis. Although this video is a playful celebration of the plasticity of moving images, the magic (of this video) primarily resides in its play with representation and abstraction of a pro-filmic space. Viola's approach to image and time relates to early motion studies where film offered a tool to analyze the physical laws of movement; in this case, however, the focus is on the electronic image and the sensory aspect of audiovisual rhythm and change.

The first image shows a pool surrounded by dense vegetation. During the seven minutes of the video the static camera is contrasted to the dynamic play with movement, stop-motion, and change, as a man (Viola) loudly takes off to jump into the water. His body freezes in midair and lingers like a sunlit ball, although the surface of the pool is still in motion, denying this unlikely presence by not reflecting the body. Owing to the mode of editing the passing of time materializes in the shifting daylight, which alters the lights and shades of the water that is now and then agitated as by invisible touch. The surface of water becomes an impossible figure of time, the locus of constant transformation mocking the relation between reflection and reflected, screen and referent. As the restrained figure starts to dissolve, Viola's reflection appears on the water and he walks out of the frame. After a series of similar reflections he finally leaves the pool to walk solemnly into the woods and out of frame. "Water constantly gives and receives new figures," although in this case the metamorphosis provided by a natural event is doubled by the constructed time-space of video editing.

The Reflecting Pole celebrates the sculptural dimension of time in moving images. Viola's manifestation of duration and change emphasizes the experience of the moving image as a temporal object. In this video the mimetic function of camera inscription meets with the sensory aspect of rhythm and the construction of an imaginary realm. The moving image is conceptually framed as an object in *statu nascendi*, as opposed to the static imprint of the photograph. Viola's elaboration of camera inscription and duration stresses the double meaning of the photographic analogy in classical film theory. The analogy between photography and film has been justified either by the photographic base of filmic representation or by the experiential difference between the moving image and the photograph. The latter claim refers to the cinematic experience of continuous change, denoting the present tense of involvement and identification. The difference between a single still image and the filmic flow of sound-images in constant change has motivated the present tense of film. In 1932 Rudolf Arnheim contrasted the photograph's weaker impact to the partial illusion of a real-time continuum provided by cinema, where images display immanent dimensions of time and volume.[5] The related psychoanalytical argument refers to the high degree of identification in film experience, which distinguishes the psychology of cinema from that of the photograph.

The film image as, in a double sense, the moving other of the photograph is primarily associated with the theory of Christian Metz. He emphasized the kinship of photography with death, opposing the nostalgia of the photograph as an image of the past with the intense presence of the film image. He grounded his argument on the hic-et-nunc effect of the moving images, where its present tense was psychologically motivated by an a priori consideration of spectator identification: "the spectator always sees movement as being present (even if it duplicates a past movement)."[6] Metz's argument is of course based on another analogy, that between cinema and language. As Gilles Deleuze noticed, Metz's emphasis on screen presence depended on a static conception of cinema as semantically equivalent to language, where the notion of *grande syntagmatique* reduced each frame to a fixed and sliced spatiotemporal unity.[7] Moreover, Metz referred to the cognitive impression of the film image as a transient moment on the screen, overlooking the temporal contingency of cinema, the plastic and vertical aspects of audiovisual layering, and the possibility of the film image to perform simultaneously as an image of the present and a trace of the past.

If Metz's theory has often been associated with the present of the film image, Bazin's theory is the most frequently quoted regarding the pastness of photographic inscription. In Bazin's work, however, the photographic analogy seems to contradict the very function of analogy as a rhetoric figure. Here, film is both firmly related to the physical base of the photographic imprint and separated from the static photograph by the essentially different experience of images unfolding on the screen. The major inconsistencies of Bazin's argument arise from his attempt to explain simultaneously the material support of photographic representation and the aesthetics and experience of temporal contingency in film. The standard reading of Bazin as a naïve realist has recently been questioned by many constructive rereadings, which look more closely at his approach to the materiality of film and the existential and affective dimensions of lived experience that may be framed and enacted in the art of moving images.[8] These rereadings and the inheritance of existential phenomenology in Bazin's work will be subject to a more detailed discussion in chapter 2.

It is now relevant to recall the contrasting or interrelating of the musical and photographic analogies in Bazin's writings. In underlining the possibility of repetition and replaying, Bazin compared the temporal art of cinema with that of music. The significant difference is not between real-time performance and the experience of listening to a record or looking at moving pictures; this difference is rather ascribed to the pure aesthetic time of music versus the lived time of film. Before Deleuze, Henri Bergson had had a major impact on Bazin's understanding of time experience in film. Bazin argued that in music time experience is evoked as an aesthetic construct, whereas in film it is based on the transfer of lived time: "musical time is immediately and by definition aesthetic time, whereas the cinema only attains and constructs its aesthetic time based on lived time, Bergsonian 'durée,' which is in essence irreversible and qualitative."[9]

Jean-Marie Schaeffer provides a third perspective on the photographic analogy. He suggests that the very lack of the photographic image—it is not analog to a perceptual flux—reinforces its impact as time-image. By decomposing the event into fixed moments, a photograph simultaneously re-presents its history of inscription. Cinema, on the contrary, "invades the spectator by the immediacy of lived time, no matter if he logically knows that the represented event already has taken place (here I presuppose that the film in question is a documentary)."[10] According to Schaeffer, there is reduced temporal impact of cinema because temporality is already part of the iconicity of the film image, "the moving image ... is *image within time*, whereas, the immobile image ... is *image of time*" (his emphasis).[11]

Departing from image and death—the most persistent of existential themes in French film theory for example (in the work of Bazin and Roland Barthes)—Schaeffer refers to the famous image of a young Vietcong soldier photographed at the very moment of his execution. He compares the photograph with the related footage of the historical broadcast:

> Each time we review this footage it is the present that fills one's chest: the man who collapses, the blood spurting as a fountain from a perfectly round hole in his temple. The photograph turns to the temporal distance. It evokes the past time, whereas the cinematic image closes the void and stresses the time as presence.[12]

Schaeffer depends both on Metz's psychology of screen presence and on Bazin's existential recognition of change mummified, although in contrast to Bazin he overlooks the troubling experience of looking at a death on film as simultaneously an inscription of an irrevocable past and the repeated gesture of, in this case, a person being killed.[13]

In the context of documentary film it is striking to note how the constructed temporality of camera movement, editing, and sound meets with that of the filmed gestures and events, which in turn are marked by the historical moment of their representation. As will be exemplified in Part II, recent work in documentary film and video testifies to an increasing interest in the material and existential aspects of the image-imprint in photography and film. Despite recurrent claims about the irrelevance of analog representation and the indexical in the digital era, these issues about image and time seem as persistent as ever.

▶
___

Documentary Approaches to Image-Affect

In *Fast Trip, Long Drop* (Gregg Bordowitz, USA, 1994) the time of the image meets with a significant reference to historical time. This is a first-person narrative on the resistance of life and fear of death, with fragmentary views of AIDS activism in the late 1980s. Gregg Bordowitz is both the principal character and the narrator, and this subjective continuity characterizes this film. This subjective voicing of a life-altering experience, however, is not the issue of an activist video. *Fast Trip, Long Drop* represents a personal crisis that should profoundly affect most people, although it primarily is a drama fueled by the anger and commitment of a community that shared the historical moment of the AIDS crisis, including the social and political consequences it had in everyday life. In this context the problem of image-affect is autobiographically motivated and personally expressed. *Fast Trip, Long Drop* is a narrative in which existential concerns and testimonial impact have to be balanced so as not to diminish the structural and historical dimension of the social problem at hand. Bordowitz's strategy was to make use of appropriation and parody, which complicates any simple notion of subjectivity and testimony. As Roger Hallas writes, there is "an ironic address which perpetually interrogates the conditions and limitations of its own testimonial performance."[14] Without individualizing and historicizing his experience, Bordowitz successfully introduces his element of time to make the viewers confront AIDS as the ticking clock of biographical time and a communal call for action.

Although there are many documentary strategies to represent historical experience, the autobiographical mode of contemporary film and video produces the most compelling results. Examples where the personal desire and imagination of the filmmaker meet with social activism and a will to grasp the historical moment incorporate aspects of film and subjectivity within a field that has traditionally been associated with the veracity of photographic representation and the persuasiveness of rhetoric discourse.

In his critical account of the ethnographic attempt of documentary cinema to represent the Other, Michael Renov has shown that audiovisual counterparts to the autobiography have a significant variety of expressions and media technologies in the field of contemporary film and video.[15] He argues that the epistemological aspect of documentary is not opposed to subjective voice, affection, and imagination. Rather, this prominent field of experimental documentary and domestic ethnography relates to earlier projects in the history of cinema, which have clearly indicated the aesthetic and critical potential of a documentary poetics. Renov's approach to image-affect calls attention to the aesthetics of film and media in the sense of how different outlooks on the world relate reflexively to representation, interpretation, and cultural framing. Accordingly, the subject of documentary is not reduced to the implied therapeutic aspect of self-representation and introspection but offers a historical perspective on ways in which the representation of the self matters to others.

In this context the theorizing of image-affect demonstrates a significant affinity with psychoanalytical theory and the experiential side of film viewing, and phenomenology is not a primary reference; there are, however, issues that are in sync with those of Emmanuel Lévinas and other representatives of existential phenomenology. Any constructive reassessment of phenomenology and film theory should at least mention the ambivalent influence of Freud and Marxism on existential phenomenology. This is one reason why it is interesting to relate the discourse on image-affect in contemporary theory to the phenomenological inheritance of classical film theory. From this perspective phenomenology may not necessarily be opposed to the social interests and critical perspectives of documentary theory.

The problem of film and indexicality is historically a discourse concerned with image materiality, although a discourse inseparable from affect. In the context of documentary studies the inevitable problem of the referential image and its existential signification has motivated approaches to the haptic in contemporary film and video. A range of studies has emerged in the wake of Vivian Sobchack's *The Address of the Eye: A Phenomenology of Film Experience*. In these attempts to study the experience of documentary film and video, an explicit interest in the phenomenology of moving images, however, does not coincide with a reference to phenomenology as a direction in philosophy, or a mode to describe subjectivity and experience. Some scholars have addressed the affective and imaginary aspects of documentary film and video where the tactile aspect of image-memories finds expressions that both depend on and defy transcendence. For example, Laura U. Marks addresses the phenomenology and semiotics of haptic visuality in contemporary film and video.[16] Despite a phenomenological reading of Deleuze, her insights into filmmakers' attempts to evoke nonaudiovisual sense experiences exclude any explicit reflection on phenomenology, and the reader is not convinced about in what sense Deleuze would belong to a tradition he openly defied. Hence, in this approach and other recent approaches to the sensory aspect of moving images, a reference to phenomenology is implied, although rarely acknowledged, argued for, or questioned.[17]

An advantage of Marks's study is her recognition of affection and sense perception in film, which belong to the experience of moving images and the implied bias toward the visual. To stage these visceral sensations conceptually and thematically, she brings attention to creative strategies in documentary. A recent book by David MacDougall goes even further to reflect on perception and being from a more pronounced filmmaker's perspective: "Corporeal images are not just the images of other bodies; they are also images of the body behind the camera and its relations to the world."[18] With a focus on ethnographic film, MacDougall approaches the matter and being of the human body in film, the inevitable constructed nature of any camera gaze, and the spontaneous appearance and conscious measurement of accidental moments in documentary.[19]

Regarding the specific aspects of film and temporality discussed in the remainder of this book, it is striking to note how these and other references related to the phenomenology of image and time center on the materiality of filmic sound-images—their existential and historical referentiality and the affective impact of both photographic inscription and *photogénie*.

In early attempts to name the new technology of photography, the adjective preceded the noun to semantically stress the essence of this new visual mode. "Photogenic" preceded "photography" in the first attempts to define the photograph.[20] Today, the notion of *photogénie* is associated with the French context of filmmaking and criticism in the 1920s, where its meaning became established as a quality of cinema and photography, providing the represented with an intensified aura. For example, in 1921 Louis Delluc wrote that "photography translates life by chance" and that "the gesture captured by a Kodak is never quite the gesture one intended to capture; it is generally improved."[21] Jean Epstein transformed *la photogénie* into a film theoretical concept, referring to the sublime realization of moving images in constant change, that is, the temporality proper to a film's becoming on the screen: "Beside all other sensory logarithms of reality, the photogenic is that of mobility. Deriving from time, it is acceleration; opposing the circumstance to the state and the relation to the dimension."[22]

Mary Ann Doane stresses the experiential signification of this notion by stressing its affinity with the very attraction of moving images—with *cinephilia* as the intuitive attitude toward the screen, "the domain of the inarticulable in the filmviewing experience."[23] Her reading of *photogénie* matches MacDougall's emphasis on the corporeal impact of the framing of found objects in the art of documentary and, more particularly, the filmic attention to bodies and faces.[24] In similar terms, Doane refers to Epstein's recognition of the directed and altering gaze of the film camera: "Epstein was exuberant in the face of the power of the cinema to convey the telltale signs of the body itself."[25]

I have mentioned some references to classical and contemporary theories, which unify on a set of questions that are "indissociable from affect."[26] This is a shifting landscape of ideas inspired by a range of perspectives and yet whose discursive topography is characterized by a common goal to inquire into the aesthetic and experiential dimensions of film as screen event. Many of these references circumvent any easy conception of surface realism or cinematic representation, highlighting the creative and experiential matters of importance for studying moving images. At a moment when many scholars refer to the digital era and the invalidity of film theory and related models of the film image, there are also creative rereadings of classical texts that motivate a return to the physical object of the sound-image and the attraction of moving images and filmic representation. Similarly, the discourse on image-affect in documentary would gain from a critical reassessment of existential phenomenology, which in turn may deepen our understanding of the aesthetics and screen experiences of documentary film.

Documentary approaches to representation and imagination may focus attention to important aspects of film form and the experience of moving images, which have been neglected in classical discourses on film aesthetics due to a narrow conception of "art cinema."

▶
_____

Film and Phenomenology

The methodological diversity of phenomenology reverberates in scholars' attempts to apply a phenomenological perspective on filmic representation and the experience of moving images. In order to motivate the relevance of phenomenology in film theory, scholars have often referred to the binary opposition between the rational and the emotional. Phenomenology stands out as the nonrational advocate for sensory data and matters of experience as "the other-side of signification," which are normally ruled out by the extrasubjective context of semiotics and psychoanalysis.[27] In 1990 a special issue of *Quarterly Review of Film and Video* was dedicated to phenomenology and media theory,[28] and this issue highlighted attention to problems of representation, subjectivity, and experience, which, during the previous two decades, had been suppressed by the perspectives of semiotics, psychoanalysis, and poststructuralism. With reference to Husserl, editor of *Quarterly Review of Film and Video* Frank P. Tomasulo suggested that phenomenology is a method and that cinema offers a subject that is particularly well suited for this mode of investigation because "it is so dependent on the explicitly *visual* experiences of time, space, perception, signification, and human signification."[29]

Although only few film books are dedicated to phenomenology, phenomenology is today listed among the major directions of film and media studies.[30] Most of these attempts are grounded in Husserl's philosophy, and a few others have turned to his inheritors and interpreters, most notably Maurice Merleau-Ponty. Hence, we cannot describe the field in one homogenous direction. For example, Bazin has frequently been considered the forerunner of a realist direction of phenomenology in film theory, although, as argued in chapter 2, there is reason to question this assumption. The methodological diversity may be illustrated by two references in stark opposition. One perspective aligns with the realist tradition commonly associated with Bazin, and the other offers a direction based on the philosophy of Merleau-Ponty.

In Allan Casebier's *Film and Phenomenology: Toward a Realist Theory of Cinematic Representation*, the early work of Husserl motivates a realist approach to filmic representation.[31] Phenomenology offers a theory of consciousness on a ground as exact and objective as that traditionally associated with science.[32] The purpose of Casebier's book is to outline an epistemology of cinematic representation where the viewer's discovery of the represented object is the issue under scrutiny.[33] The dominant position in film theory holds that cinematic representations are epistemologically related to the spectator's language, ideological beliefs, and aesthetic sensibilities or to the unconscious thought processes such as desire and expectation. Casebier rejects this idealism because it denies any objective reality beyond the construction of representation and spectators' reception of it. One of his major arguments is that cinematic representation, here understood as the visual and auditory presentation of the world—objects and events that exist and unfold beyond the image—guides the viewer's discovery of the mediated realm. In consequence, and owing to the film's existence as a given object beyond perception/film experience, cinematic representation cannot be conceptualized with respect to spectator schemata. The following may sum up the core themes of his proposal: the independent existence of the filmed object beyond representation and the primordial impact of appearance; "line, pattern, size and shape relations, camera movement are hyletic data" that become discrete and integrated properties of perception.[34] Hence, what counts is the presented realm on the screen, discovered by the spectator as "a flesh and blood reality."[35]

Such a description of a transcended realm seems to make no difference between fiction and documentary film. Casebier, however, dedicates one of the last chapters to documentary experience. In his critique of documentary theory, exemplified by the work of Bill Nichols and Michael Renov, Casebier considers the distinction between unmediated and mediated perception to be "unuseful in analyzing perception."[36] By this he means that Husserl never conceived of perception as unmediated and that perception is never complete, because the perceived object "appears to us in incomplete form."[37] In Nichols's and Renov's opinion, however, this distinction is primordial to the truth claim of traditional documentary and the common belief that "what you see is what there was" (Nichols) and that the mediating process through which "the pro-filmic" (Renov) is transformed is a process that usually is invisible to the viewer of a documentary film. In Casebier's opinion this relation between the construction of the pro-filmic space and the presence of a historical reference is a mere product of the idealist/nominalist framework. Instead, he suggests that a phenomenological perspective would focus on the referent as the sensory reality of film experience. It does not matter if the filmic form at hand is reflexive (such as in Rouch's *Chronique d'un été*) or conventional/transparent (such as in Wyler's *Memphis Belle*), "part of what it is to be a filmic documentary is to take and use motion pictures of the referent."[38] In documentary experience the viewer's perception is automatically guided to the referent, which would therefore deny "the idealist freedom to construct the object of the documentary."[39]

Not surprisingly, in documentary, Casebier deals with photographic representation and the sensa of real events transcended in film. A constructive aspect of his critique is the assumption common in poststructuralist analyses that reflexive form automatically would question the impression of a sensory reality and that the relation between form and reception would be arbitrary. Casebier looks beyond the text to stress the pragmatic side of film viewing, audience expectations, and the indexing of documentary genres as set by producers, directors, distributors, and screening contexts. The reference to Carl Plantinga and Noel Carroll, however, only confirms the obvious importance of these external factors. There is no additional analysis regarding the sensory and affective impact of screen realities per se, or the expectations that documentary and the marketing of nonfiction film usually trigger.

Arguing in polemical terms for a final expunction of the idealist/nominalist framework in film studies, Casebier seems today to have few inheritors. Meanwhile, this attempt for a realist theory of cinematic representation is an important example of the limited, yet existing transcendental phenomenology in film theory.[40]

Vivian Sobchack's *The Address of the Eye* stands out as a critical antidote to the former, integrated as it is within the idealist/nominalist position so affectively rejected by Casebier. Her theoretical approach to film experience is based on the philosophy of Maurice Merleau-Ponty, who critically modified the theses of Husserl and Martin Heidegger, in order to posit the existential and semiotic aspects of the *Lebenswelt* and *Dasein* (here understood as an intersubjective, historical, and social sphere of experience). From this perspective phenomenology provides tools to describe the emotional and existential side of film experience. Hence, Sobchack's perspective stands out as an explicitly subjectivist approach beyond the text-centered and enclosed model of semiotic analysis. She refers to Merleau-Ponty's claim that the act of consciousness is already impregnated with language, meaning, and the presence of the other; that intersubjectivity necessarily rules out the idea of a universal self, because language makes intentional acts to exceed *my* experience: "This semiotic phenomenology irreducibly links the structure of language and the activity of embodied being, focusing on the lived-body speaking the *Lebenswelt* (the lived world) and even occasionally 'singing' it."[41]

In an essay dedicated to nonfictional film experience, Sobchack analyzes the content of documentary consciousness.[42] With reference to Jean-Pierre Meunier (a Belgian psychologist heavily influenced by Merleau-Ponty), she suggests a distinction between our existential attitude toward the home movie, the documentary, and the fiction film. Sobchack emphasizes that the home movie and the documentary film are legitimated by the trace status of nonfiction footage: "Thus documentary consciousness is structured as a particular temporal relation between the present and the past...."[43] The private *film souvenir* of the home movie works as a mnemonic sign, orienting the viewer's identification toward the experienced event referred to by the fragmentary record. Fiction film usually requires a process of identification that is dependent on a fictive diegesis. According to Sobchack the general characterization of documentary consciousness relies on the narrative contextualization of nonpersonal image-memories, which results in an existential referent to the world through the viewer's cumulative comprehension of the representation at hand.

The important difference between Sobchack and Casebier is that she refuses to see each mode of cinematic identification as propelled by any preconstituted status of the film. Cinematic identification is understood as "a general comportment and attentive attitude toward the screen that is informed by personal and cultural knowledge."[44] Hence, there may be "a shift in the structure of our identification," caused by a change in our attitude toward the screen (we start to enjoy the presence of an actor rather than the character he portrays) or by a nonfictive contamination of the fictive diegesis.[45] Sobchack offers a modified theory that opposes the metaphysical *doxa* of classical phenomenology, while reconsidering perception as embodied vision. Also, her work is an important attempt to present existential phenomenology as an alternative to the psychoanalytical model of spectatorship and cinematic identification.

In the remainder of this book I argue that the problems of image and time in aesthetic theory and film studies cannot be separated from the tradition of existential phenomenology. This context of thought is predominant in classical film theory and has been affirmed as well as questioned in early experimental approaches to cinema. Phenomenological notions of inscription and transcendence reverberate in classical discourses on photographic representation, with important existential and cultural significations for common expectations and beliefs associated with documentary representation. The sociocultural realm of film and media and the intersubjective experience of moving images, however, also complicate the use value of phenomenology as a method.

Promises and Pitfalls of a Phenomenological Perspective

Cinema is a product of artificial perception, imagination, and constructed narration, which in problematic ways transgresses the categories of a phenomenological analysis: *consciousness/ego–noetic act–noema*.[46] In classical approaches to the phenomenology of moving images, such as the 1920s experiments with visualized rhythm, there is, nevertheless, an incentive for a theoretical recognition of the affective as well as physiological sensation of moving images and, therefore, for an aesthetic phenomenology of cinema. This is a context where the fascination with the physical medium of film intermingles with experiential aspects of moving images. For example, reflections on rhythm and duration stress the interrelation between the constructed time of the image and the time of the movie theater.

Although these early conceptions of the film image lack any explicit theoretical framework, and despite the arbitrariness of aesthetic preferences, they focused on the formal and experiential aspects of moving images that generally are overlooked in more recent studies of cinema. The reason we overlook these aspects is that we customarily focus on either the general features of spectator psychology, such as cognitive aspects of how the narrative logic of story time is understood, or the formal aspects of the ways in which symbolic meaning is achieved. Phenomenology may be an alternative approach that would account for the affective side of film experience. But the question remains how such a perspective could be useful today, and how exactly it could be modified to avoid the solipsism of classical phenomenology.

Objections can be made whether a perspective traditionally concerned with *the thing in itself* would be able to account for the formal and narrative side of the mediating process, and not only with the transcended realm of moving images. Can phenomenology provide a perspective beyond the fallacy of introspection and transcendental idealism? Moreover, film culture and film viewing are always dependent on historical and sociocultural factors. Despite the private dimension of film viewing, cinema is something we experience with other people. This social aspect initially seems to imply the intersubjective experience, but then how would a phenomenological perspective account for the sociohistorical dimensions of film culture?

These are methodological questions whose answers would demand a separate volume. The present discussion will be limited to some problems that are of immediate importance to the possibilities and limitations of phenomenology as a method for studying moving images and film experience. Vivian Sobchack's work demands special attention at this point because *The Address of the Eye* presented a theoretical framework that was based on Merleau-Ponty and existential phenomenology—in analyzing the structure of experience from within the subjective act of perception.

From the perspective of transcendental phenomenology the viewer would conceive of film in terms of appearance, independent of any imagination and ascribed meanings. If so, how is it that when talking about film we often disagree on *what* was shown? How can we neglect that perception involves interpretation and constructed frames through which we react to sensory qualities as well as semantic information and symbolic signs?

These problems are acknowledged in *The Address of the Eye*. Film viewing is described in terms of an existential and social experience where the viewer's active reception and the framing of the world that is both subjective and mediated interact. Her major concern is the spectator's perceptual and emotional response to the screen. Similar to Merleau-Ponty's antiessentialist and semiotic direction, Sobchack is less concerned with cinematic qualities per se than with how spectators respond to the filmic process of mediation. The ways in which the camera relates to the pro-filmic space are more important than the ontological status of the filmed. What matters is the camera's intended gaze: "This is a vision that knows what it is to touch things in the world, that understands materiality. The film's vision thus perceives and expresses the 'sense' of fabrics like velvet or the roughness of tree bark or the yielding softness of human flesh."[47] Transcendence is conceived of as instrumental mediation, as a mode created and performed through technological devices, and ultimately realized within the viewing situation.[48] The realist attempt of cinematic images partly belongs to film technology and partly to spectator expectations and attitudes toward the screen.

Sobchack's purpose of mapping points of intersection between "the seeing that a film performs before us and the seeing we perform before it"[49] relates to the metaphoric title of the book, "The Address of the Eye," which can be clarified in relation to the following three assumptions. First, a film is a site of multiple relations between acts of seeing and acts of being seen. In addition to the film viewer's directed gaze we may consider the perceptual activities that materialize on the screen: the visualization of touch and smell, or the *mise en scène* of subjective points of view. Hence, the address of the eye corresponds both to the loci of sight involved in the viewing situation and to the perceptual skills of cinema.

Second, *body–subject* and *film–body* are core notions in Sobchack's reading of Merleau-Ponty. The theme of the film–body is based on his critique of the Cartesian notion of perception as pure transcendence and the uncritical a priori of vision. Although discrete and subordinated in cinematic representation, Sobchack finds the cinematic body–subject to literally match Merleau-Ponty's concept of the object–subject duality of existence. Just as my act of seeing often involves myself as a seen object, "the film's 'body' is always implicated in its vision."[50] Sobchack argues that the film's body is normally unrecognized, but it is present as a subjective instance that is primordial to the performed perceptual acts on the screen. These mediated modes of perception are referred to in terms of a bodily presence that becomes interrelated with the audience's physical presence in the movie theater. In its most organic sense, the film–body designates the relation between the film's perceptual modes and its technological body. Usually, its perceptual organs remain hidden or transparent, but they may be noticed when the apparatus has been revealed on purpose or by chance.

Third, the interaction between film and audience creates what Sobchack calls "a transcendental space," which exceeds the individual body and its perception of a specific situation. This space is therefore marked by a relative independence, representing a spatiality that is always "inhabited and intersubjective."[51] Sobchack argues that perception (natural and cinematographic perception alike) inevitably relates to a subjectivist positioning, a judgment, a point of view, or an interpretation of some kind.[52] Her primary focus is on the perceptual and expressive performance on the screen and our perceptual and affective response to this event. "Film is always presenting as well as representing the coming into being of being and representation,"[53] she writes, and film is defined in line with how it is experienced, "as always in the act of becoming."[54] Cinema offers a double site of perceptual activity, "the dynamic, synoptic, and lived-body situation of both the spectator and the film."[55]

In opposition to transcendental theories, *The Address of the Eye* criticizes any simplified relation between film and viewing. Rather, this relationship is understood as a reversible structure of perceptual and expressive activity, and cinematic vision is singled out as different from ocular vision. Aspects of film recording are juxtaposed to the possibilities of cinema to refigure the inscribed and to rearticulate its meanings by sound, framing, editing, and narration.

Despite this explicit orientation toward semiotic phenomenology, *The Address of the Eye* leaves us with some puzzlement. The suggested model of film viewing risks ending up in a conceptual system that seems mysteriously enclosed between two existential loci of perception, that of the film and that of the viewer. The question remains whether phenomenology may at all provide a method for analyzing moving images.[56] More specifically, Does Gestalt theory—an important reference in Merleau-Ponty's work—really increase our understanding of film experience? So far, *The Address of the Eye* stands out as the most ambitious and consistent attempt to promote a phenomenological theory of film experience, although the methodological argument is less convincing.

For example, there is a problem with the bias toward vision, a bias that also can be found in Merleau-Ponty's *Phenomenology of Perception*, although he recognizes vision as a perceptual mode beyond seeing in the literal sense of seeing with one's eyes. Drawing upon this recognition of embodied vision, *The Address of the Eye* nevertheless succumbs to an exaggerated emphasis on the act of seeing and being seen. This visual a priori of Gestalt theory, of background and foreground relations that also were primordial to Merleau-Ponty, may raise an objection regarding his reference to psychology, which seems rather archaic and outdated from the perspective of more contemporary research.

This bias toward the visible seems to have been an issue of self-reproach, because in her recent book *Carnal Thoughts: Embodiment and Moving Image Culture*, Sobchack explicitly refers to filmic perception as a screen event that appeals to all senses.[57] The aim of the book is to provide a phenomenological description of embodied experience in more general terms of the animation of the human body, which of course is a subject that also goes beyond cinematic experience. The overall methodological objective is to promote phenomenology in terms of a strategy of thick description.[58] There is reason to discuss the use value of this method, which Sobchack claims to be relatively user friendly, and to pay attention to her reference to autobiography and anecdote as means to trigger an inquiry into more general problems of subjectivity as a socially mediated process.[59]

Similar to Marks's book *The Skin of the Film*, *Carnal Thoughts* emphasizes film experience as grounded in the flesh: touch and smell as well as sound and sight are evoked by the virtual time-space of moving images.[60] The method of phenomenology is promoted in similar terms:

> The proof of an adequate phenomenological description, then, is not whether or not the reader has actually had—or even is in sympathy with—the meaning and value of an experience as described—but whether or not the description is resonant and the experience's structure sufficiently comprehensible to a reader who might "possibly" inhabit it (even if in a differently inflected or valued way).[61]

I argue that the phenomenological description is radical in its methodological self-sufficiency because it attempts an analysis of experience from within subjective experience (in this case the film scholar herself). Obviously, there is no analysis of moving images that is not directed by subjective preferences and the emotional and intellectual impact evoked by the film. However, different from an interpretation or reading propelled by a theoretical perspective, or a structural analysis of genre, narration, and audiovisual form, Sobchack's analysis aims at a generalized explanation of film experience based on her impressions and emotional response to the screen.

Sobchack critically acknowledges "the gap that exists between our actual *experience* of the cinema and the *theory* that we academic film scholars write to explain it—or perhaps, more aptly, to explain it away."[62] The alternative seems to be an excessively subjective position, where the kinesthetic subject is traced within the scholar's experience. At one point Sobchack refers to her emotional response to Jane Campion's film *The Piano* (New Zealand, 1998):

> I want to ground my previous discussion "in the flesh." In my flesh, in fact—and its meaningful responsiveness to and comprehension of an actual film, here *The Piano*. However intellectually problematic in terms of its sexual and colonial politics, Campion's film moved me deeply, stirring my bodily senses and my sense of my body. The film not only "filled me up" and often "suffocated" me with feelings that resonated in and constricted my chest and stomach, but it also "sensitized" the very surfaces of my skin—as well as its own—to *touch*.[63]

This passage can be read as a mere celebration of the intense affection that cinema is capable of provoking, although it also indicates a problematic move toward a solipsist position. How can a phenomenological description based on the analyst's—*my*—film experience improve our general understanding of viewing improve? Despite Sobchack's rejection of Husserl's phenomenology and her emphasis on social context, this belief in the phenomenological description seems to endanger the analysis in the direction of introspection. Although the intersubjective aspects of film experience are important to Sobchack, the phenomenological description tends to be either exclusively personal or just too descriptive: you describe the filmic event and your emotional reaction as thoroughly as possible, and that is the end of it.

Based on a post-Husserlian concept of perception and experience, Sobchack's project is first oriented toward the intersubjective and social realm of film viewing. This seems to be a necessary premise for a contemporary approach to film and phenomenology, indicating how phenomenology still may provide an inspiring context of thought. As Sobchack is correct to emphasize, Maurice Merleau-Ponty was one of the initiators of semiotic phenomenology. He was sensitive to the intersubjective frames through which perception has to be filtered (language and other sociocultural structures of everyday experience), although, as I will show in a later section, the sociocultural structures of everyday experience are subject to analysis in more recent work of social psychology.

Sobchack's research attitude is informed by existential introspection. Moreover, her methodological argument depends on a feminist perspective. In opposition to the typical "male" perspective of analytical reasoning, this "female" counterpart—the carnal understanding of the screen event— is presented as a promising alternative. A related project is found in Giuliana Bruno's *Atlas of Emotion: Journeys in Art, Architecture, and Film*, an evocative piecemeal history of tactile and sensory vistas in film, architecture, paintings, and cartography.[64] An exhaustive list of spatial and corporeal metaphors adds to the logical chaos of Bruno's atlas, where, similar to the argument in *Carnal Thoughts*, the suggested feminist perspective on embodied space is rooted in the most pristine of Cartesian dichotomies, that of the male intellect vis-à-vis the female body.

Instead, I argue that Sobchack's major contribution consists in a thought-provoking theorizing of the film-audience line from the perspective of existential phenomenology. *The Address of the Eye* provided a productive attempt to apply the phenomenology of Merleau-Ponty to cinema. Sobchack differentiated the embodied vision of cinema from that of the viewer, which is different from Merleau-Ponty's analogy between cinema and human perception. Finally, there are other essays where she clearly avoids the solipsist "I/eye" ritual, in order to stress the social and cultural of existential matters in cinema. "Toward a Phenomenology of Nonfictional Film Experience" and "Inscribing Ethical Space: Ten Propositions on Death, Representation, and Documentary" exemplify how phenomenology may provide a theoretical perspective for studying film and media.[65] These essays were of particular importance for this book, and I will return to them in the classical topic of image and death.

In the context of documentary where reality is evoked in terms of social and historical experience, the prospect of reducing film experience to a matter of physical sensation seems troubling. However, as I hope to show in the following discussions, phenomenology—in the sense of semiotic phenomenology—may provide a helpful framework for the present consideration of documentary time.

[2] *The Time-Image and the Trace*

Cinema not only puts movement in the image, it also puts movement in the mind. Spiritual life is the movement of the mind. One naturally goes from philosophy to cinema, but also from cinema to philosophy.... The encounter between two disciplines doesn't take place when one begins to reflect on the other, but when one discipline realizes that it has to resolve, for itself and by its own means, a problem similar to one confronted by the other.

:: Gilles Deleuze, "The Brain is the Screen." An Interview with Gilles Deleuze, trans. Marie Therese Guirgis, in *The Brain is the Screen: Deleuze and the Philosophy of Cinema*, ed. Gregory Flaxman (Minneapolis: University of Minnesota Press, 2000).

To grasp the paradox of instant and flux in moving images could be compared to the vain attempt in philosophy to locate the instant within the flow of consciousness. Identifying the paradoxical instant is therefore a problem where the phenomenology of time meets with classical attempts to specify the ontology of cinema. Attempts at identifying this paradoxical instant have resulted in describing both film in analogy with human perception and film in analogy with machine perception beyond and independent of the subject. In this chapter I will depart from the point of intersection between phenomenology and cinema, which illuminates the diverse conceptions of cinematic temporality in film theory and the aesthetic and affective impact of film as time-image and trace.

Gilles Deleuze's *Cinema* has greatly contributed to the analysis of moving images, but his film theory coincides with a critical response to the phenomenology of Merleau-Ponty. Without denying or questioning Deleuze's obvious critique of phenomenology and metaphysics, there will be reason to illuminate his dependence on André Bazin and his recognition of film as screen event. Not only Henri Bergson played an important role in Deleuze's immediate experience of the mobile section. Bazin was an equally important reference for his analysis of duration and qualitative change in cinema. I argue that the most striking echo of existential phenomenology in Deleuze's *Cinema* is the recognition of the sensory and affective impact of film as screen event.

The following reading of Bazin will relate to the debate on aesthetic phenomenology in postwar France, which is a context beyond consideration in the common account of Bazinian realism. A major assertion of the following discussion is that Bazin's film theory has less to do with realism than with the recognition of image and time and related aesthetic and existential problems in cinema. Bazin was primarily interested in the experience behind the image, duration and change (the unfolding and becoming of events on the screen), and the material and existential aspects of the image-imprint.

The works of Bazin and Deleuze are obvious references for any account of cinema and temporality, although a coupling of Deleuze's ideas and existential phenomenology is provocative, considering his critique of phenomenology and classical philosophy in the large. Moreover, Paul Ricœur's approach probably represents an even greater challenge for film theory, given the absence of film and visual culture in his phenomenology of time, narrative, and memory. I will, however, argue that Ricœur's hermeneutical approach to the phenomenology of memory and the creative interrelation of time experience and narrative imagination does apply to problems of representation and historiography beyond the domain of the written word.

▶——————————————————————

Cinema and Time Experience

The temporal quality of cinema, cinema's transformation of still images into continuous movement on the screen, and cinema's complex production of meaning are aspects that make film an attractive subject for philosophical reflection. With its simultaneous enactment of *métabolè* (qualitative change) and *kinésis* (motion), the instant and flux, cinema is a phenomenon that, similar to Aristotle's description of the circle, "is made up of contraries. For to begin with, it is formed by motion and rest, things which are by nature opposed to one another."[1]

This contradictory relationship within the film image resonates in a classical philosophical problem: the paradox of the instant, or the specious present, which in the tradition of Occidental thought has always been ascribed to the enigma of time experience.[2] The paradox of the instant deals with the relationship between temporality and consciousness and the question whether time belongs to the realm of physics or to subjective experience, which Aristotle posed in the following terms: "Whether if soul did not exist time would exist or not, is a question that may be fairly asked?"[3] Augustine provided one of the first psychological models of time consciousness, relating memory to the experience of the past, perception to the presence, and expectation to the experience of the future.[4]

The problem of time experience relates to another conceptual dualism, that of the instant (*Aion*) vis-à-vis the flux (*Chronos*).[5] We are inevitably embraced by time, and moments follow upon each other "one damn thing after another,"[6] but from everyday experience we recognize just as intuitively how experience is a process of multiple temporalities, how reflections and daydreams easily transgress any supposed linearity of time. Logically it is not possible to grasp time as indivisible moments, because while reflecting upon the present moment the time already belongs to the past.

Edmund Husserl's theory of time consciousness suggests a solution to this problem. In his famous analysis of time experience, Husserl recognizes the complex simultaneity between the enduring act of consciousness and the extension of the temporal object (the melody), while also describing the *retentional* and *protentional* movements that vertically cut through the horizontal progression of time experience.[7] He suggested that each perceived moment bifurcates in a continuum backwards and forwards through the immediate memory of the tones just heard (retention) and the expectation of the tones just about to be heard (protention).[8]

From a deconstructivist or poststructuralist horizon Husserl's model represents an abstraction that hides its process of reduction in the pretension to describe the enduring flow of consciousness. Husserl overlooked the fact that his *Querschnitte*—the point in perception where present, past, and future coincide—was but "an ideal limit useful for the clarification of the structure of consciousness, but not itself a momentary act."[9] Shaun Gallagher suggests from this critical perspective that it is rather Martin Heidegger's concept of *Ereignis* ("Is it happening?") that seems to resonate in, for example, Jean-François Lyotard's reassessment of time and being: "the present, in its presenting, happens, but cannot be grasped in its happening."[10]

In the contemporary context of semiotic phenomenology the philosophy of time meets with a strong recognition of discourse because we only understand time through the ways in which this enigma has been culturally, socially, and historically articulated. For example, Dominique Janicaud argues that time is a nominal unity, and as such it cannot be grasped beyond the understanding of a temporal measure. Yet phenomenology reminds us of the inevitably polymorphic dimension of time, in terms of an existential opening of horizons: "To temporalize is to fuse rhythms and styles that permit the reinvention of a chronological understanding. Time experience by itself is nothing but the referential unity of such understanding."[11] Rejecting Husserl's mysterious notion of consciousness, Janicaud suggests that time experience should be analyzed with regard to specific practices of time measurement, that is, diverse modes of measuring time and the role such techniques have played historically and culturally in the conception of time and space. Time cannot be experienced without the distinctive role of a revelatory number, because, he writes, "without index, inscribed traces, marks and displays, duration would simply not exist."[12]

Similar to Janicaud, I argue that a phenomenological approach to cinematic temporality should acknowledge the creative possibilities of framing, extending, freezing, or fragmentizing the filmed event or gesture. The accomplishment of time measurement in film relates in decisive ways to the affective impact of tempo and rhythm. Looking back at film theories influenced by existential phenomenology, *time measurement* accords with a common theme of lived time in moving images, which perhaps has less to do with transcendence than with the cinematic invocation of a temporal dimension. For example, this invocation of lived time is evident in the recorded sound of heartbeats and in the cinematic representation of the passing or halting of time.

The notion of time measurement brings attention to the point of intersection between the phenomenology of time and the phenomenology of cinema, which is a reason why philosophers have been attracted to film, and film scholars to philosophy. Gilles Deleuze is an important reference in this context. Similar to Paul Ricœur, Maurice Merleau-Ponty, Emmanuel Lévinas, and Jacques Derrida, he preferred to elaborate a designation of the aporia of time itself, rather than present a final answer to the metaphysical question at hand.[13] In their comments on the Husserlian paradigm they seek in various ways to map the limitations of this model, while still, to some extent, approaching the same set of questions.[14] So Deleuze refers to the paradoxical instant and the question whether cinema mimics this classical philosophical argument. As Mary Ann Doane argues, his contribution consists in the idea that cinema reveals Zeno's fallacy and, we may add, the mistake of Husserl. The mobile section corresponds with the viewer's experience of movement and change, not a section of immobility.[15]

▶
_____

A Model of Perception

We commonly refer to *Cinema* by Gilles Deleuze as a film book in two volumes: *Cinema 1: The Movement-Image,* which brings attention to the linear narration and figures of image-affect in "classical cinema"; *Cinema 2: The Time-Image,* a celebration of postwar art film, whose narrative structure and layering of sound and image offer radically new crystalline figures of perception, time, and memory. Although he criticizes the linguistic focus of Christian Metz and explicitly stresses the unfolding of sound-images rather than the structural logic of an enclosed narrative, Deleuze's analysis of cinematic time remains grounded in the forking narrative paths or surprising events of ruptures and blanks that contribute to the expressive power of film narration. In *Cinema 2* the emphasis on narrative time is evident in the major coverage of Orson Welles and his practice of temporalization through memory that "begins with *Citizen Kane.*"[16] Like André Bazin, Deleuze celebrates Welles's shot in depth and its power to contain several *sheets of time* in one single *now point*. Deleuze's comments on *Citizen Kane* were motivated by Welles's narrative use of a particular device through which the time-image is evoked as a figure of simultaneity that presents the linear succession of "childhood, youth, the adult, and the old man."[17] Among others, Deleuze also refers to Alain Resnais, in whose films the mysterious work of the human brain is represented by means of cinema's sublime powers to unveil "the cartography of mind." In these narratives memory is represented beyond, and independent of, the subject.

Deleuze's *Cinema* also accommodates a strong recognition of cinema as experienced. The dynamic relations internal to the image presuppose the viewer's involvement to complete the cinematic sign at hand. The durational impact of Yasujirō Ozu's contemplative framings of objects, his cinematic still lifes, is an example that goes beyond the logic of narrative time:

> At the point where the cinematographic image most directly confronts the photo, it also becomes most radically distinct from it. Ozu's still lives endure, have a duration, over ten seconds of the vase: this duration of the vase is precisely the representation of that which endures, through the succession of changing states.[18]

About the static framing of objects in Ozu's films, this comment brings attention to the duration of a take that bridges the time of the image and the time of film viewing. In Raymond Bellour's terms, this example offers, as it were, "a pure time-image within the temporality of the movement-image."[19] Here, the temporal ordering of story events or the implied symbolism of a sequence that compresses the narrative process into one single framing does not motivate the time-image. Instead, a static framing whose excessive mode of duration appears to invoke a transgression between the time of the image and the time of film viewing provokes a shift in rhythm.

This and other examples in *Cinema* indicate that Deleuze recognizes cinematic movement in relation to film viewing. To grasp the full implication of this recognition, we have to, in turn, understand the philosophical argument at the core of Deleuze's film books. Regarding the paradoxical instant, Mary Ann Doane characterizes the difference between Bergson and Deleuze in the following terms:

> Zeno's fallacy finds its technological embodiment in the cinema—in its spatialization of time, its investment in the reality of instants.... Deleuze claims, on the other hand, that the movement needs to be thought in relation to the spectator rather than in relation to the apparatus, and that, for the spectator, movement is immediately given in an "intermediate image."[20]

Hence, Deleuze's time-image expands into a philosophical argument beyond its historical and aesthetic meaning in *Cinema 2*. Aside from a critique of both Zeno's paradox and Husserl's *Präsenzzeit,* the cinematic paradox of infinite series also serves as a critical response to Merleau-Ponty's existential phenomenology "where the paradox of infinite series characterizes the relationship between a perceiving subject and being (or reality)."[21] It is precisely the relation between movement and instant, between "immobile sections of movement" and "mobile sections of duration," that offers the point of departure in *Cinema*.[22] Cinema provides a model of perception, according to which the film frame metonymically refers to the mental image of a past event, inscribed by the mnemonic process of our brain. This mental image is a prerequisite for natural perception, because this image conditions and coincides with our perceiving/framing of a present event. In analog relation to its inscribed object, the film image offers a perceptual process beyond the notion of natural perception, because the cinematographic apparatus continuously produces an illusionary movement through its interaction of different instantaneous images *(prises de vue instantanées)*. In film experience this illusion coincides with the movement of the inscribed object. Deleuze suggests that the ambiguous location of the image within the unfolding of the film automatically stages the enigma of time, because the film image generates an infinite series of pasts and futures within each instant.

Deleuze's discussion accords with certain qualities that we ascribe to the film image, such as movement, rhythm, interval, and the interacting layers of images and sound. Moreover, it is also possible to interpret interval in terms of the relation between the film and the viewer; for example, in Deleuze's vocabulary the center of the image ("image centre") stands for the interval between "an action and a reaction."[23] Compared to Janicaud or Ricœur, who both argue that time is unthinkable except as mediated, Deleuze refers to Bergson in stressing the immediacy of time. However, as already suggested, the reference to Bazin and existential phenomenology is evident in Deleuze's approach to cinema and temporality. The interrelation between Bazin, Deleuze, and Ricœur is less improbable considering their anchorage in French postwar philosophy than their incongruent interests may indicate. It is more than likely that the cinephile Deleuze paid close attention to Bazin's essays in the review *Esprit*—a review that, thanks to the contributions by Paul Ricœur and others, was dedicated to phenomenology.[24] Before a closer explanation of Ricœur's hermeneutic approach to the philosophy of time, the present account of time experience in film demands a historical detour to the aesthetic theory and phenomenology of postwar France.

▶

Aesthetic Phenomenology and the Time-Image

In Husserl's philosophy *aisthésis* is mirrored in the concepts of *Sinn* and *Sinnlichkeit,* which generally signify the action or faculty of sensing or perceiving. Here, the notion of sensa—"unitary *sensile* experiences, sensory to contents such as the data of color, touch, sound and the like"—could be related to aspects of cinematic perception, such as the measured length of a shot (defined by editing and dissolves), a split-screen device producing a vertical montage effect, or the use of lighting, color, and sound.[25]

Such a use of Husserl's notions, however, would be erroneous because, according to his phenomenology, there cannot be any qualitative difference between, for example, a filmed tree and the tree in itself. Still, in the aesthetic debate of the twentieth century, Husserl's notion of sensa echoes in the concern with the rhythmic essence of a work of art.[26] In this context rhythm was commonly identified as the prerequisite of the overall structure of an artistic expression: a unfixed location of meaning and transmitted aesthesis, where the act of contemplation met with the imaginary realm of artwork.

In 1953 a book by Mikel Dufrenne, *Phénoménologie de l'expérience esthétique (The Phenomenology of Aesthetic Experience),* sought to fill a significant gap in Husserl's phenomenology, that between our perception of the world and our perception of aesthetic objects.[27] Dufrenne's aim was to highlight the artificial act of perception offered by paintings and other objects of art. He addressed the dynamic interrelation between our experience of art and the individual artwork.

Dufrenne questioned the Husserlian concepts of the transcendental ego and the thing in itself, and in opposition to Husserl, who would have rejected the notion of aesthetic experience, he addressed the experiential aspects of art and the viewer's contribution to its realization.[28] He argued that an art object becomes an aesthetic object the moment it is seen and appreciated as such. In the context of cinema Dufrenne's notion of the sensory depends not only on the qualities of the film image but on viewers' attitude toward the screen, their shared horizon of expectations and knowledge of cinema, and the directed interest of their gaze. Still, the aesthetic object is claimed to have a relative independency beyond artistic intention and reception. In *The Phenomenology of Aesthetic Experience* this relative independency is referred to in terms of the ontological self-sufficiency of the aesthetic object, which separates the aesthetic object from other perceived objects through the presence of form: "Form is form not only in uniting the sensory but also in giving it its *éclat*. It is a quality [*vertu*] of the sensory."[29] Moreover, Dufrenne writes that "the aesthetic object appears to us as a whole. It is an object unified by its form. But the form is not only the unity of the sensory; it is also a unity of meaning. This form is, however, above all the principle which informs the sensory by delimiting it."[30]

Dufrenne's account of the viewer's participation in the becoming of an aesthetic object is often drowned in romantic exclamations, such as, "I coexist in this world of the work of which I am a witness.... I obey the time of the music, I wait for the characters in the novel to reveal themselves."[31] What is more interesting considering Dufrenne's phenomenology is the recognition of aesthetic perception as opposed to natural perception. In other terms, and about cinema, this notion of aesthetic experience would be in tune with the conception of film as a mediated act of perception.

In the cultural debate of postwar France, Dufrenne's phenomenology added to the predominant concerns with ontology, existentialism, and theories of perception. Despite important differences, Bazin's film theory is in line with Dufrenne's aesthetic phenomenology, in terms of Bazin's interest in the artistic re-mediation of lived experience in film and the experience behind the image. Bazin's ambivalent reference to realism, however, has propelled the predominant description of his work as a realist theory of cinema.

Jean Mitry was one of the first theorists to criticize the fallacy of transcendental realism in Bazin's writings. *Esthétique et psychologie du cinéma,* which Mitry wrote in the early 1960s, aimed at a theoretical recognition of aesthetic as well as experiential aspects of film.[32] Mitry hoped to achieve a psychology of film experience. Gestalt theory, which was equally an important reference of Merleau-Ponty's *Phenomenology of*

Perception, reverberates in his concern with perceptual aspects of form and background. Similar to Dufrenne, Mitry considered the aesthetic object and the reception of it as two equally important dimensions for an inquiry into aesthetic experience in general and into film experience and the artistic practice of filmmaking. Aside from the influence of Merleau-Ponty and Dufrenne on Mitry's work, his argument is marked by the obvious presence of linguistics and semiotics. The ideas of Ferdinand de Saussure, Émile Benveniste, and Christian Metz with their different theories of signification resonate in inconsistent ways throughout *Esthétique et psychologie du cinéma.*

Bazin's emphasis on photographic representation and the existential signification of this automatic inscription, which provide the photograph and the film image with an ontological identity radically different from other modes of visual representation, provoked Mitry. In Mitry's opinion the camera does not reveal reality in itself. Depending on specific artistic choices and the use of the apparatus, the camera represents a subjective framing of the world: "[A] photograph is the product of a photographer. With a particular reality to record, the cameraman makes a certain choice: he chooses his frame.... The image is obviously dependent on the agents producing it."[33]

Mitry questioned Bazin's work in terms of a realist theory and argued that the experience of film primarily depends on the significant function of rhythm and montage in cinema.[34] He admitted that temporal relations in the film image may be revealed through elaborate modifications of the frame and that a durational quality may be apperceived in terms of a measured unit of space-time, although this would not be a quality specific to cinematic perception. Rather, it is the mere consequence of our eyes' ability to discern the changing proportions of movement in space. The sensory aspect of rhythm in moving images would therefore ultimately depend on the physiological fact that "the eye measures time through spatial modifications."[35]

Then how do Bazin's writings correspond with transcendental realism and to what extent is the identity of image and world important to his film aesthetics? Recent rereadings of Bazin try to look beyond this critique and try to find new perspectives on his conception of photography and film, ontology and film style.

▶

Visceral Moments and Persistent Memories

André Bazin, in pejorative terms, has been singled out as the originator of a realist tradition in film theory.[36] This assumption is primarily grounded on his preference for certain stylistic approaches in filmmaking, such as the long take and depth of focus, which accomplish the "embalming" of an object or a gesture in the full authenticity of its original splendor. Bazin associated this accomplishment with the signature of specific auteurs. For example, in his comment on von Stroheim's films reality is claimed to "lay itself bare like a suspect confessing under the relentless examination of the commissioner of police."[37]

"Reality lays itself bare" and similar expressions have caused Bazin's critics to see the window metaphor as emblematic for his film theory.[38] Allan Casebier, who refers to the realist theory of Bazin, argues that Bazin's a priori recognition of the antecedent reality behind the image is in tune with Husserl's concept of the thing in itself. Hence, the framed object or event is claimed to transcend in photographic and filmic representation. Although Bazin uses expressions and terms that no doubt would legitimize a reading of his essays in light of transcendental phenomenology, such an approach results in a simplified and erroneous understanding of his film aesthetics. Also, this approach overlooks the important connections between Bazin's writings and the crucial position of existential phenomenology in the intellectual debate and cultural activities of postwar France.

Similar to Dufrenne's framing of aesthetic experience, Bazin's apparent interest in the relation between image and reality is informed by realism as an artistic achievement and as an existential issue beyond both ontology and style. In Philip Rosen's opinion the idea of reality transcended is by no means the unique principle of Bazin's work and should rather be related to his fascination with "the processes by which human subjectivity approaches the objective."[39] Bazin brought attention to photography and film as modes of representation "that satisfy once and for all and in its very essence, our obsession with realism."[40] In similar terms Dudley Andrew refers to Bazin's dependence on photographic representation "as an essential string in the genetic code of cinema," which reveals Bazin's interest in the psychology at play behind the image as experience.[41] The realist label is questioned and so is the idea that the meaning of realism in Bazin's essays would coincide with a stylistic category. Rather, Andrew suggests, "it is an automatic effect of photographic technology drawing on an irrational psychological desire."[42]

Daniel Morgan has looked more closely at two propositions underpinning the standard reading of Bazin. First, the ontological identity that Bazin ascribes to film is based on the definite relation between the photographic imprint and the photographed world. Second, the ontology of the photographic image depends on the "commitment, via the mechanical nature of the recording process of the camera, to the reproduction of an antecedent reality."[43] The first proposition resulted in a narrow understanding of Bazin's conception of realism, whereas the second proposition motivated scholars to explain Bazin's conception of realism in semiotic terms and with reference to Peirce and the index argument. In Morgan's opinion both readings result in a simplified understanding of Bazin where the notion of realism is misread and the very ambiguity of his argument is overlooked. Bazin's texts are marked by the inability—or unwillingness—to provide a consistent description of the image at hand, a hesitation that is mirrored in the remarkable number of metaphors: "mummy, mold, death mask, mirror, equivalent, substitute, asymptote, etc."[44] "The flower" and "the snowflake" also add to the list, and Morgan is right to stress the ambivalence caused by these metaphors in Bazin's description of the photographic image: "Photography affects us like a phenomenon in nature, like a flower or a snowflake whose vegetable or earthy origins are an inseparable part of their beauty..."; it is "something more than a mere approximation, a decal or approximate tracing."[45]

To understand this ambivalence in Bazin's argument, we should not overlook the important influence of existential phenomenology. For the present account of cinema and temporality the following two issues are of importance: (a) Bazin's recognition of cinematic duration as lived time and (b) his reference to the phenomenology of the trace. The first issue relates to the pleasure or compelling experience of looking at events unfolding on the screen, of time passing as it were. The second issue touches on the index argument, although Morgan overlooks the difference between the index and the trace. The affective implication of the image as a mnemonic sign depends, of course, on the indexical status of photographic inscription, whereas the trace primarily relates to a philosophical problem of image and memory that cannot be reduced to the semiotic problem of the index.

Bazin's film theory closely relates to the philosophy of time. The temporality of the photograph meets with the psychological effects of duration and change in moving images. Bazin's presumed realism is commonly related to his preference for specific stylistic devices of space-time continuity and duration. The aesthetics of spatial depth and the temporal continuity of a long take have therefore often been confused with the acclaimed transparency of camera inscription. In Bazin's phenomenological acknowledgment of lived duration, however, there is always the recognition of aesthetic accomplishment. The photographic registration of an event is coupled with creative strategies to stress the time of the image. From this perspective realism in *Nanook of the North* (Robert J. Flaherty, USA, 1922) would be less about whether the representation of the Inuit family is a convincing documentation of a social realm, than Flaherty's creative ability to measure the interval of an event and to frame the unfolding of drama. When Bazin refers to the achievement of a specific waiting period in *Nanook of the North,* he stresses its physical impact in terms of screen time and lived duration:

> What matters to Flaherty, confronted with Nanook hunting the seal, is the relation between Nanook and the animal, the actual length of the waiting period. Montage could suggest the time involved. Flaherty however confines himself to show the actual waiting period, the length of the hunt is the very substance of the image, its true object.[46]

In this case realism is achieved by a mode of framing through which the time of the image transfers the existential meaning of actively awaiting the right moment. Suspense augments as time passes, bridging the time of the image with the time of film viewing. In this and other examples André Bazin accounts for the measure of a take and the experience of gestures unfolding in real time, which is accomplished through the creative variation of change and stasis within a single *plan séquence.* This is not to exaggerate the mimetic relation between natural perception and cinematic perception, because Bazin's approach to temporal continuity includes the possibility of abstraction and defamiliarization. In Part II, I will consider the abstract feature of isochronal representation. *Real-time approximation* could be a useful term for examples where duration is staged to invoke a sensation of time passing, while also introducing ambiguity into the image.[47] In filmic contexts far from Flaherty's dramatized ethnography, there will nevertheless be reason to return to Bazin's account of lived time, important documentary issues of *mise en scène,* and the ethical implications of framing social space.

Aside from the visceral impact of time passing, Bazin's approach to the aesthetic experience of cinema never omits the impact of film as an art of record. The notions of the mold and the death mask mirror the importance he gives to photographic inscription and the indexical relation between image and referent. The argument, however, cannot be reduced to the truth claim commonly ascribed to photographic and filmic representation. Among the recent rereadings of Bazin, *Rites of Realism* offers a collection of essays that account for the ritual and performative aspects of representation and reenactment, beyond the problem of verisimilitude.[48] The temporal contingencies of film represent a major theme, which Ivone Margulies addresses in terms of visceral signifiers for the real, and which is further clarified by one of Bazin's essays, "Death Every Afternoon."[49] Pierre Braunberger's documentary *La Course de Taureaux* ("The Bullfight," France, 1949) seems to have struck Bazin as a powerful combination between this visceral signifier and the psychological impact of the unfolding now of the represented event. In this essay Bazin paid attention to the archival status of film that permits an endless repetition of the filmed event. Once represented, the event in question turns into a mnemonic object that may be looked at and reviewed over time. In opposition to any banal notion of the camera as a window on the world, however, the filmed event is not reality transcended. On the contrary Bazin celebrates the art of editing and the craft of a skilled editor to capture something of the ambience at the site of recording. He recognizes the creative accomplishment of the editor, who in reconstructing the bullfight managed to invoke the physical realism of the spectacle—"the mystical triad of animal, man, and crowd."[50] What follows is an elaborate reflection on the aura of the imprint: the irrevocable registration of an actual event and the this-is-happening aspect of cinema, which differentiates film from photography. The bull is dead, but on the screen it is brought to life and (potentially) killed again and again in eternity. Hence, Bazin is less occupied by the historical referent than by the cinematic enactment of death and the reframing of death, the metaphysical kernel of both the bullfight and the film.

From the perspective of existential phenomenology Bazin's account of the uncanny experience of watching repeatedly the not-yet-now of a past event brings attention to the difference between the index and the trace, which tend to be confused in the predominant discussion about cinema and temporality. Traditionally the conception of film as a time-based medium and a temporal art refers to the photographic base of filmic representation, the cinematic record of unfolding moments, and the experience of the sound-image as index.[51] The discussion about indexicality is commonly marked by the confusion of the imprint and the trace; the latter not only denotes a material vestige of the past but also coincides with a recurrent theme in Western philosophy. In her reassessment of film and indexicality, Mary Ann Doane comes close to a distinction, although she does not address the phenomenology of the trace. She argues that the standard reference to Charles Sanders Peirce tends to reduce the index to the photographic imprint, whereas Peirce himself would rather underline its function as a hollowed-out sign:

> In Peirce's description, the index is evacuated of content …. It designates something without describing it; its function is limited to the assurance of an existence. Hence, indexicality together with its seemingly privileged relation to the referent—to singularity and contingency—is available to a range of media.[52]

This sign function beyond description is in tune with Emmanuel Lévinas's suggestion that the trace is a "disarrangement expressing itself" and therefore "not a sign like others."[53] In film the trace has the complicated status of referring to the inscription of images and sounds, to the uncanny presence of the past invoked by photographs and archive film, as well as to the banal sense employed by historians and documentary filmmakers, according to which the trace is the source material, the fragmentary texts or images, out of which events in the past may be reconstructed as narratives. In cinema the trace is also subject to creative strategies of *mise en scène* and narrative imagination. The staging of and framing into different vestiges and images of the past provide effective means to transform a material indication of "this has been" or "time passing" into a representation of deeper symbolic and affective meaning. In this sense the temporal contingency of a vestige, imprint, or recorded sound in film may be invoked as the "assurance of an existence," in the sense outlined above.

Originally, the trace has less to do with the materiality of the vestige, than with its uncanny presence of absence. The trace is a trace of something, and therefore it stands out as an intentional object whose mode of being is equivalent to its function as inscription of the past within the present. In Bazin's essays the existential recognition of the trace as a presence of absence is far more complex than a mere confirmation of the indexical status of a photographic image. The bullfight example brings attention not only to the filmic attraction of repeating and reliving a gesture or event in the past but to the meaning of film as archive memory. This idea is more explicitly articulated in a short review on Nicole Védrès's archive film *Paris 1900* (France, 1950), where Bazin compares the enactment of personal memory in Marcel Proust's novel *À la recherche du temps perdu* with the nonpersonal memory of archive film. In the film the aesthetic pleasure results from a distancing, because *these memories* do not belong to the viewer. They invoke an act of reminiscence beyond personal memory: "cinema is a machine to recover time in order to lose it more easily."[54]

In line with the influence of existential phenomenology, it is important to note that Bazin's consideration of the trace goes beyond a mere reflection on appearance and transcendence. Bazin's account of the trace is not even limited to the visual a priori of the vestige, because the trace is not necessarily dependent on what is actually shown. Philip Rosen draws attention to these extravisual markers of indexicality with reference to Bazin's commentary on *Kon-Tiki* (Thor Heyerdahl, Sweden and Norway, 1950).[55] Moreover, he shows how Bazin accounts for the referent from the side of imagination and expectation: "It is precisely the activity and desire of the subject—'our obsession with realism'—that makes indexicality the crucial aspect of the image for Bazin."[56]

Bazin explains the success of Heyerdahl's exploration film by emphasizing the brute quality of amateur images and the significant omission of drama in the film, because out of practical reasons the crew member who for the moment was in charge of shooting had to stop filming as soon as something unexpected or dangerous happened. The cinematic drama of Kon-Tiki consists in the denied vision of these moments, which makes the film "itself an aspect of the adventure. Those fluid and trembling images are as it were the objectivized memory of the actors in the drama."[57] He refers to the authenticity of this film in terms of the affective meaning of its technical mistakes, which is in tune with the impact of the negative image: "It is not so much the photograph of the whale that interests us as the photograph of the *danger*."[58]

In the following I aim to contextualize the trace as a persistent theme in the philosophy of time and an issue especially dear to existential phenomenology. Moreover, regarding the overlapping albeit different problems of the index and the trace in documentary it would be interesting to address related issues of archive memory and the narrative construction of time, which is inevitable in any representation of the past.

▶
The Trace: Archive, Imagination, and Chronofiction

Bazin acknowledged the status of the film image as archive memory. The existential implications of the film image as mnemonic sign are crucial to Bernard Stiegler's critique of Husserl. Stiegler brought attention to the fact that Husserl's *Zeitobjekt* and the role it plays in his description of time experience referred to an ideal conception of the melody, which overlooked the feature of its recorded counterpart. From this perspective the cinematic *Zeitobjekt* opens up to the sociocultural aspects of cinema as a technology of memory.[59] Moving images provide artificial memories to our imagination and perception. These images and sounds provide souvenirs of past events, but they are usually unmemorable on a personal and subjective level. In Stiegler's opinion the archive memory of film represents a tertiary memory that posits the historical interval between the moment of recording and the reception of these sound-images over time.[60]

For the present discussion of time experience in film I borrow this notion of the tertiary memory that brings attention to the fact that in time each film somehow turns into a fragmentary document of the historical moment in which it was made. More important, Stiegler's notion also relates to the creative possibilities of documentary to stage problems of history and memory. Questions of film as archive memory represent one important aspect of the trace in cinema, although to discuss the meanings of the moving image as mnemonic sign or related problems of film and historiography we will have to look more closely at the crucial position of the trace as a classical discourse in the philosophy of memory as well as the meanings it opens up in film regarding the aesthetics of the time-image and narrative imagination. Paul Ricœur is an important reference in this context. The later part of his work, dating from the early eighties to his last major achievement in 2000, *La mémoire, l'histoire, l'oubli (Memory, History, Forgetting),* represents an important reference for any critical reassessment of existential phenomenology and for studying the representation of history and memory in the large.

Memory, History, Forgetting departs from a dual figure of time in Baroque iconography, which illustrates the major set of problems in Ricœur's book. It symbolically relates to his overall attempt to bridge the problem of time and memory in classical philosophy with the practical challenges and poetic possibilities of narrative time in historiography and fiction. Ricœur argues that time is unthinkable beyond mediation, although he solely insists on the mediation through a fictional or historical text. Before a closer account on how *Memory, History, Forgetting* may relate to problems of time in documentary, Ricœur's hermeneutic outline of the phenomenology of memory seems helpful regarding the present reassessment of the trace in film theory.

In Baroque iconography history is thought of as being cramped between the creative process of writing and the never resting, destructive god of time who tries to tear a page out of the book of history as he sweeps by. This figure of time materializes in a statue that Ricœur discovered at the Wiblingen Monastery in Ulm, Germany, and which he describes in the following terms:

> In the foreground, Kronos, the winged god. An old man with wreathed brow: his left hand grips a large book, his right hand attempts to tear out a page. Behind and above, stands history itself. The gaze is grave and searching; one foot topples a horn of plenty from which spills a cascade of gold and silver, sign of instability; the left hand checks the act of the god, while the right displays history's instruments: the book, the inkpot, and the stylus.[61]

Philosophically, and regardless of the fact that our present toolbox of historical representation contains more than the written word, the symbolism is still apt regarding the frustration involved in the project of narrating and depicting the past, to grasp the meanings of historical events while simultaneously trying to keep up with the present. Also, the destructive act of Chronos calls attention to the effacing of vestiges and, more indirectly, to abuses of archives and historical representation.

Ricœur's book offers a critique of historical judgment. The trace (*la trace*) is a bearing theme that Ricœur addresses through a series of inquiries ranging from Plato and Aristotle, to Augustinus, Kant, Husserl, Sartre, and Bergson.

According to Ricœur the problem of the trace originates in the classical "confusion conveyed by the expression 'memory-image,'" and hence it belongs to the relation between memory and imagination. He argues that the persistent enigma of the presence of the past, as illustrated by the metaphor "the slab of wax," originates in the work of Plato. About *Theaetetus,* however, Ricœur argues that memory is bound up with forgetting: "Whatever is impressed upon the wax we remember and know so long as the image ... remains in the wax, whatever is obliterated or cannot be impressed, we forget and do not know."[62] Hence, already in Plato the possibility of the erroneous memory is subject of consideration, because of the tight relation between image and the metaphor of the imprint (*tupos*) where error is assimilated to an erasing of marks, "or to a mistake akin to that of someone placing his feet in the wrong footprints."[63] Speaking of the present representation of the absent thing, Plato emphasizes the role of the image (*eikōn*) and tends to enclose the problematic of memory within that of imagination. In turn, Aristotle draws attention to "the representation of a thing formerly perceived, acquired, or learned," implying that the problem of the image belongs to that of remembering and knowledge—"memory is of the past."[64]

True to his method of critical synthesis, Ricœur's definition of the trace depends on a compromise between the affective and imaginary realm of appearance outlined by Plato and the Aristotelian model that implies the social realm of language and the trace in terms of recollection—the intended action of remembrance. I am particularly interested in the creative and intersubjective aspect of Ricœur's approach to the trace in historical representation. In the three-parted volume *Temps et récit (Time and Narrative)* he discussed the role of *emplotment* that organizes the contingencies of time and being into a whole.[65] The hermeneutic inquiry is concerned with ways in which philosophers, historians, and authors of fiction have acknowledged and exemplified this narrative structure. Hence, the telling of time belongs to both historiography and poetics. In line with the semiotic direction of Ricœur's phenomenology, experience involves not only oneself but also the presence of other subjects. It is a mediated process where a social, intersubjective realm is predominant in the response to what Husserl designated as *Lebenswelt,* and Heidegger as *Dasein.*

Ricœur implies that narrative is the mediating dimension between time and the ways in which time is understood in practical life. Embracing this reversible movement between narrative and time, this circle that embraces narration and temporality implies a broadened sense of narrative, signifying both fiction and history—*history* as the reconstructed event historians offer to our understanding of the past. In this general sense, *intrigue* designates the power of the narrative to refer to time experience and the meanings time has in our lives. Time cannot be grasped beyond these intersubjective meanings, which in turn inspire and inform the construction of stories: "time becomes human to the extent that it is organized after the manner of a narrative; narrative, in turn, is meaningful to the extent that it portrays the features of temporal experience."[66] Ricœur stresses the power of mimesis in narration to articulate existential questions of time through poetic figuration. This notion of mimesis, however, goes beyond fiction and the creation of stories per se, by denoting a mimetic movement from everyday life to discourse, and back to the world again.[67]

Most important in this argument is the impact that narratives have on practical life. In *Time and Narrative, Volume 3,* this idea is developed with reference to Heidegger's conception of historical time.[68] To put it simply, *historical time* is the time of our shared experiences, mediated through the constructed discourses of history. This is the sphere in which the linear force of material time is vertically punctuated by a multitude of subjective stories. In this context the trace becomes an ethical possibility, linking the experience of the past to the responsibility of the present, in order to mediate, to interpret, and to provide narrative enactment. Ricœur suggests an ethical synthesis between the creativity inherent in any construction of intrigue and the responsibility toward the past that should be demanded from this narrative reinvention.

This ethical approach to the trace relates to his celebration of the narrative possibility of "telling history alternatively."[69] By this Ricœur refers to narratives where, beyond the macroperspective of historiography, historical experiences and events find an alternative articulation. In opposition to Hayden White's argument, Ricœur does not suggest that all historical narratives are equally remote from the actual event of the past. To stress the inevitable construction of historical events is not to claim that they are all fictive or untrue. Rather, the communicative ethos of narration is related here to the possibility of poetic narration to give voice to historical experience, to impinge a microperspective on the linear axis of official history.

Despite this possible link between *Time and Narrative* and aspects of historical representation in documentary, the relevance of Ricœur's phenomenology is limited by the fact that he exclusively discusses temporal figuration in reference to written narratives. The same problem marks *Memory, History, Forgetting*. Although important aspects of preservation versus erasure/oblivion enter through broader issues of historiography and the documentary trace, it is striking to note how Ricœur overlooks the constructed image-memory provided by film and media. The perfect symmetry between narrative and temporality excludes other processes of temporalization. Aside from the literal manipulation of tempo and space-time relations in moving images, the persistent theme of the trace in cinema provides for the relations between the present and the past that belong to narrative techniques and audiovisual strategies that appeal to our affection and imagination.

Janicaud, who depends on the philosophy of Ricœur, but who questions Ricœur's bias toward narration and the written text, argues that every process of temporalization is "chronofictive."[70] His critique suggests a technological take on the impact that diverse measuring instruments have historically had on our conception and culture of time. I am less interested in the narrow sense of time measurement, which refers to quantitative measures for a precise evaluation of linear time, than in the intuitive estimation of duration and the sensory judgment of a temporal dimension. In existential phenomenology the latter, wide sense of time measurement was acknowledged, including Bazin's thoughts about lived time and aesthetic modes to posit this existential impact of image and time in cinema.

Aside from the cinematic aspects of the time-image, Ricœur's phenomenology of narrative time would also overlook the complex relation between narrative imagination and historical representation in documentary. Documentary films are commonly driven by the incentive of a quest, because many of these narratives hope to provide a revelatory insight into a social or historical realm. This documentary aim is in tune with Ricœur's notion of narrative figuration, which in a filmic context would relate to the production of image-memories through montage, narration, and *mise en scène*. In the context of documentary, however, a reference to *Time and Narrative* will automatically upset Ricœur's categories of historical and fictive narratives. Applied to documentary film, his phenomenology requires a deepened consideration of the intersected processes of creative form, narrative imagination, and historical representation in moving images.

The Trace Remediated: The Critical Potential of Chronofiction

Brian Glassic, one of the characters in Don DeLillo's *Underworld,* makes the following statement one dull night in a motel room:

> I watched TV in my motel. I lived responsibly in the real. I didn't accept this business of life as a fiction, or whatever Klara Sax had meant when she said that things had become unreal. History was not a matter of missing minutes on the tape. I did not stand helpless before it. I hewed to the texture of collected knowledge, took faith from the solid and availing stuff of our experience. Even if we believe that history is a workwheel powered by human blood—read the speeches of Mussolini—at least we've known the thing together. A single narrative sweep, not ten thousand wisps of disinformation.[71]

Although we may disagree with the drastic expression of a single narrative sweep, media representations contribute to a shared horizon of cultural and historical references. Brian Glassic's statement is a forceful reminder of the inevitable social implications that must be considered in this context of film and the emplotment of historical time. In media representations of the past, montage and narrative devices reframed, contextualized, and rendered significant the images and recordings of historical events. In various ways these social and ideological aspects of film as archive memory play a decisive role in our expectations and response to documentary representation, while also being subject to thematic enactment in film and video.

Hence, the present reassessment of the trace demands a special recognition of the complex relation between film and historiography and the social and political role of moving images as archive memory. Somehow, as we enter the empirical realm of visual culture the trace has to be demystified. For good and bad, media representations shape our conception of the past. Yet, in order to focus on the formal and expressive possibilities of historical time in documentary, I have chosen to leave the dystopic implications aside, which is a practice in line with Ricœur's idealist and ethical recognition of recollection and narrative imagination. The trace represents a persistent figure of time in cinema and in documentary film and video in particular. "The trace signifies without making anything appear," and yet it bears witness to something that happened and even to the passing of time itself.[72] Although the spectacular aspect of the image-imprint depends on an excess of visibility and indexicality, it does not automatically become an affective sign of the past.

In concert with Jean-Paul Sartre and Maurice Merleau-Ponty, Ricœur emphasizes that for the trace to stand out as image-memory, language, interpretation, and even knowledge are required. There must be something with which to fill the trace to make it count as the past. This is where Aristotle's "memory is of the past" meets with the material side of the trace in historiography. History is a science of traces, and it is the trace that "orients the hunt, the quest, the search, the inquiry."[73] In documentary there are many ways in which the temporal contingency of the trace orients the quest, however different this quest may be. The trace is evoked frequently in documentary film and video, where the vestige, photograph, moving image, or recorded sound may be framed to conjure up the presence of the past. The poetic enactment of the image-imprint brings attention to the memory objects of cultural preservation and the fragile texture of vestiges that are victims to the destructive power of Chronos. For example, in *Toute la mémoire du monde* (Alain Resnais, France, 1956) the material vestige meets with the cultural and historical practice of memory and preservation in the portrayal of la Bibliothèque Nationale in Paris. Similar to *Les statues meurent aussi* (Chris Marker and Alain Resnais, 1950) this film offers a reflection on the historical vestige and the destructive aspects of time passing and human neglect. Resnais accounts for the long and complicated itinerary that awaits each book, poster, or image from the department of cataloging and indexing to the particular shelf where it is predestined to contribute to the overall memory of the library, or simply to dust and fall in oblivion.

Sites of memory such as the museum or the library bring attention to the film itself as a historical object. The practice of photography and film represents not only a culture of production, reproduction, distribution, and public exhibition but also a culture of preservation and classification. In the broader context of documentary filmmaking the compilation of archival footage is pivotal to the film culture at hand. As Catherine Russell writes, "all too often, the archive serves as visual evidence of history, with the role of found footage reduced to the textual authority of the documentary fact."[74] Documentary, however, also involves projects where the archive is manifest in both a material and a symbolic sense. Here, the compiled material is not offered as a mere trace of the past but as a trace of another trace. The sociocultural and historical context, from where this documentary ready-made is taken, still clings to the inserted fragment.

The archival status of film adds an important dimension to the mode of transition associated with the trace in classical philosophy. The ambivalent status of the trace resides in its simultaneous denotation of passage and mark: it represents a temporal transition between the present and past, remaining a static imprint of an irrevocable event. As I intend to show in the remainder of this book, the chronofiction provided by documentary usually fuses with more or less outspoken attempts to narrate historical events or to stage thematically problems of cultural memory, testimony, and oblivion. Regarding the affective impact of the trace, the suggested approach to cinema and temporality will first have to consider the psychological aspects of time in moving images and the related methodological problem of how to analyze the experience of documentary film.

*Frame-Breaking Events and Motifs
beyond Representation*

The following sections will focus on the time-image and the trace as events of defamiliarization or visceral chock, consequently upsetting both film viewing and any presumed analogy between the phenomenology of cinema and the phenomenology of time experience. Maurice Merleau-Ponty implicitly confronted the issue as he stressed the sociocultural dimension of spectator expectation. He argued that a stylistic anomaly of film form is not something immanent to experience.[1] One may add that, however exceptional a stylistic anomaly, the film should not be isolated from the cultural and social context and standards in reference to which the film was made. Time experience in cinema raises questions whether, when, and how a specific screen event stands out as an anomaly. How is it that some sequences, camera movements, and so forth strike us as either pleasant or disturbingly hard to watch?

In order to approach the time-image as a significant screen event, I will refer to the notion of the *frame-breaking event,* which I borrow from Erving Goffman's phenomenology of everyday life. In his discussions Goffman combines situations in social life with a perspective on structural mechanisms on the side of representation, stage (or screen) performance, and the cultural realm of social interaction and intersubjective perception. In documentary where experimental figures of isochronal representation, repetition, or altered speed are further marked by a significant reference to real events, people, and places, there is the possibility of frame-breaking events where unexpected modes of representation meet with motifs at odds with visual taboos or in line with voyeuristic pleasures.

The classical problem of image and death offers a relevant point of departure. The philosophy of time is intrinsically related to and even propelled by human's awareness of his or her death. The inevitable limitation of biographical time and the natural yet enigmatic transformation of life to death are problems that have always been pivotal in human's reflection on time. The relation between image and death represents a problem intimately connected with that of temporality in theories on photography and film. Bazin's reference to the phenomenology of image and death is exemplified in chapter 2, where I discuss the philosophy of time inherent in his notion of the *mummy complex* and the inscription of change as the *metaphysical kernel* of film. Roland Barthes, who dedicated *Camera Lucida* to Jean-Paul Sartre, referred to the existential meaning of the photograph in terms of a pure *this has been*. In this context image and death are related to our ritual use of photographs to recall the face and gestures of dead relatives and friends. The affective meaning of image and death, however, goes beyond the family album and the irrevocable past of the photograph. With reference to Alexander Gardner's image of Lewis Payne—a young man sentenced to death, portrayed in handcuffs at his cell, and with a scornful look in the camera—Barthes described the temporality of this image in the following terms: "He is dead and he is going to die."[2] Hence, the past tense of a photograph may simultaneously suggest the *not yet now* of a future, the outcome of which we already know.

Image and death stands out as a trope of time in photography and film where it is closely aligned with chock, thrills, and repulsion or with motifs and events that defy representation. Aside from its obvious connection to the discourse of the trace, image and death is more generally a crucial issue in the context of film and phenomenology because it opens up to the psychology of image-affect.

▶──

The Phenomenology of Image and Death

In 1979 Amos Vogel made the following observation, which is still of relevance:

> Now that sex is available to us in hard-core porno films, death remains the one last taboo in cinema. However ubiquitous death is—we all ultimately suffer from it—it calls into question the social order and its value systems; it attacks our mad scramble for power, our simplistic rationalism and our unacknowledged, child-like belief in immortality.[3]

Ever since the execution genre of classical cinema, new modes of death in moving images have been added, although the framing of somebody *actually* dying or being killed remains highly provocative. No matter how banal the common motif of death and dying may appear to the viewer of fiction film, nondiegetic deaths and documentary representations of inert bodies remain a highly disturbing motif.

The staged violence and death in fiction film belong to the diegetic realm of movies and television series. The sudden appearance of an actual death, however, contaminates the fictive space-time in terms of an authentic ending of lived time and the eerie transformation from moving body to inert object. Vivian Sobchack refers to this event as a documentary moment because it represents a fictive event that coincides with the record of an actual death. To exemplify the impact of a documentary moment, Sobchack points to the hunting and the killing of a rabbit in *La règle du jeu* ("Rules of the Game," Jean Renoir, France, 1939).[4]

There is a significant difference between the representation of animal death and human death, which is similar to the difference between death in fiction film and in documentary. From a psychoanalytical perspective Akira Mizuta Lippit argues that the phenomenology of image and death depends on different taboos, restricting animal and human representation, and fiction film and documentary.[5] To bring attention to the *reality effect* provoked by animal injury or death in dramatic narrative films, he departs from the importance ascribed to the disclaimer *no animal was harmed*. The effect may be less pronounced in documentary, although, as Lippit convincingly shows, a significant combination of anxiety, attraction, and visual taboo marks the examples from Thomas Edison's 1903 actuality *Electrocuting an Elephant* to Georges Franju's 1949 essay film *Le sang des bêtes (Blood of the Beasts)*.

The Edison example would clearly relate to Bazin's essay "Death Every Afternoon," because aside from the psychological aspect of the anthropomorphized death of Topsy there is also the spectacular event of filmic metamorphosis.[6] The recorded choreography of the elephant's electrocution offers a combined spectacle of cinematic temporality— movement, stasis, and movement again; dramatic change and a potentially endless repetition of a past event—and the existential drama of life coming to an end. In *Blood of the Beasts* allegory complicates the psychological aspect of image and death depending on the viewer's ability to read it as a commentary on the French complicity in the Holocaust. Nevertheless, the stark contrast between text, music, and uncompromising images of animals being slaughtered brings attention to the shocking impact of an isochronal representation of death.

The image of somebody dying or being killed represents a poignant trope of time, where the irrevocable ending of lived time is screened without any deeper insight into the question of death and decease. In cinema death may simply be recorded and replayed in terms of the transformation from vivid gesture to immobile object. In the context of existential phenomenology the change from being into nonbeing represents a recurrent subject of discussion. For example, Emmanuel Lévinas stresses the ethical signification of the human face turning into mask, according to which death appears in terms of transformation from movement to stasis, or, more correctly, as annihilation and the end of being.[7] Sobchack approaches the same set of questions while emphasizing the experiential difference between the symbolic enactment and visual excess of death in fiction and the shocking and confounding counterpart of documentary.[8] She argues that the recording of death stands out as the most poignant of indexical signs because it is a sign that exceeds visibility: "The representation of the event of death is an indexical sign of that which is always in excess of representation, and beyond the limits of coding and culture: Death confounds all codes."[9] The most provoking figure of death is not the image of a dead body but a body transforming into corpse: "the moment of death can only be represented in a visible and vigorous contrast between two states of the physical body: the body as lived-body, intentional and animated—and the body as corpse, as flesh unintended, unanimated, static."[10]

The Zapruder film with its amateur record of Kennedy's assassination offers a famous illustration of human death as cinematic metamorphosis, although one may object that Sobchack overlooks the iconographic status obtained by this and similar archival images of historical deaths. In a spectacular way the Zapruder film matches no doubt the attraction described by Bazin and others of looking repeatedly at the inscription of death, the irrevocable moment in time when a person ceases to exist. However, a new dimension is added to this image when it is framed as a famous archive memory, firmly embedded in our shared collection of historical events. For most people the recurrently shown footage of the Zapruder film is probably less striking in terms of an image of death, than that blurred and incomplete piece of evidence whose meaning was last defined by Oliver Stone in *JFK* (USA, 1991).

Still, Sobchack intends a more general signification of image-affect, image and death, and the existential and cultural status of death as documentary screen event. Death is a motif that is both excessively visual and impossible to represent. She acknowledges the gut-feeling aspect of wonder and belief as we face the screening of an actual death. The framing of violence and death posits the image as indexical sign invoking the existential meaning of the trace, and hence the motif of death emphasizes the status of documentary footage as "ethically charged."[11] At this point we may recall the ambivalent role of photographic representation in the aftermath of September 11, 2001. Like many other newspapers and journals *Time Magazine* published a whole series of images from Ground Zero in New York, disturbingly well-composed pictures of disaster. Included in this collection was an image of people jumping from their offices in World Trade Center—tiny figures on their way down, photographed in midair and literally in the transit from life to death: an unbearable image, grotesque and horrifying beyond words. Sobchack's essay is helpful in stressing the ethical dimension of the trace: "Before the event of an unsimulated death, the viewer's very act of looking is ethically charged and is, itself, the object of ethical judgment: The viewer is held ethically responsible for his or her visual response."[12]

Vogel's reflection quoted above belongs to a review of *Des Morts* (*Of the Dead*, Jean-Pol Ferbus, Dominique Garny, and Thiery Zeno, Belgium, 1979). This film challenges the visual taboo of death in a series of sequences where death and the metamorphosis from human form to organic object appear in unflinching takes, forcing the viewer to contemplate the pale, immobile complexion of the dead, the funeral preparation of corpses, the decomposing mask that was once the face of an old woman, a severely injured man covered with tubes, or a view from within a cremation chamber where a body is being consumed by flames and crumbles into ashes.

The statement of interviewees and textual markers emphasizes the allegorical drive of this montage, which aims at an open-ended reflection on meanings of death and the funeral rituals of different cultures. The film provides a stark example of death as visual representation and death as an imaginary realm that differs according to various cultural standards. There is a decisive use of contrasting between the communal engagement in, and respect of, the dead in Thailand, Mexico, and South Korea and the isolated, industrialized, and repressive culture of death in the Western world represented by the United States and Belgium. Although *Of the Dead* is marked by the typical direct cinema ideal of recording the real to unveil a social truth, it zooms into the normally insupportable image of death and decay and offers persistent framings that question the suggested transparency of photographic representation. The ethnographic gaze is brought to the fore in scenes that portray the death rituals of other cultures, although it is contradicted by a poetic mode of contemplation where the cameraman's personal engagement in the mourning of others results in a respectful celebration of the living. *Of the Dead* is a subversive attempt to inquire into the limits of cultural acceptance, while forcing the viewer to consider the very act of film viewing. The allegoric juxtaposition of death rituals in different corners of the world brings attention to the fact that the anxiety evoked by representations of the dead depends on the social and cultural codes and contexts that inevitably direct expectations and sense perception. This relative quality of image and death is already a poignant theme at the outset of this film.

At a funeral home somewhere in California a man dressed in white addresses the camera: "The days after the remains have been taken out, the body is cosmetized and dressed." A full view shows the covered body and the hand of the dead man: "I will cosmetize this hand…. I first clean out the nails." Music accompanies the title, and the hand is shown in close view as each nail is being made. Then, the skin is painted in a true-to-life color. The next sequence shows mountains and jungle in the north of Thailand. A Hmong village is introduced, followed by the wake of an old woman. In stark contrast to the dead man at the Californian funeral home, her bed is surrounded by life: a man sings about the fatal disease that ended the woman's life, and a daughter cries at her side. In this context when a pig and several other animals are slaughtered, animal death is not framed as an image of death but a depiction of the living paying tribute to the Gods and the deceased. Different from the desperate roar of the dying horse in *Blood of the Beast,* the final howl of the dying pig naturally blends with the cry of the weeping daughter. Not even in the later sequence where the funeral ceremony is represented and the face of the dead woman has decayed beyond recognition does the image evoke as much anxiety as the clinical, cold, and dehumanized counterpart of the Western funeral home and autopsy room.

The variety of death as visual motif and cinematic event in *Of the Dead* questions any attempt to define the existential meaning of image and death. Again, the representation of death as a disquieting trope of time in moving images depends on conventions and expectations related to style and to expressive strategies to invoke death as a frame-breaking event.

▶ ────────────────────────────────

Negative Experience and the Manufacture of Frame-Breaking Events

How may the anxiety provoked by images of death or related screen events be grasped and explained? In what sense may phenomenology illuminate the social and psychological mechanisms, because of which this affects film experience? The predominant directions in film and phenomenology do not have an answer to these questions. The merit of Sobchack's essay is that she accounts for the image of death as an existential matter and a tradition of visual representation. The phenomenological description pairs with an outlining of image and death as a genealogy in visual culture, and the chocking appearance of actual death on the screen and the impact of a cinematic sign effect are related. In film experience, however, the documentary moment remains a blunt concept because it brackets the social realm, historical context, and related aspects of audience expectation and genre conventions. Regarding the problem of spectator psychology the reader will notice a similar limitation in this book. For reasons of demarcation and because of the book's focus on the aesthetic and existential aspects of documentary representation, the discussions that follow do not include research on reception and film viewing. There are, however, related theoretical references that may be helpful, indicating a possible development in this direction. For example, Erving Goffman's *Frame Analysis: An Essay on the Organization of Experience* offers a theoretical model with important implications for understanding documentary moments and related events.[13]

Goffman's approach to the social space of stage performances could be compared to phenomenological attempts such as that of Mikel Dufrenne (discussed in chapter 2). Goffman's notion of *selected attention* represents another link to phenomenology because it deals with the subject's involvement in the world, and more specifically, it relates to Husserl's teacher Brentano, who addressed the relation between the content of perception and "the reality status we give to what is thus enclosed or bracketed within perception."[14] A work of social psychology, *Frame Analysis* is nevertheless an attempt that is a step closer to more recent perspectives on semiotic phenomenology. In Goffman's opinion social structures of everyday life rather than transcendence govern our involvement in social situations and representations. Pragmatic, but not relativist, he departs from the assumption that experience has less to do with ontology or with the biological processes of the brain, than with how socially constructed meanings and the culture of social activities shape our expectations and the concepts through which we understand and react to given situations.

The problem of the documentary moment could be related to Goffman's discussion on the psychological mechanisms of a negative experience. A negative experience results from a subject's encounter with a situation that does not fit the (socioculturally) set frame, through which she interacts with a given situation. *Frame* in this context is understood as a socioculturally constructed preconception that governs our definition of a specific situation and, therefore, our cognitive understanding and emotional reaction. Instead of living the situation and experiencing what it offers the subject becomes disturbingly aware of a frame-breaking event, which in turn may evoke a reflection on her being in this situation.

Moreover, this frame-breaking event may provoke thoughts about how and why this situation came about in the first place. To exemplify the impact of negative experience, Goffman tells the story of a man who suddenly hears music that differs from his conception of auditory harmony and the criteria he ascribes to music: "He cannot follow along, he cannot get into the music; and so the unpleasant constraint of sitting out an experience while sitting in it."[15]

For the present consideration of time in moving images two important aspects of this example bring attention to the important sociocultural dimension of everyday experience. First, the musical object is a cultural product and an expression whose label *exotic music* is ascribed to it by a specific context of performance as well as by the relative notion of auditory harmony.

Second, the qualities of the performance break with the listener's preconstructed frame of perception, through which he considers the music. He finds himself to be in the middle of a *black-box situation,* in which his perception unexpectedly fails to make sense. Moreover, this negative experience involves a meta-awareness of the very extension of the tune, which stresses the unpleasant constraint of sitting out an experience while sitting in it. In this context *frame* denotes the activity of perceiving a sound, visual representation, or performance because we always experience through a socioculturally shaped and shared frame of references, knowledge, and values. Frame also points to the notable impact that the intersubjective activity of framing has on rendering a perceived situation meaningful. This process is not only about understanding and decoding but also a sensory and emotional interactivity with situations, because "frame organizes more than meaning; it also organizes involvement."[16]

Obviously, the frame-breaking event may correspond to many everyday situations, and consequently, Goffman's model consists of a complex web of categories and subcategories to map the multiple process of frame activity. In the following, *negative experience* will be used in the specific sense that it obtains in the context of performance:

> This sort of experience is to be found in pure performances—for example, exhibition sports, such as wrestling and roller derby, and dramatic scriptings, whether live, taped, photographed, written, or drawn.... In these shows any device that recaptures attention, or at least demonstrates that the uninvolving events in progress are not the real performance, has a special value. Here, note, a particular kind of frame break will largely figure, the kind that therapists and interrogators exploit when they verbally and calmly draw attention away from the anticipated story line to the framing mechanisms presupposed in its maintenance; in brief, self-referencing *reflexive* frame breaks.[17] (original emphasis)

In this context negative experience refers to a frame-breaking event anticipated within the performance at hand, or in the audience. Owing to the less interactive situation of the movie theatre I primarily associate this notion with the reflexive frame-breaking devices in cinema. Bertolt Brecht's notion of the *Verfremdungseffekt* would relate to this definition of the negative experience. Yet different from Brecht's intentional/functional prescription to the play writer, actors, and stage designer, Goffman's notion of the negative experience regards both the manufacture of an artistic expression and the social realm of spectatorship. In Goffman's opinion the primary locus of negative experience is the social situation, the face-to-face encounter. Still, our frame of reference may just as well break down in receiving representations, narratives, and diverse kinds of performances. A negative experience may be provoked by changes in the spectator's attitude or by the deliberate production of a frame-breaking event within the performance.

Goffman charts a social context where the intersubjective dimension of negative experience is particularly poignant and where this effect may also be intentionally provoked for dramatic, aesthetic, and poetic purposes. Moreover, changes in the spectator's attitude to the stage/screen affect her frame activity. An example related to film experience could be the unexpected laughter of a fellow viewer during a moment in the film that most of the audience would regard as tragic or deeply moving. In this and similar situations the frame-breaking event is entirely provoked by the audience's "unauthorized increase in lamination of the frame."[18] The unexpected laughter and similar examples would point to the fact that film experience depends on not only the representation itself but also the mood and attitude of the viewer. On the other hand Goffman points to situations during stage performances where the spectator's make-belief in a staged fiction suddenly gives way to the awareness of the material world outside the diegetic universe. A clip from *New York Herald Tribune* (Paris edition, October 3, 1951) is a poignant example that is in tune with Sobchack's description of the documentary moment:

> Orson Welles banged Desdemona's head so hard on the bed in the murder scene from "Othello" here last night that members of the audience began murmuring protests. Mr. Welles said after the performance that he guessed he just got caught up too realistically in the spirit of the play. Said Gudrun Muir, who played Desdemona: "It was in a good cause."[19]

Goffman also recognizes the creative possibility of a stage performance to intentionally provoke a negative experience, that is, the expressive potential of time measurement in representations and stage performances, and not least how it is experienced. In the encounter with a pure performance, he argues, we cannot examine but one frame element at a time. *The brackets* represents a frame element that refers to the usually clear-cut brackets, both temporal and spatial, which are immanent to dramatic scripts and performances in general, dependent as they always are on a set duration, or the temporal finitude of a narrative.[20] Here, we recognize a voluntary shift in the use of the term *bracket* and *bracketing*. Different from its signification in classical phenomenology, where the activity (conscious and unconscious) *to bracket* certain experienced qualities is opposed to the intentional act of *positing* or *intending*, the brackets here signify the spatiotemporal realm and the physical duration of the drama. Also, Goffman's discussion includes the possibility of violating the temporal brackets in order to generate negative experiences, which may have diverse dramatic and symbolic functions in a play or a film.

In Part II, the notion of the frame-breaking event will be related to the expressive function of temporalization in documentary. In the context where screen attraction supposedly coincides with a thrill of the real, the frame-breaking event is often propelled by a combination of manipulated space-time (duration, tempo, rhythm, and repetition) and the enactment of the sound-image record as a trace of a historical and social realm. Classical as well as more recent examples of experimental documentary will bring attention to the creative possibilities of time measurement in documentary and the thematic enactment of the trace. The malleability of time and space in film and the impact of manipulated space-time in moving images belong to the neglected aesthetic aspects of documentary cinema. For example, *Des Morts* explores a visual taboo and a classical existential theme of image and death, but the subversive quality of this film primarily results from a radical mode of contrasting the different death rituals and of using effects such as long, static takes of motifs that already represent a provocation to the eye.

Hence, time measurement in film may in itself provoke a frame-breaking event such as the duration of a static framing, which coincides with or outlasts the filmed event. The ascribed authenticity of the long take may immediately be questioned by strategies to visualize the artificial status of a monocular framing or to linger on nondramatic views deprived of spectacular action. Goffman's account of the manufacture of negative experience seems relevant in this context because it concerns the dynamic interrelation between, on the one hand, aspects of desire, expectation, and potential changes in screen attitude and, on the other hand, the aesthetic, discursive, and narrative possibilities of moving images.

Frame-breaking events may also result from more explicit conflicts between appearance and context or between images of different sociocultural meanings. Compilation techniques may be used to confront fictive images with archival footage or to contaminate a record of official history with the private documentation of a home movie. Goffman's notion of negative experience may also relate to wider issues of cultural memory, such as the role of photography as an important and yet incommensurable tool to document the past. For example, the photographic detail may represent a provocative claim to represent beyond representation, or the photographic imprint may be accused of reducing a complex historical event to a spectacular sight of horror and death.

▶

Documentary *Mise En Scène:* A Double Sense of the Imprint

Of the Dead and other examples brought attention to the classical association between death and photography. The related problem of photography and historical events that defy representation has been a subject of particular interest for scholarly work and documentary projects dedicated to film and historical trauma. The Holocaust remains the preferred topic in this context, although this is a crucial problem for any approach to historical trauma and cultural memory in film and media.

In the discourse of Holocaust photography the use and misuse of truth-claiming images have been discussed in relation to the role of photography and film in representing and commemorating the Shoah. A range of problems cling to these images that were photographed, or reproduced, to demand "retrospective witnessing."[21] In 2001 a French exposition on Holocaust photography propelled an extensive debate worth mentioning in this context, because it illuminates the controversial archive memory of documentary images. The Paris exposition was entitled *Mémoires des camps*, and the related publication included an analysis by Georges Didi-Huberman of four photographs taken by members of the *Sonderkommando* at Oświęcim. The *Sonderkommando* consisted of prisoners whose function was to lead their fellow prisoners into the gas chamber and then to collect and dispose of their remains. The *Sonderkommando* was regularly changed, and the first task of the new group was to help in executing their predecessors.

In his commentary on these images, Didi-Huberman stressed their historical and imaginative signification in terms of photographic record and the implied testimony of a photographic act accomplished against all odds. The exposition and, more notably, Didi-Huberman's emphasis on the importance of the image-object and its appeal to imagination were questioned by, among others, the psychoanalysts Gérard Wajcman and Élisabeth Pagnoux. For example, the critics questioned the way Didi-Huberman's analysis of the images put him in the place of the witness. They argued that his description of what the images show, suggest, and fail to show annihilated the temporal distance between presence and past and resulted in an exaggerated focus on the image-object as fetish. To address these images as photographic and aesthetic objects cannot result in anything but a morally dubious voyeurism.[22] In response to this critique Didi-Huberman wrote *Images malgré tout,* where he clarifies his position in relation to the predominant discourse of Holocaust photography.[23]

A general merit of *Images malgré tout* is that it challenges the fallacy of total relativism in postmodern claims that there is no truth. Didi-Huberman agrees with Wajcman's suggestion that "what cannot be seen has to be shown," but he questions Wajcman's conclusion: "What this means is that there is no image."[24] Didi-Huberman aligns with Jean-Luc Godard and Claude Lanzmann in that the Holocaust per definition forces us to rethink our relation to the image, although he challenges their radical inferences, too. Lanzmann, who refused any archival record for his film *Shoah* (France, 1985), argued that there is not a single image to represent this event. With reference to *Histoire(s) du cinéma* (Jean-Luc Godard, France, 1988–1998) Didi-Huberman explains the position of Godard: "all these images do not speak of anything but this (although 'speak about' is not the same as to tell), and that is why he revises tirelessly our entire visual culture with reference to this question."[25] *Nuit et brouillard* (*Night and Fog,* Alain Resnais, France, 1955), where both photographs and vestiges of the concentration camp are framed as traces of the past, would represent a middle position most closely related to Didi-Huberman's recognition of the limited testimony of photographs and, yet, his belief in the image *after all*.

The analysis of the four photographs departs from the well-established assumption that the Shoah is an historical event that defies visual representation. There are very few pictures taken by prisoners, and in reproducing the images taken by the Schutzstaffel or the film sequences and stills shot by the allies at the end World War II, we seem to abstract the human tragedy from the actual experience of the camps. Hence, Didi-Huberman relates to Holocaust photography and its discourse of the unimaginable. Affirming the general insufficiency of archival images to represent the past, he is nevertheless eager to stress the historical value of photography and film and the potential of these images to serve as a material support of memory. In this case he inquires into the testimonial function of four particular images, which, despite their limited outlook on the past, refer to the reality of the concentration camp from the point of view of the prisoners. The photographs, preserved at the Oświęcim Museum of Auschwitz–Birkenau, were taken with a camera hidden in a pan and show the burning of corpses and a group of naked women being led toward the gas chamber. A heavy black frame is predominant in the first and second photographs, as if the images were shot through the opening of a building. Didi-Huberman offers a lengthy account of the fact that the photographer had to hide in the dark to take these pictures and that the building in question is most likely to be the gas chamber. His description of this image turns into a dramatic narrative of the very moment of inscription, as if the value of the image-trace is to be found in the courage of those prisoners who decided to tear a fragment of their hell in order to testify to the atrocities of Oświęcim:

> The terrible paradox of this *dark room:* In order to bring the camera out of the pan, to prepare the view-finder, to approach it to his face, and to take a first sequence of images …, the photographer had to hide in the gas chamber, which was hardly—perhaps not entirely—emptied of its victims. He retreated into darkness, which thus protected his point of view. He ventures to change position and moves forward: The second shot is a little more frontal and slightly closer to its target. Hence, it is more hazardous, but also, paradoxically, better composed: a neater picture. As if for an instant the terror was subordinate to the necessity of his mission, to *tear* an image. It shows the task of his fellow workers, to deprive the corpses of their last human features. The gestures of the living mirror the weight of the corpses and the task to be fulfilled: to pull, drag, and through away....[26]

Everything is contained in the image, Didi-Huberman suggests, although it would be more correct to explicitly acknowledge the testimonies provided by Primo Levi and other survivors who tried to give voice to their experiences and whose narratives influenced the imagination of Didi-Huberman. *Images malgré tout* includes a historical account of the preservation and reuse of these four photographs, where historians have isolated details and deprived the images of the physical distance between photographer and action. In several cases the significant black frame, which mirror the awkward situation of the photographer, has been retouched.[27] Another paradox is that, in order to improve the images' testimonial function, historians edited the image into *a better picture* without realizing that the imprint of the prisoners' point of view was omitted. The recurrent manipulation of the photographs exemplifies the complex relation between historiography and the status of the image-imprint as a trace of the past.

The provocative aspect of *Images malgré tout* resides in Didi-Huberman's research attitude and his focus on the image-object itself. The testimonial function ascribed to the photograph and the problematic approach to visual aesthetics and imagination appalled critics. Regarding the present consideration of image and time, the major problem is that Didi-Huberman overlooks the difference between the photograph as inscription and the photograph as trace. Although he clearly refers to Jean-Paul Sartre and Maurice Merleau-Ponty in his emphasis on imagination, he does not explicitly address the importance of extratextual knowledge and narrative imagination when insisting upon the immanent meaning of the image. Despite the opening line of his essay, "In order to know, one has to imagine," he uncritically reproduces this reference to existential phenomenology.[28]

We have already seen how Bazin emphasized the act of looking at the image and the intersection between trace, memory, and imagination. In their account of the trace, Sartre and Merleau-Ponty referred to the same three-parted scheme; the relation between trace and image-memory is less about transcendence than the added meaning that is needed to animate the image as trace: "These traces in themselves do not refer to the past: they are present; and, in so far as I find in them signs of some 'previous' event, it is because I derive my sense of the past from elsewhere...."[29] This emphasis on extratextual knowledge is also pivotal in Barthes's recognition of the photograph as sign effect. His notion of image-affect in *Camera Lucida,* the "punctum," is not immanent to the photograph. The punctum appears in the encounter with *certain* images: "Many photographs are, alas, inert under my gaze"; Barthes concludes in regard to the image that "reaches" and "animates" him.[30] Barthes's photograph essay is dedicated to Sartre's *L'Imaginaire,* in which Sartre argues that a transgression from past to present cannot take place without something with which "to animate that piece of paper in order to lend it a signification it did not have before."[31] Hence, in relation to this semiotic insight into existential phenomenology Didi-Huberman's analysis represents a narrative process where the image-object becomes enacted as a trace of the past.

I was inspired by this concern with the image *after all,* related issues regarding archive and memory, and, not least, the recognition of cinematic strategies to stage the image as a trace of the past. Whether we agree with Didi-Huberman or his critics, in a documentary context the debate is important in demarcating the problem of historical representation and imagination. *Images malgré tout* brings attention to the possibilities and limitations of narration as an act of recollection—a problem that may be related to the staging or enactment of the trace in documentary.

A recurrent theme in *Images malgré tout* refers to Sartre's notion of the image as *action* rather than *image-object*. The trace has less to do with transcendence or truth than with the activity of the viewer to imagine the past. In this case the impact of the photograph as trace involves primarily an ethical appeal to the viewer, in order to engage with and respond to the image as archive memory.

At this point there is reason to address the double sense of the imprint in film, which may appear as a frame-breaking figure of time. In chapter 2, I mentioned that the problem of the trace was crucial to the classical philosophy of memory. Paul Ricœur has shown how the relation between the theme of the *eikon*—the image-memory in the sense of a present representation of an absent thing—and the imprint, *tupos,* aligns with the conflict between Plato's view that memory invokes the past event as presence of absence and Aristotle's statement that "all memory is of the past."[32] In moving images and film narration the problem is further complicated by the multiple claim of photographic inscription as material support, testimony, and the possibility of playing and replaying the recording of a past event. Moreover, the materiality of the vestige may itself be subject to representation. Sometimes the camera zooms into the scars and vestiges of the past, making them visible in landscapes, buildings, or a human face. In this sense the photographic marker of time takes on a physical, spatial dimension. Lanzmann explored this possibility, and he rejected the photograph in favor of cinematographic strategies to map the sites of former Nazi camps and the faces, gestures, and testimonies of survivors and former guards. Regardless of the deliberate exclusion of archival footage, *Shoah* accomplishes a veritable *mise en scène* of the *tupos:* ruins, old train rails, and a remarkable framing of facial expressions and body language.[33] The mode of filming and recording is also marked by the historical moment in which the film was made. Hence, the typical *cinéma vérité* mode of Shoah represents another trace of time.

In this context it is important to consider audiovisual strategies to map the voids and gaps of history, in order to evoke the painful loss of memories or even the inability to remember. As exemplified by Laura U. Marks, absent images (video black or black leader) are common in intercultural film and video where private history and public memory fuse in attempts to represent events repressed by official history or by the traumatic experience of the social actors.[34] Hence, the trace is not necessarily operating on the level of images and physical objects but in fragmentary signs of faces, sounds, and reconstructed views, which are simultaneously linked to and separated from the past.

Aside from the filmic unveiling of vestiges in a landscape, the impact of the *trace of the trace* is perhaps even more intense, or at least more visually poignant, when the human body is in focus. Examples are provided in *Shoah* and *Night and Fog* through the bodily appearance and facial expressions of victims in the former and through the stark references to physical violence in the latter. In *Night and Fog* the photographic record of the Holocaust shows terrifying vestiges of affected bodies, such as a mountain of eyeglasses, cut hair, and the marks made by nails on the ceiling of a gas chamber. These vestiges are imprints that provoke our imagination of suffering, giving brute evidence of violence and endless terror. Although *Night and Fog* is a film that critically posits the cinematic reinvention of the past, it is hard to overlook the persuasive impact of inscribed evidence, of historical time.[35]

On the screen, shots of physical wounds and dead people directly appear as a kind of marked landscape. In this case the camera scrutinizes the trace of an irrevocable fact: bruises that indicate violence; the fixed stare of somebody whose memory is blocked by traumatic experience; the gruesome, disembodied remains of war victims; or just the delicate net of wrinkles in a face that indicates the inevitable linearity of biological time.

The literal framing of the imprint is perhaps most striking in cases where we actually see a body being affected, that is, when the indexical sign coincides with a representation in approximate real time. Pornographic representation is most commonly associated with this effect of indexicality because the fragmented body landscape of insistent close-ups suggests the unfolding of an event in real time. A related example, which nevertheless works out differently as an instant shock effect, would be the unexpected violence of a body being hurt in front of the camera. This is the case with Harun Farocki's ingenious approach to the image-imprint in *Nicht löschbares Feuer* ("Inextinguishable Fire," Germany, 1969). Sitting at a table, Farocki quotes the statement of Thai Bihn Dahn, a Vietnamese man who experienced a napalm attack on his village in 1966. The following statement precedes an allegoric visualization of napalm burns:

> How can we show you napalm in action? How can we show you the injuries caused by napalm? If we show you a picture of napalm injuries, you will close your eyes. First you will close your eyes to the pictures, then you will close your eyes to their memory, then you will close your eyes to the facts, and then you will close your eyes to the entire context. If we show you a person with napalm injuries, we will hurt your feelings. If we hurt your feelings, you'll feel as if we'd tried napalm out on you, at your expense. We can give you only a hint of an idea of how napalm works.

The camera closes in on Harun Farocki's wrist, where he burns himself with a cigarette. In Jill Godmilow's remake *What Farocki Taught* (USA, 1998), which is presented as a copy of Farocki's film, it is striking to note how the filming of the cigarette burn is reframed—the framing of the imprint is once more doubled.

In film, aspects of recording, reframing, and narration posit the image-imprint as a dramatically refracted sign, disclosing its existential impact as presence of the past. In the context of reframed vestiges and marks in landscapes and faces, the trace constitutes a recurrent iconography of *pastness,* which often fuses with violence and death. Yet the affective impact of the trace goes beyond the notion of visual imprint. Sound plays a pivotal role, and as a sign of affection and memory in documentary, the trace is not necessarily dependent on photographic representation.

Part II. Experimental Figures of Time

[4] *The Interval and Pulse Beat of Rhythm*

In *Introduction* I suggested that rhythm represents a problem of special importance for the conception of the moving image as screen event. Rhythm stands out as a classical problem in aesthetic theory and most notably in relation to the temporal arts of music, dance, and theater, where it represents an element of importance for the overall expressive structure. Also, rhythm plays a decisive role in the audience's affective response to the performance. In moving images and film narration a literal aspect of *time measurement* is added by the immanent relation between photogram and cinegram and by the metric composition of montage and framing. The cinematic interval depends on both the construction of sound-image rhythm and the viewer's sensory judgment of a temporal dimension. According to the suggested framework of this book the time of the image depends on the perceived "brackets" (Goffman) or "revelatory number" (Janicaud) caused by framing, editing, and other devices. In film, rhythm provides an unfixed location of meaning that appeals to, and may have a more or less dynamic effect on, the viewer.

Opposing any perspective based on transcendental phenomenology, the experimental cinema of the 1920s embraced different practices that unified in a fascination with photographic representation, perception, and the expressive and imaginary qualities of the world mediated and transformed in moving images. The creative exploration of the optics and rhythms of cinema nonetheless applies to the notions of aesthetic phenomenology that were introduced in Part I and which may still provide insights into the formal and sensory work of space and time in moving images.

The scholarly discourse on cinema, sense perception, and visualized rhythm has been biased toward a narrow canon of avant-garde films, neglecting the related experiments of cinematic practices and screen events beyond art cinema. The scholarly discourse has almost entirely omitted the genre of science film, and few scholars have associated the aesthetic pleasure of moving images or the imaginary realm of cinema with this field of experimental filmmaking. Owing to the epistemological ambition of educational cinema, science film represents a film culture considered incompatible with the production and reception of film as art. Science film, however, represents a field in which film experiments challenge the limits of natural perception and whose amateur innovations have greatly contributed to the history of experimental cinema.

Scientific ideals often influenced the recurrent use of the musical analogy in film criticism and avant-garde manifestos of the 1920s, and science filmmakers elaborated techniques to visualize processes invisible to the human eye. These experiments often resulted in imaginary realms beyond natural perception and closely aligned with those of avant-garde cinema.

▶
Experimental Approaches to Time Measurement

In film history there are many examples that illuminate the mutual influences between experimental and documentary cinema. Obviously, experimental cinema applies not only to canonized avant-garde films but also to the elaboration of film form within a range of film cultures, including amateur, ethnographic, and science film. Aside from the accomplishment of avant-garde movements and individual film artists, transgression and exchange between experimental practices of this era have received less attention. In the work of Dutch amateur filmmaker J. C. Mol it is striking how avant-garde ideals met with scientific elaborations of the film image and that aesthetic experience also applied to the screenings of science film.

In the beginning of the 1920s J. C. Mol started to experiment with cinematography as a tool for scientific inquiry. His experiments resulted in a body of work representing a remarkable hybrid example with overlapping aspects of amateur, science, educational, industrial, and avant-garde film. In 1924 Mol initiated the Bureau voor Wetenschappelijke Kinematografie ("The Bureau for Scientific Cinematography") in Bloemendaal outside Haarlem. He gave hundreds of lectures in classes of adult education. Although Mol was a self-taught scientist and filmmaker, his experiments in microcinematography made him a pioneer of this technique.[1] Numerous contributions to journals of amateur photography and film testify to Mol's fascination with visual technologies and camera perception.[2] Films such as *Ontlukeinele bloemen* (*Opening Flower*, J. C. Mol, The Netherlands, 1928) and *Van bol tot bloem* (*From*

Bulb to Flower, J. C. Mol, The Netherlands, 1931) exemplify the aesthetic impulse that may be found even in the wryest of science films. Moreover, manipulated views of flowers sprouting and dying offer a filmic counterpart to today's digital morphing where the natural event has been temporally compressed to perform as a comprehensive yet uncanny transformation.

Uit het rijk der kristallen (From the Domain of Crystals, J. C. Mol, The Netherlands, 1928) shows chemical substances transformed into sparkling crystals. In 1929, at the invitation of Abel Gance, this film was shown at an avant-garde theatre in Paris where it was referred to as the latest craze of *cinéma pur.* This screening also anointed Mol a celebrated member of the Dutch Film League. The unlikely event of an amateur filmmaker and science lecturer entering the highbrow context of avant-garde art reminds us that the usual distinction between art cinema and science film did not apply to the experimental cinema of the 1920s.

The history of experimental film has often been subsumed under or equated with the history of avant-garde cinema, that is, "the artists in each period have been reified as knights of film art, fighting heroically, individually, only loosely bound together in a movement at the level of distribution, exhibition, and reception."[3] The present account of Mol's work—representing a single corpus of films achieved outside a commercial film industry—would seem to support this way of thinking. But for Mol, cinema was primarily a scientific and pedagogical means of research and education. His film experiments grew out of an amateur's will to master technology and control production and screening.[4]

Reviewing Mol's films, we nevertheless find it striking how his experiments parallel avant-garde projects of that era. Both science film and art cinema provided conceptual inquiries into camera optics and the space-time malleability of moving images. Despite obvious differences a comparison of Mol's rhythmic rendering of microcinematographic views with, for example, Walter Ruttman's work on absolute film and the city symphony reveals a shared fascination with cinematic perception. In Walter Benjamin's opinion the mimetic impulse of filmic representation gives way to *a new tactility,* that is, the desire to reproduce movement is conflated with the desire to document the cinematic movement itself.[5] The appreciation of nature represented and transformed by cinematic perception is typical of experimental cinema in the early twentieth century, including the experiments of amateur filmmakers inquiring into the materiality and malleability of the moving image. The experimental approach to cinematic vision points to the paradoxical coexistence of a perception that presents itself as becoming perception or a vision beyond the parameters of binocular vision. As Rosalind E. Krauss suggests, the modernist enthusiasm with the photograph consisted in the belief in its vision as "an extraordinary extension of normal vision, one that supplements the deficiencies of the naked eye."[6]

In Jan-Christopher Horak's outline of the history of experimental cinema, Mol is paired with the French surrealist filmmaker and marine biologist Jean Painlevé.[7] Aside from their shared interest in science and cinematography, an affinity for film style is also apparent. Some of Mol's films reveal a playful reflexivity reminiscent of Painlevé's humorous narratives, although the surrealist's celebration of marine animals or bloodsucking bats surpasses the educational intent of Mol's films and public lectures. Mol's science cinema was foremost a pedagogical tool for the lecture hall and a means to carefully document and measure events and objects in nature.

Although Mol did not explicitly refer to the avant-garde writings and manifestos of his time, it is striking how the notions of visualized rhythm and the transformation of the real in moving images represent common denominators between avant-garde cinema and science film.

▶

Visualized Rhythm and the Promise of a New Art

The fascination with the moving image as rhythm and sensory pulse beat is apparent in many manifestos, essays, and film critiques. The musical analogy appears early in the history of French film criticism, but a more outspoken theoretical application is notable during the second half of the 1920s. For example, the composer and film critic Émile Vuillermoz was interested in achieving and perceiving cinematographic music. He wrote that cinema resembles music in that cinema is an art form in which a line of thought is mediated by leading motifs, changes in tempo, and rhythmic highlights. Similarly, a filmmaker must find a suitable phrasing, a significant rhythm: "He [the filmmaker] must calculate the length of his sequences and know what length he may give to his arabesque without risking what might be called the viewers tonal sensation of his composition."[8] Vuillermoz related the cinematic possibilities of visualized rhythm to the fact that film and music offer a unity in time and space in addition to containing temporal extension. Vuillermoz also stressed that the experiences of film and music depend on similar physiological reactions and that "after all, the optical nerve and the auditory nerve have the same faculties of vibration."[9]

Similar ideas reverberate in the theory and cinema of Germaine Dulac, who stands out as one of the most passionate advocates of a *symphonic cinema*. In her texts from 1925 and onward she often stressed cinema's rhythmic structuring of durational units. These ideas were formalized in her attempts in 1927–1929 to cinematographically interpret music by Debussy and Chopin: *Disque 927, Arabesque,* and *Thèmes et variation.* In an article from 1927 she emphasized the cinematic counterpart to the affective sensation of musical rhythm:

> Visual rhythm in correspondence with musical rhythm makes the cinematographic movement to stage the signification and force of movement in general. This is a qualitative fact of harmonic duration that has to be transformed into, if I dare to describe it as such, sonorities constituted from the emotions contained within the image itself. In cinematographic measurement, visual rhythms correspond to musical rhythms (which lend weight and meaning to general movement). These visual acts, as valuable as the lengthy harmonic passages, transform themselves, I dare say, from the sounds derived from the emotions found within the image itself.[10]

Not only was film claimed to resemble the transcendent and affective impact of musical sound, but it also offered the composed structure of a symphony.

In 1919 filmmaker and critic Albert Guyot offered some suggestions for elaborating a cinematic measure. Mathematics was, according to Guyot, the common trait of music and cinema.[11] Representing two modes of temporal art, film and music both depend on elaborated methods of measurement, he would argue, and consequently, a composer as well as a filmmaker is "a man who knows how to count. When he does not count, he measures. Just as in music, mathematical precision is at the core of cinema."[12]

In relation to the filmic experiments of J. C. Mol it is striking how this mathematical ideal echoes some years later in the context of the Dutch Film League. The Amsterdam *Filmliga* manifesto called for a cinema in opposition to commercial film culture, arguing that only in one of a hundred occasions "do we see *film*. Usually we see nothing but *cinema,* crowds, the commercial regime, America, kitsch."[13] To counter the threat to *real film,* the manifesto promised a series of public screenings and, therefore, the possibility of a new culture dedicated to *film:* "Saturdays during the coming season of 1927–1928, about 12 matinees will be shown in Amsterdam, among which we will show one important new film every week to a genuinely artistic-minded audience."[14]

Aside from the expected avant-garde rejection of mainstream cinema the manifesto also sought international support of experimental film. The first issue of *Orgaan der Nederlandsche Filmliga,* published in September 1927, presented two foreign correspondents: Mannus Franken, from Paris, and Simon Koster, from Berlin, who were to report all screenings and other film events of interest to the *Filmliga*. This issue, edited by Menno Ter Braak, Joris Ivens, L. J. Jordaan, Henrik Scholte, and Constant van Wessem, promoted a fresh approach to film critique, film and audience, and film technique. For example, regarding accepted ideas about *film realism,* El. D. De Roos emphasized that film experience should go beyond notions of realism, reality, or unreality and acknowledge a new, formal conceptualization of *filmic reality (film realiteit)*.[15] This materialist celebration of the moving image is further expressed in Ivens's essay, "Film Technique. Notes on the Succession of Film Images."[16] This short piece on the constructed entity of tempo and the use of rhythm and duration stresses the metric and *composed* texture of absolute film. Ivens praises the experiments of absolute film for conceptualizing the organization of the moving image into "an almost mathematical movement" ("bijna mathematische gang") and for extending the formal possibilities of filmic inscription and projection.[17] Rather than differentiating art from science, the Dutch Film League actively questioned this dichotomy.

Let us recall the literal signification that time measurement obtains in the avant-garde cinema of this era. Attempted visualizations of sensory perception and the subconscious relate with the common appropriation of musical terms in film criticism and theoretical notes of this era. Theorists and filmmakers, however, acknowledged the technology and experience of *cinematic perception,* which is different from phenomenology and Husserl's analysis of the subject's apperception of a material world, the *sensa* of the thing in itself. With cinematic perception we move into a fascination with a modern technology, which, similar to photography, complicated and transformed the relation between natural perception and representation in visual art.

Film was primarily recognized as a time-based medium, dependent on the artistic elaboration of rhythm and tempo. This emphasis on the constructed meter of film involves the recognition of pulse, duration, and change and of film as an expression closely affiliated with the human nervous system—heartbeats as well as the quick change of mental life in dreams and hallucinations. Aside from the futurist visions of human and machine, and surrealist projects to map the subconscious, these assumptions and experiments posit film in terms of measure and interval— a kinetic event that requires the viewer's sensory reception. Put differently, cinema was the great promise of a visual poetry, with a direct appeal to the viewer's imagination and desire. Just like music the ultimate cinematic expression would directly interact with the viewer's emotions.

The suggested kinship between music and film was rooted in the idea of *pure visual rhythm*. As artists and theorists celebrated the expressive potentiality of film, strategies were outlined to translate auditory rhythm into a cinematic choreography. The discourse of rhythm includes various *Gesamtkunstwerk* such as *Parade* (France, 1917), a ballet by, among others, Erik Satie and Guillaume Apollinaire. Also, in the debut of the Dada movement in Paris, led by Tristan Tzara, performances such as *Vaseline symphonique* (1920) offered theatrical shock effects through conceptual explorations of the spatiality of vocal rhythms.[18]

Subsequently, within French and German experimental cinema between 1921 and 1925 some films were explicitly aimed at a visualization of musical rhythm, such as *Ballet mécanique* (Férdinand Léger, Man Ray, and Dudley Murphy, France, 1924), *Entr'acte* (Réné Clair, France, 1923), and *Cinq minutes de cinéma pur* (*Five Minutes of Pure Cinema*, Henri Chomette, 1925, France). Hans Richter, Walter Ruttman, and Viking Eggeling offered graphic approaches to rhythm in *Rhythmus 21,23,25* (Hans Richter, Germany, 1921–1925), *Opus I–IV* (Hans Richter, Germany, 1921–1924), *Horisontell-vertikal orkester* (Viking Eggeling, Germany, 1919), *Diagonalsymfonin* (*Diagonal Symphony,* Eggeling, Germany, 1924), and *Opus II–IV* (Walter Ruttman, Germany, 1926).

In addition, the emphasis on rhythm and tempo is of course pivotal in the work of Sergei Eisenstein and Dziga Vertov. One of the crucial notions of Eisenstein's montage theory, the *monistic ensemble,* references the samisen music of Japanese Kabuki theatre. This music is characterized by its organization of multiple auditory elements to match the dynamic coexistence of auditory and visual levels in cinema. Hence, rhythm is a tool to control the creation of meaning as well as the affective response of the audience, and the ideal realization of tempo will transfer the images in discrete units of an overall discourse. The successful interaction of the pulse beat of the film with that of the viewer—the experience of rhythm and the becoming of a significant whole—is an experiential dimension that Eisenstein elaborated in theory and in practice.[19]

Opposing Eisenstein's ideal of discrete units of rhythm is Vertov's concept of *interval*. This concept refers to the intersection between film shots, a differentiated zone of becoming through which the film's images in constant change provide a significant meter: "The school of kino-eye calls for construction of the film-object upon 'intervals,' that is, upon the movement between shots, upon the visual correlation of shots with one another, upon transitions from one visual stimulus to another."[20] In *Chelovek s kino-apparatom* (*Man with the Movie Camera,* Dziga Vertov, USSR, 1929), dissolves, split-screen devices, and distorted perspectives orchestrate the cinematic components, and rhythm becomes the conceptual leitmotif: the rhythm of montage, the inscription of rhythms before the camera, the rhythm within the fragmented structure of the frame, and the rhythm within the relation between the fictionalized camera eye and the viewer's experience. Vertov's contribution to the discourse on visualized rhythm can be found in this reflexive concern for the cinematic, which innovatively is accomplished through a playful conceptualization of filmmaking and film experience.[21]

▶
Science Film and the Aesthetics of Abstraction

Driven by an epistemological desire, the science filmmaker offers visual analyses that lead beyond any clear-cut distinction between documentation and abstraction. Regarding the scientific context of production and the educational aim of these representations, this ambivalent status of visual documentation recalls the analytic images of Marey's machines, such as *the myograph,* with which to graphically schematize the phases and speed of muscle contractions; *the odograph,* with which to record the number and frequency of steps; as well as the tool of chronophotography and *the photographic gun.*[22] In Marey's work analogical representation and graphic abstraction fuse in a way similar to the ambivalence of cinematic vision between photographic inscription and the plasticity of moving images.

In Mol's work the educational study of, for example, a mosquito and the spread of malaria, in *Malariafilm* (The Netherlands, 1924), meets with a contemplation of plants and crystals in cinematic transformation. This *aesthetics of abstraction* partly coincides with the flatness, segmentation, and planar division of space that, according to Lisa Cartwright, characterizes experiments with both cubism and microcinematography in the early decades of the twentieth century.[23] Cartwright considers this stylistic similarity between art and science beyond any "personal influence or historical coincidence": rather, this similarity mirrors an overall "cultural response to the epistemological instability of human observation and to the sight of the human body," because representations in the modern era are marked by "the notion of the body-in-process and its streamlined physiological time-image."[24] Mol's approach to cinematic abstraction, however, involves more than the transverse section of a magnified specimen or the depiction of microbes invading the system of a living being.

Mol wrote many articles for amateur journals on photography and film, which provide some insight into his thoughts about filmmaking and science. During the 1920s he published articles in *De Camera, Focus, De Hollandsche Steden, Het Lichtbeeld,* and *Lux-De Camera.* These journals primarily deal with technical details such as the use of different lenses, coloring devices, objectives, and techniques such as how to use soft-focus photography[25] or photograph ice crystals.[26] Between 1926 and 1927 Mol wrote articles that reflected his increased interest in lighting devices and exposure time for photography and film as well as interest in trick-film techniques such as slow motion *(De vertraagde film).*[27]

In this context it is striking how the notion of time measurement both interrelates and differentiates the film experiments of science film and avant-garde cinema. In an earlier section, I referred to avant-garde theories and experiments wherein the cinematic rendering of space and time was associated with the transcendental performance of music: the meter of film invokes subconscious movements of dreams and hallucinations as well as a viewer's physiological, embodied response to moving images. Although the play with fast forward, reverse motion, and slow motion in avant-garde cinema reverberates in some of Mol's films, time measurement takes on a literal meaning in his experiments. The possibility of extending, reversing, and compressing a preordained movement in time and space on the screen becomes a pedagogical device in order to analyze and explain natural processes. The results of these scientific inquiries nevertheless are cinematic abstractions that stress the moving image as plastic form.

By 1923 Mol referred to the *crucial position* of cinematography in modern society and, more specifically, to the possibilities of its application in science: "cinematography has already, and with promising results, served in the fields of technology and science."[28] In his article entitled "A Filmic Practice," Mol described the new Ernemann camera. This German invention by Hans Lehmann—a camera capable of shooting five hundred frames per second—is better known as *Zeitlupe* (Dutch, *tijdloupe*). In his successive attempts to refine the cinematic depiction of plants growing in real time, Mol used this technique. Describing the *tijdloupe* for the readers of *Focus,* Mol had great hopes for its scientific use and expressed his fascination with the screening of processes invisible to the human eye: "It is hard to foresee what scientific services are to be expected from the tijdloupe."[29] Although the principle of this space-time abstraction is simple, he remarked that its fascination lay in how cinematography makes it possible to screen this altered form.

Mol's combined passion for nature, camera technology, and the optics of cinema resembles that of Jean Painlevé. Mol found inspiration in Painlevé's films, which he praised for their level of abstraction. Yet he disliked the irony and playful personification in Painlevé's documentation of marine life.[30] In 1930 Painlevé founded the Association for Photographic and Cinematic Documentation in Science and developed techniques to shoot footage underwater. Moreover, he considered himself a popular film-maker too, and films such as *L'Hippocampe* (*The Seahorse,* France, 1934) were celebrated as surrealist film art.[31] Different from the ironic tone of Painlevé's films (which are at once science films and mock documentaries), Mol's projects of documentation and measurement are more closely affiliated with traditional educational film. Where Painlevé showed an ironic distance to the truth claim of science cinema, Mol remained obsessed with the microcosms of plants and minerals.[32]

Despite this suspicion of a reframing and allegorization of the natural world, many of Mol's films express a desire of the gaze and a poetic contemplation that lead beyond the putative transparency of educational cinema. These, together with a dose of humor, are apparent in *De tijd en de film* (*Time and the Film,* The Netherlands, 1928)—one of Mol's more conceptual approaches to the time of the film image. The first part of the film offers a veritable screen lecture on cinematic time.[33] A military parade shot in normal speed illustrates the *natural movement*. An intertitle explains:

> A film consists of a series of thousands of little pictures. If when projected the same number of pictures is shown on the screen each second, as the number of pictures which was taken in a second, we see *the natural movement* on the screen.... If we take the pictures more quickly, however, the movements on the screen are retarded; it looks as if time is going more slowly.[34]

An orchestra parades in slow motion, followed by a sprint and a horse and carriage in equally slowed tempo. "In the same way, time can also be accelerated," the text proceeds, and on the screen appear the comic gestures of bricklayers and construction workers in speeded-up action. The most spectacular illustration is shown after the intertitle: "One can even make time go back: then the movements are reversed." Amsterdam bikers go backward, cars and people are screened in reversed street views, the sport of hurdles gains in drama through the uncanny perception of remote action, and, finally, a little boy "builds" a banana by pulling small bites from his mouth until the fruit is rewrapped in its peel.

This illustration of the manipulated space-time of cinema is followed by a study of plants and opening flowers. "Everything in nature accelerates," Mol suggests, pondering on the beauty of flowers "accelerated tens of thousands of times." Then follows the metamorphosis of the chrysanthemum, star of Bethlehem, campanula, carnation, and passionflower. The organic and, to our eye, static life forms of the flowers are here animated and visualized in captivating sequences of manipulated space-time.

In the early 1930s Mol elaborated his technique of filming the growing and fading of plants. These attempts to represent natural processes reflect the science filmmaker's experimentation with time measurement and the visualization of rhythm. In order not to disturb their natural rhythm, Mol set the plants in a room flooded with daylight. A clock controlled the coordination of curtains and camera flashes, and one frame was exposed every quarter-hour. Hence, during twenty-four hours, only four to six seconds of film were shot.[35]

The endless variation of flowering and fading plants, which during the 1930s more or less dominated the production of Mol's film company Multifilm, testifies to a peculiar obsession with cinematic techniques to measure the life of plants. *From Bulb to Flower* (The Netherlands, 1931) was ordered by Haarlem tulip cultivators' organization, Het Centraal Bloembollencomité. It represents the spectacular mass cultivation and harvest of tulips and hyacinths. Variations of the *tijdloupe* motif are combined with more typical industry film shots of men and women in the fields sorting and packing bulbs and flowers.

Some of the trick-filmed sequences of *From Bulb to Flower* are recycled in *Het Wonder der Bloemen* (*The Miracle of Flowers,* J. C. Mol, The Netherlands, 1935). These two films approach cinema as a device measuring natural processes (the flowers) and artificial processes (industrial production and film production, respectively). In contrast to the tourist views and commercial publicity of *From Bulb to Flower, The Miracle of Flowers* offers a celebration of the flowering plant as screen attraction. Sequences of opening and closing flowers are interrupted by images of Mol as he (in true Vertov style) manipulates the exposure time or looks at film rushes. A 1935 version of *Time and the Film,* this film reveals the secrets of temporal manipulation and the accomplishment of film production.

With these examples in mind we see how the pedagogical purpose of educational film makes room for a pure fascination with enchanted close-ups of flowers opening in approximate real time. The scientist's gaze, marked by analytical distance and clinical scrutiny, seems to be replaced by a delight in buds, petals, stalks, and pistils in vital motion. Moreover, these screen attractions seem to be loaded with erotic overtures, welcoming a Freudian interpretation and reminding us that the symbolic power of *the figural* operates even in the screen cultures most differentiated from art film.[36]

Ontlukeinele bloemen/Opening Flower. Collection Nederlands Filmmuseum.

Ontlukeinele bloemen/Opening Flower. Collection Nederlands Filmmuseum.

This is not to suggest that Mol's representation of flowers makes irrelevant or contradicts the educational purpose of explaining and depicting botanic life. Rather, the close view of "climbers seeking support," or the flowers of Eremurus that "appear each at the right time and in the right place," equally appeals to the desire for knowledge and the aesthetic pleasure of the moving image as plastic form. Watching a flower of Eremurus sprout in a manipulated tempo is a fascinating study of metaphysical order and uncanny regularity that has nothing in common with the static presence of the flower in the field. Hence, in this sense the experimental imagery offers a critique of the film image as mimetic representation and documentation of the real. We may learn something about the world, but the attraction of Mol's films consists in a world rendered unfamiliar and transformed into a screen event.

▶

Invoking the Form and Tempo of Unseen Events

The *tijdloupe* and other devices inspired Mol to carry out abstractions of natural processes and to develop an educational use for the time-image of cinema. In turn, his microscopic views of crystals resulted in a structural minimalism, which, even compared with the work of Walter Ruttman and Hans Richter, was more radical in questioning the mimetic strive of cinematic representation. In 1928, with the microcinematographic study *From the Domain of Crystals*, Mol became a celebrated representative of avant-garde cinema. When this film was offered at a special screening organized by Abel Gance at the avant-garde theatre Studio 28 in Paris, the film was shown on an unusually large screen by three projectors running in synch.[37] This was *cinéma pur*, the avant-garde circle concluded, and consequently, the film was also a great success later that year at the seventh *Filmliga* program in Amsterdam where it was presented as *absolute film*. The following comment testifies to the enthusiastic reception of microcinematography as art:

> We are convinced that his [Mol's] experiments are very important in this transitional stage of the Filmliga, for all change that will liberate the cinema from the tyranny of the stars will have to start by studying the simple principles of what is seen, the movements registered by the camera-eye. The difference between "art film" and "science film," however useful otherwise, is not relevant in this case, as we are as yet unclear about where "art" begins and "science" ends.[38]

The film offers a twelve-minute study on crystals, combining a work on abstract rhythm with the transformation of crystals into microcosmic landscapes. Different from the screening of organic life in abstracted real time, this microcinematographic framing of chemicals seems to express the moving image as pulse beat and transformation of a plastic shape. A version of this film with an elaboration of form and color, *Kristallen in kleur* (*Crystals in Color,* The Netherlands, 1928), testifies to an even closer bond with the experiments of Ruttman and other avant-garde filmmakers.

Full attention is given to the cinematic exploration of texture and surface, and intertitles indicate merely the name of the represented substance. Hence, the visual attraction of this film goes beyond documentation in the sense of scientific gaze or epistemological desire. Through microcinematography the magnified crystals become moving, organic patterns. Intertitles introduce "methylal," "boric acid," "calcium chlorate," "sal-ammoniac," "calcium citrate," "soda," "asparagine," "uranium nitrate," "silver nitrate," and "caffeine," but the depicted substances seem provocatively alien to their names. The material referent suggested by, for example, "sal-ammoniac" is subordinate to the purely visual pleasure of abstract form in constant transformation.

From the Domain of Crystals is *absolute* because natural objects are perceived differently and by more than our eyes. Crystals become virtual landscapes that appeal to the imagination and desire of the viewer, and there is also the pleasure of recognizing familiar shapes in abstract forms. Ice crystals in spectacular bloom turn out to be boric acid; wobbling rounds, a school of jellyfish perhaps, are asparagine; and uranium nitrate approximates a desert after having been sculpted by a storm. The radical imaging within this film consists in its rhythmic unfolding of abstract patterns, whereas the pedagogical ambition of this science film is reduced to a mere listing of names. Hence, exploring and exposing the border of the visible world, Mol accomplished a structural minimalism strongly aligned with avant-garde ideals of embodied, visualized rhythm.

To sum up this theoretical and historical contextualization of time measurement and sensory rhythm in the experimental cinema of the 1920s, J. C. Mol's films explore the space-time relationship of moving images beyond notions of realism and narration. The magic of these screen events resides in the play with documentation and abstraction of a profilmic realm. Throughout the history of cinema attempts have been made to frame the frame of the camera eye, in order to measure a body's movement in space, or to reinvent the temporal extension of a natural event into abstract patterns. Such projects of experimental filmmaking, however, are not restricted to the field of avant-garde cinema. We commonly associate experimental cinema with the innovative achievements of individual film artists, whose images represent a programmatic alternative to mainstream

Microcinematographic view of chemical substance. *Uit het rijk der Kristallen/From the Domain of Crystals*. Collection Nederlands Filmmuseum.

cinema and the formal standards set by a commercial film industry. In experimental cinema the craft of filmmaking takes on new meanings and provides conceptual tools (at times, even a theoretical framework) to explore the specific medium of the moving image and related techniques of photographic representation.

Mol's films offer illuminating examples of the practices and conceptions at the core of experimental cinema. His films from the 1920s and early 1930s delimited the historical framework of this case study: the shared concern for visualized rhythm and space-time abstraction in the science film and avant-garde cinema of this era. Mol celebrated the beauty of the natural world, but it would be more correct to say that his films transform the world into spectacular screen events. Similar to the experimental work of Henri Chomette or Walter Ruttman, his films posit the aesthetic experience of cinema as a time-based medium. His pedagogical ambition and experiments to extend camera techniques represent a film culture different from the predominant narrow equation of experimental cinema with avant-garde film. Anonymous illustrations for public lectures, microcinematographic experiments for the laboratory, publicity for chocolate and tulips, industrial films, whimsical examples of slow motion, obsessive views of opening flowers, and microscopic representations of crystals screened in avant-garde theatres form the radically different culture of Mol's film production.

Aside from recognizing aesthetic experience in the context of science film and educational cinema, the example of Mol represents an experimental figure of time that seems illuminating for a reassessment of phenomenological issues in early film theory. Although these experiments contradict any simple analogy between cinema and perception, their inquiries into filmic representation and the possibilities of depicting natural processes bring attention to meanings of documentary time in the sense of screen attraction and embodied experience. Time measurement offers a useful notion in this context where critics brought attention to the constructed meter of film and the instrumental elaboration of cinematic rhythm, to realize a sensory pulse beat, to control image-affect, and to reach the musical ideal of a transmitted interval that directly appeals to the pulse, duration, and change of mental life. From the perspective of science film the avant-garde conceptions and practical elaborations of the musical analogy in the 1920s are strikingly aligned with the literal approach to time measurement in Mol's attempt to film the life span of a plant or to depict crystalline shapes beyond human perception. The musical analogy implied a recognition of science and mathematics: similar to the composer the filmmaker "must know how to count and measure," the French critic Albert Guyot argued, and according to the Dutch *Filmliga* the greatest challenge of film art resides in elaborating strategies to "study the simple principles of what is seen." By choosing a biased perspective on visualized rhythm and time measurement, the theory and practice of experimental cinema in this era—which defied any definite opposition between art and science, fiction and documentary—may provide interesting incentives to ongoing discussions regarding the representations and audiovisual attractions of contemporary screen cultures.

[5]   *Screen Events of Velocity and Duration*

From the perspective of existential phenomenology it is interesting to note how the reflection on film and temporality has been biased toward duration and continuity, at the expense of rhythm, change, and repetition. For example, André Bazin was primarily interested in cinematic duration and the quality of lived time that may result from the tension between change and stasis within a single take. The inheritance of existential phenomenology in the work of Bazin and others includes a romantic recognition of the human gesture—a confidence in cinema to transmit directly the experience traced in faces and gestures. For example, Maurice Merleau-Ponty quoted Roger Leenhardt, who argued that different from the novel, "which offers the ideas of man," the cinema shows gestures and expressions and ways of regarding things and other people who characterize our being in the world. Leenhardt suggested that in cinema there is a specific temporal mode for each gesture, for example, a brief moment for the amused smile, a moderate duration for the indifferent face, and a long duration for sadness and suffering.[1]

Leenhardt's assertion refers to the affective and symbolic function of time measurement in film. The function of tempo is pivotal to any representation in moving images, fiction film and documentary alike, although the timing of a facial expression or a gesture may seem even more important for a film, where the story is subordinate to representing a social space and where actors are encouraged to proceed in their daily activities, to address the camera or to act as if they are oblivious of the film team. Duration represents a temporal dimension in line with the preferred focus on contemplation in aesthetic theory and existential phenomenology. To consciously experience duration in film, however, we have to demarcate and single out the take in the overall montage. In moving images duration represents one aspect of tempo and interval, which, similar to the filmic experimentation with speed, is dependent on rhythm and change.

Images of velocity more seldom seem to have been subject to phenomenological reflections on manipulated tempo and image-affect in cinema. Different from the representation of an everyday gesture in real time, speed presents a more radical challenge to the popular conception of the documentary image as a representation of the real. Whether the effect of acceleration belongs to the filmed event or results from the pace of the camera, the figure of velocity tends to blur the image and tends to make the mediating process as conspicuous as the referent. The authenticity associated with shaky images indicates that a fragmentary film or video recording of, for example, a violent street scene offers speed with a seemingly increased truth claim.

In the history of cinema there have been important attempts to manipulate the tempo of filmed events and locations. In this context urban space has provided a recurrent motif for reflexive inquiries into camera perception and montage. The city has survived as a recurrent motif in the art of moving images, more generally. The symbolic and iconographic overlap between the rapid change of urban space and the cinematic play with stop-motion, acceleration, and deceleration remains a preferred subject of formal experimentation and poetic expression in film and video. Yo Ota's work contains examples of interest for considering velocity as a frame-breaking event. His 16-mm films exemplify the legacy of this format in the history of experimental cinema. In particular, *Incorrect Intermittence* (Yo Ota, Japan, 2000) applies time measurement in a way that parallels the scientific aims of J. C. Mol and the discourse of visualized rhythm discussed in chapter 4.

▶

Urban Space: A Motif of Flux and Transit

Traditionally, the city film provides cinematic inquiries into the visual attractions of unexpected events, spectacular buildings, fancy shop windows, flickering lights, people in motion, and the racket and speed of machines and vehicles.[2] These immanent rhythms of the city have always provided a gratifying motif for experimentation with cinematic temporality. Whether the experiments belong to the canon of city films, they offer images where documenting urban space meets with a self-referential, reflexive inquiry into camera optics and the space-time of moving images. In this sense the experimental cityscape in film explores the creative tension in photography and film between mimetic representation and visual abstraction. For example, Walter Ruttman's work on rhythm and framing in *Berlin die Sinfonie der Großstadt* (Berlin, The Symphony of *a Great City,* Germany, 1927) playfully masks and transforms the content of urban views. In the experimental cityscape the transient movements and chaotic sounds of urban space fuse with the auditory and visual pleasures of the movie screen, so that viewing the film both resembles and radically deviates from that of urban *flânerie.* The experimental cityscape posits *the haptic* of film viewing, streetwalking, and sightseeing as something that cannot be reduced to vision alone but implies the other senses as well.[3] As a filmic motif, urban space permits the perceptual skills of cinema and the flux and transit of the cityscape to find an integrated form. The urban site is at once subject to social representation and formal experimentation, where the latter aspect stresses the abstract feature of camera views and the plastic quality of images pitched to surreal speed.

The double attraction of urban views and cinematic perception already marked the reception of early cinema. As Tom Gunning emphasized, filmmakers and audiences were attracted not only by cinema's true-to-life representations but also by the exhibition of spectacular views, mediated by an apparatus.[4] The first film shows have not surprisingly been described as *big city affairs* with the inherent paradox of people entering the movie theaters "from busy city streets in order to see projected on the screen—busy city streets."[5] Aside from the entertainment in recognizing a specific location, the spectator had the chance to identify a familiar face, or maybe even to recognize herself in the crowd. When the camera moved into the street, city life was not simply documented; it offered the means to explore the cinematic apparatus and to study apperception.[6]

Early moving pictures of urban space, such as *Paris: Champs-Elysées* (Lumières, France, 1899–1900), *New York: Broadway at Union Square* (Lumières, France, 1899–1900), and *Russia: Moscow, rue Tverskaïa* (Lumières, France, 1899–1900), or panorama films like *Panoramic View of the Brooklyn Bridge* (Edison, USA, 1899), *La Tour Eiffel* (Edison, USA, 1900), and *Champs de Mars* (Edison, USA, 1900), depicted random events with a preference for the perceptual thrills of modern architecture. For example, *La Tour Eiffel* shows the visual and vertiginous experience of a mounting view of Paris, shot from the elevator. Similarly, crowded streets were transformed into spectacular impressions of urban space. The aesthetic contingency appears in these images, where the represented cityscape turns into a malleable motif through the play with the frame and the framed, between the duration of a shot and the real time of the filmed event. The early city views usually paid more attention to skyscrapers and bridges than to motifs of flux and rhythm, and movement was evoked in the vertiginous perspective of towers, in the framing of smoke and steam rising from chimneys and vehicles, and in the representation of artificial lighting.

In the early twentieth century, New York was a recurrent motif in the films by Edison and the American Mutoscope & Biograph Company. *Coney Island at Night* (Edwin S. Porter, USA, 1905) exemplifies how a new time-exposure technique made it possible to represent the spectacular illumination at Luna Park and Dreamland by night. Owing to the technical challenge of filming by night, the cityscape depicted in the three-minute film is reduced to the lights decorating each facade, merry-go-round, and Ferris wheel. Together with single patches of light blurred by a sudden movement, the filmic panorama presented a world of illuminated shapes, dots, and dashes. *Demolishing and Building Up the Star Theatre* (Frederick S. Armitage, American Mutoscope & Biograph Company, USA, 1901) is another example that more explicitly relates to the elaborate tempo of city films. The demolition of the theater at 13th Street and Broadway was filmed from a Biograph office across the street, and a time-lapse technique was used to control exposure every four minutes. Different from the strategy used by Mol to present and analyze a development invisible to the human eye, time-lapse was used to mock the historical destruction of a Manhattan theater. Aside from the spectacular demolition the passersby in front of the building also became part of this figure of reversed motion.[7]

In the early city film the aesthetic contingency was produced deliberately and in line with, among others, "the school of straight photography" (Alfred Stieglitz), or other modernist ideals and influences. For example, the intertitles of *Manhatta* (Paul Strand and Charles Sheeler, USA, 1921) are based on the poetry of Walt Whitman: "High growths of iron, slender, strong, splendidly uprising toward clear skies...." Those poetic cadences, according to Jan-Christopher Horak, "seem to counterpoint the film's visual rhythm."[8] Despite its typical display of buildings, bridges, ships, and trains, *Manhatta* produces a play of geometric shapes realized by camera angles and by varying the length of the shots.[9] During the 1920s filmmakers explored the relation between the urban structures, movements, and sound, and the rhythm produced by montage and spatial composition. The dynamic flexibility of cinematic perception was explored in these representations of the metropolis, where the concept of the *city symphony* testifies to the predominant use of the musical analogy in the film criticism of that era. *Berlin* is of special interest because it offered, as Helmut Weihsmann suggests, "an abstract film-essay ... a rhythmic decomposition" of urban space that poetically mirrors the rhythms of city life itself.[10] In these and related examples the documentation of the cityscape combines with aesthetic and expressive aspects of tempo, as the device of altered speed and stop-motion transforms the urban motifs into figures of acceleration and restrained motion. *Berlin* could be compared to the work of rhythm versus duration in *Rain* (*Regen,* Joris Ivens, The Netherlands, 1929) or to the montage technique and tricks of lap dissolves, slow motion, stop-motion, and reverse motion in *Man with the Movie Camera* (*Chelovek s kinoapparatum,* Dziga Vertov, USSR, 1929) where city activities are both represented and abstracted by a similar wit of a "cinematic meta-mechanics."[11]

Aside from the urban motif with its implied and added dimensions of rhythm, the experimental cityscape is characterized by the frequent transgressions of mimetic representation, where the veracity ascribed to photographic representation becomes subordinate to the elaboration of cinematic form. Noel Burch once suggested a distinction between the *Edisonian* and *analytical* fascination with the apparatus of cinema.[12] The first mode refers to cinema in a simulacrum of life, and the second aims at the desire of, among others, Étienne-Jules Marey and the early Lumières to use the camera as a scientific tool with which to map and measure the world. Burch was aware that these positions overlapped in early cinema: the attraction consisted both in the represented event and in the aesthetic experience of the film image.

Then, in what sense do the city films of the 1920s correspond with later examples of the experimental cityscape? In William Uricchio's opinion, the American avant-garde of the 1930s realized urban views that in many respects referred to the European city film. For example, Jay Leyda's *A Bronx Morning* (USA, 1931), Irving Browning's *City of Contrasts* (USA, 1931), and Herman Weinberg's *Autumn Fire* (USA, 1931) incorporate the continental view of the city "as a dynamic physical and social experience rather than simply as a space to be described and documented."[13]

The structural film of the 1960s and 1970s contributed in important ways to the history of experimental cityscape. For example, in *Lost, Lost, Lost* (USA, 1976) Jonas Mekas explores urban space through a subjectivist narrative where the documentary agency of recording was "haunted by the specter of Méliès," by the playful tricks of a visualized and self-referential representation.[14]

The following example from contemporary Japan adds to the history of the experimental cityscape. *Incorrect Intermittence* offers a metacinematic study of tempo and change and a figure of velocity.

▶ ──

Incorrect Intermittence: A Figure of Velocity

Incorrect Intermittence (color, six minutes) consists of three interrelated parts or *scenes* that are unified by three different locations in Tokyo: a railway crossing, a shopping street, and a temple. An electronic soundtrack has been added to the silent 16-mm footage. The thematic arrangement of the urban sites and the clear beginning and ending of the film constitute an open-ended narrative, inviting the viewer to fulfill its meanings. The discontinuity between the shots combines with the overall impression of a rhythmic whole, which is caused by the use of time-lapse technique and altered camera speed. The fact that some sequences are shot in color and some in black and white adds to the pulsating tempo of this film. In Ota's experiment, editing is not the primary tool, yet *Incorrect Intermittence* shows the emphasized rhythm of a montage film. To obtain this paradox of continuity, duration, change, and speed, Ota recorded each location at the interval of hours, and sometimes even days, by using different filters and by alternating the camera speed. The result mirrors aspects of both duration and speed while using real time as an editing tool.

Incorrect Intermittence explores the process of filmic inscription and the plastic and tactile quality of moving images. It represents an inquiry into the abstract space-time of cinema where Ota plays with the physical fact that time is "a function of movement in space."[15] Although similar figures of tempo and change could easily be realized in digital media, Ota's aim is to stage the materiality of 16-mm film. In this sense, the rhythmic rendering of a railway crossing is not only a cinematic manifestation of tempo and speed but a reflection on the image-imprint. The use of 16-mm film signals a critical counterpractice beyond the restraints of commercial film culture, which exemplifies the overlapping structures of visual technologies, the pragmatic status of new media, the reoccurring conceptions of the time-image, and the creative reinvention of old tools in contemporary contexts. In using the familiar city film motif as a point of departure, Ota experiments with the ambivalent border between photographic representation and plastic abstraction and between mechanical production and artistic manufacture that has always characterized the moving picture.

Similar to the Mol example in chapter 4, Yo Ota's work is in tune with the notions of aesthetic phenomenology regarding the interest in images as objects of perception, while suggesting a materialist take on cinematic temporality that would oppose the assertions of transcendental phenomenology. Ota's work corresponds with the experiments of science film, in that his projects often exceed a cinematic deconstruction of natural events by an explicit turn to the concrete, mechanical aspect of camera inscription. The artistic dream of Yo Ota is that of a scientist: "to realize a perfect figure of cinematic temporality," that is, to screen "unexpected appearances of time and space" and "to map differences between natural and artificial vision." Aesthetic and phenomenological issues of image and time take shape in Ota's films, and the titles often refer to his inquiry into the temporal contingency of cinema: *An Intermittent Succession* (1980), *A Relative Time-Table* (1980), *Topological Time* (1981), *5400 Seconds* (1986), *Installation Time* (1989–1990), *Distorted Television* (1997), *Incorrect Continuity* (1999), and *Incorrect Intermittence* (2000). The problems of visualized rhythm and interval are often accounted for through experimentation with speed and repetition. Ota tries to reinvent and to cinematographically stage these issues beyond the practice of montage and narration. Consequently, voluminous aspects of time and space are produced through elaborate manipulation during filming. For example, a change in tempo becomes an event free of any narrative function, and traditional editing techniques are replaced by the use of devices such as filters and time-lapse. Moreover, Ota attempts to highlight the interface between the constructed time of the image and the prescribed time of its screening. In line with the experimental cinema of the 1920s, this attempt is propelled by Mol's fascination with the phenomenology of film viewing.

Incorrect Intermittence represents an example that would contradict the binary opposition between continuity and change that has commonly been ascribed to the experience of, respectively, the long take and montage effects. *Incorrect Intermittence* produces a figure of velocity that involves both images blurred by speed and moments of contemplation. The repeated views where the documented site transforms into an abstract pattern add to the contemplative status of the film.

Because of the alternative mode of filming urban space, *Incorrect Intermittence* results in a rhythmic flow of city views that is in synchronization with the music, which, despite the obvious space-time discontinuity, creates an impression of a continuous sequence. The opening part of the film is composed of images shot from a commuter train and a crossing where the train rushes by—a motif especially dear to the classical city views of the early twentieth century.

The following scene has a variety of shots filmed at the same street, where the pace of passersby is pitched into a surreal speed. There are moments when the image slows down, which allows the viewer to distinguish faces in the crowd or the gait of a person. In a traditional shot of this shopping street in Tokyo, the pitched view or the alternation between footage in color and black and white would provoke a *frame-breaking event,* in Goffman's sense of an event, which radically differs from the viewer's conception of filmic representation. Even in relation to a city symphony from the 1920s, and despite the archaic framing of a train, the minimalist approach of *Incorrect Intermittence* deviates from the thematic organization of urban views and the visual tricks expected from the classical city symphony. In Ota's film the stressed relation between the profilmic space and the manipulation of camera inscription makes the urban space a mere material for cinematic experimentation. When the tempo slows down, the referent—a particular site in Tokyo at a particular moment—materializes on the screen. The title *Incorrect Intermittence* refers to this rare moment of normal screen-time, which introduces a break in the upbeat tempo of the film.

The final minutes of the film show a sanctuary with a Buddha statue surrounded by people who successively approach to pour holy water on the statue and to polish it. In line with the previous sequences, the temple scene is marked by spatial continuity and a rhythmic collage of people and their expressions and gestures. Although the fugitive nature of moving images represents the leitmotif of *Incorrect Intermittence,* a contemplative quality is nonetheless obtained by the mode of altered speed.

Regarding the premises of montage in the 1920s, the film stands out as a hybrid example of discontinuity and fragmentation (in this respect closer to Dziga Vertov, than to Sergei Eisenstein) and the experience of continuity (though in contrast to Bazin's reflection on lived duration). In the attempt to define the visual singularity and expressive possibilities of cinema, the work of rhythm, sound, and color in *Incorrect Intermittence* echoes the radical experiments of earlier city films. Similar to the fugitive movements

Incorrect Intermittence. Courtesy of Yo Ota.

Incorrect Intermittence. Courtesy of Yo Ota.

Incorrect Intermittence. Courtesy of Yo Ota.

of urban space in other city films, the filmic experimentation with speed in *Incorrect Intermittence* highlights the infinitesimal border between the distinguishable images of an urban location and its transformation into plastic views.

Incorrect Intermittence illustrates the work of altered tempo in film. The classical parallel between the outlook from a moving vehicle and the flux of images on the screen brings attention to a view that is both contemplative and blinded by velocity. The play with photographic inscription versus filmic abstraction results in sequences that only momentarily capture the documentary image, in the sense of an image providing a thrill of the real, while satisfying our obsession with realism.

▶
To Screen the Passing of Time

An interesting remark by Henri Bergson concerns the impossibility of measuring duration. When we try to quantify the passing of time, we impose an artificial division of the temporal phenomenon called *duration*. Therefore, duration is unthinkable beyond any acknowledgement of consciousness and lived experience.[16] In cinema the crucial point of intersection is precisely between the space-time of the image and the duration in which both the film and film viewing are embraced. Duration cannot be measured beyond our qualitative judgment of time passing.

Applied to film experience, Martin Heidegger's reference to the "*ek-static* dimension of Time" could be related to the dynamic unfolding of sound-images on the screen: "Zeit ist nicht, sondern zeitigt sich" ("time is only graspable in terms of a process of becoming").[17] The experience of time in moving images depends on this ecstatic dimension. Heidegger's emphasis on time as a process of becoming seems even more apt in cinema, where space-time relations materialize through "raptus," "transport," and "Schwung."[18] Hence, with Heidegger we may conclude that the Aristotelian signification of *ekstase* (physics) and the notion of *ekstatikon*, which denotes "destabilization," "transposition," and "deviation," unveil in the filmic elaboration of rhythm, interval, and speed. As Deleuze emphasized with reference to the still lives in Yasujirō Ozu's films, a static framing, however, may introduce an *ecstatic* change within the unfolding of a film. The temporal extension of a shot may be acknowledged in terms of volume or, as Eisenstein put it, "the experience of unexpected conflicts such as conflicts between an event and its duration."[19]

Similar to the figures of rhythm and tempo provided by the city film, the problem of duration has been a subject of formal and thematic experimentation in cinema. Andy Warhol's pop films represent a radical approach to the screening of time. *Kiss* (USA, 1963; fifty minutes of different couples kissing), *Sleep* (USA, 1963; a six-hour film, composed by six shots, of John Giorno sleeping), *Eat* (USA, 1963; Robert Indiana spends forty-five minutes eating a mushroom), *Blow Job* (USA, 1963; a thirty-five-minute static close-up of a man who is being given a blow job; the orgasm demarcates the end of the film), and *Empire* (USA, 1964; the Empire State Building framed continuously for eight hours) set the standard for the materiality of extended screen-time in later projects of structural film.[20] The conceptualization of duration is even more striking in a short film such as *Mario Banana* (Andy Warhol, USA, 1964). It is a silent 16-mm black-and-white film, showing a front-on shot of the famous drag queen Mario Montez, who is dressed in an elaborate wig, with flickering eyelashes and painted lips. She looks seductively in the camera as she peels, licks, and eats a banana. Throughout this four-minute film the static framing of this consummate allegory posits our voyeurism through an elaborate transgression of the time of the image and the screen-time.

As one of the important forerunners of structural film, Warhol conceptualized the space-time of cinema through radical figures of duration. P. Adams Sitney refers to duration as the temporal gift from Warhol to structural cinema and suggested that "he was the first filmmaker to try to make films which would outlast a viewer's initial state of perception."[21] David James emphasizes the metacinematic dimension of Warhol's films, which refers as much to the phenomenology of spectatorship as to a deconstruction of the mediating process per se: "His is thus a meta-cinema, an inquiry into the mechanisms of the inscription of the individual into the apparatus and into the way such inscription has been historically organized."[22]

Warhol's play with filmic representation and the unfolding of an event in real time posits the materiality of a static camera view, and the exhaustive lack of action or monotone repetition may appear as the radical negation of cinema. His cinematic minimalism, however, theorizes the very foundation of film as a temporal event, exposing the measured time of the screening and the abstract feature of the frame. *Sleep* consists of a static take of a man sleeping that lasts six hours (there are in fact six shots, but the editing is barely noticeable because of the length of these one-hour shots)—a radical example of isochronal representation and a view closely related to the static glance of a surveillance camera. The attentive viewer may observe changes in the sleeper's face that are caused by camera adjustments in combination with discrete muscular spasms. The barely discernible transformation creates a tension between the frame and the framed and a continuous play of light and shadow. According to Sitney the final freeze-frame emphasizes the texture of the grain and causes a flattening of the image, which affirms the self-referential aspect of this representation.[23]

Duration in film is not necessarily a matter of *durée*, in the sense of extended screen-time. A poignant impression of time passing may crystallize within a few seconds. It may take on an instant sensitivity as with Chris Marker's sleeper in the photo novel *La Jetée* (France, 1962), where, in cinematic simulation, a montage of stills suddenly bursts into a rare excess of movement. A close-up of the woman asleep is followed by eleven shots that are rhythmically shown in dissolves, as the sound of birds' twittering intensifies. At the eleventh image the photogram reveals itself as cinegram: She opens her eyes, twinkles, and smiles. The viewer is confronted with a figure of lived duration realized during the brief but highly intense course of an *Augenblick*.

The Warhol example offers a point of departure particularly apt for a reconsideration of the phenomenology of duration in moving images, because it defies the transparent representation and the naïve concept of realism that has commonly been associated with the long take. In stressing the artifice of the camera framing and the abstract quality of isochronal representation, Warhol's cinema opposes the assumption that has often been associated with André Bazin and the critique of his work. It, however, would be a mistake to reduce Bazin's reflection on duration to an issue of cinematic realism, because the argument is primarily about Henri Bergson's notion of lived duration and its existential implications for cinema.

A static framing of an event or a gesture indeed stresses the very length of a moment, so that the duration of a shot or the sensation of time passing becomes the primary focus of film experience. With reference to the hunting scene in *Nanook of the North* Bazin brought attention to the cinematic possibility of representing the unfolding of a moment: "the length of the hunt is the very substance of the image."[24] Bazin referred to the experience of waiting for an anticipated event to happen, and he celebrated the possibility of cinema to depict and transfer this universal experience.

Bazin argued that in *Nanook of the North* the length of the waiting period represents *the substance* of the image, but, as Warhol's films exemplify, the extended take may outlast action and defy drama, so that the very length of the shot becomes the primary attraction. The static camera or the long take represents devices with which to alter the ambience and meaning of the filmed event. Strategies to frame the passing of time and the interval of specific gestures add to the overall rhythm of the film and provide an effective means to stress the camera gaze and the manipulated space-time of the moving image. With reference to *Citizen Kane* and Orson Welles's use of depth of focus, Bazin touched upon this abstract quality of cinematic duration: "depth of focus reintroduced ambiguity into the structure of the image."[25] The emphasis on ambiguity brings attention to the possibility of cinematic duration as a frame-breaking event. A temporal thickness with implications both for the narrative and for the viewer's affective response to the screen may be obtained by exaggerating the length of a shot and by emphasizing the frame and the camera gaze. The clock-time gag represents a classical example of isochronal representation in fiction film, where it offers a means to collapse story time into screen-time. In a moment of indecision about a planned robbery in *Bande à part (Band of Outsiders,* Jean-Luc Godard, France, 1964), Franz, Arthur, and Odile have a minute's silence to make up their minds: "A minute's silence can be very long. A real minute can last an eternity." The following minute passes slowly indeed, and the additional gag to remove all sound further emphasizes the length of the scene.[26]

In documentary the poignant event of time passing often seems to result from the assumingly spontaneous performance of the social actor. For example, the drama of the testimonial act owes much to the expected authenticity of the subject and her address to the camera and response to the interviewer off screen. A pause for effect, a frown of irritation, and signs of intimidation or hesitation may, together with camera angles, mode of framing, and editing, result in a significant slice of time. Isochronal representation in documentary may produce a disquieting ambiguity within the image, as when the extended shot and static camera make us aware of our intruding gaze. In this sense the static framing and excessive length of the shot are an intimidating reminder of the social and ethical implications of voyeurism in cinema. *No quarto da Vanda (In Vanda's Room,* Pedro Costa, Portugal, 2000) is an interesting example of the manifestation of this disquieting ambiguity in documentary. *In Vanda's Room* is the result of the year Pedro Costa spent in the poor Fontainhas district outside Lisbon, where he filmed the home and everyday life of Vanda Duarte. In the use of sound and the mode of representing the actors and events as if there was no camera or film team, *In Vanda's Room* is influenced by the stylistic ideals of direct cinema. Different from the enacted spontaneity and crisis structure that characterized the work of many direct cinema filmmakers, *In Vanda's Room,* however, consists of static shots that tend to outlast the action and gestures of Vanda and her friends. Together with the elaborate composition of scenes, Costa's long takes result in a stark documentation of a social environment. The overall rhythm of the film is achieved in order to match symbolically the desolate circle of drug addiction, poverty, and illness that marks the life of Vanda Duarte. Everyday life seems to consist of an endlessly repeated series of events that are as inevitable as predictable and whose dullness is emphasized by the static camera and the excessively extended view: waking up, smoking heroine, trying to find money, buying drugs, smoking with friends, and collapsing.

Similar to Frederick Wiseman's film *Domestic Violence* (USA, 2001), *In Vanda's Room* applies a radical figure of isochronal representation to force the viewer to see and respond to the life and social environment of people and problems that remain disturbingly unseen or neglected in modern society. The almost-three-hour film is a screen event to be endured both physically and morally. *In Vanda's Room* is the opposite of a participatory observation, because the actors never address the camera and the cameraman remains off screen. The film offers a thoroughly artificial framing of a social realm and a camera gaze at once completely passive and committed, which returns the gaze of the viewer in a highly disturbing way. The viewer becomes engaged in an everyday limbo where drugs have become the one and only reason for being. There are scenes of three to five minutes where time simply passes. One of these takes shows Vanda in bed. She is very ill, and the persisting framing of her fits of coughing in a dark, cramped room evokes compassion but a compassion that combines with a sickening awareness of smell and buzzing flies.

In this film, where duration takes on both an existential and a plastic signification, audiovisual representation offers a means to not only document but represent symbolically the pace of life in the shantytown. The ending interferes almost as a chock. A black screen and music provide a moment of reflection: an ending defying any conclusion. The appearance of this final nonimage can be related to the semantic function that Béla Balázs ascribed to the passing of time caused by a similar device, the fade-out:

> The slow darkening of the picture is like the melancholy, slowly softening voice of a narrator and after it a pensive silence. This purely technical effect can produce in us the sadness of farewells and of the impermanence of things. Sometimes its effect is like that of a dash in a written text, sometimes like a row of full stops after a sentence, leaving it open, sometimes like a gesture of leave-taking, a mournful gaze after something that has departed for ever. But at all times it signifies the passing of time.[27]

Balázs's reflection on the fade-out stresses the affective aspect of tempo in film. With cinematic devices such as a decelerated movement, a lingering framing, or the literal enclosure of a fade-out, the ambience of the narrative may be symbolically achieved. As Merleau-Ponty suggested the function of the interval in film is both sensory and signifying.[28] Hence, aside from the tactile manifestation of duration in the Warhol example, these events of temporal extension posit a transgression between the time of the image and the time of film viewing that impinges on our understanding of, and emotional response to, the narrative.

In Vanda's Room offers a radical example of time measurement, indicating that the time-image of documentary may be less about cinematic realism than about the accomplishment of framing, timing, and overall rhythm.

▶
_____

Real-Time Approximation: An Ambiguity within the Image

Real-time approximation may be a suitable term for the frame-breaking effect caused by a take whose length matches the duration of the filmed event. It, however, has less to do with the static camera or the long take as such, than with the relative signification of cinematic duration: the various expressive functions and psychological effects that figures of extended time may have in film. Isochronal representation does not automatically result in a frame-breaking event, although when the viewer is consciously aware of time passing on the screen she may reflect on metafilmic aspects such as the artifice of camera framing, the length of the shot, or film viewing. Isochronal representation may also produce a moment of deceleration in the overall rhythm of the film—a change of tempo with important symbolic and narrative implications.

Scholars have paid attention to the expressive function of this space-time manipulation but have exclusively referred to fiction film and the role of duration in relation to *mise en scène*. An illuminating example is offered in *Jeanne Dielman, 23 quai du Commerce, 1080 Bruxelles* (Chantal Akerman, Belgium, 1975). For representing the dull and lonely life of a mother and part-time prostitute in *Jeanne Dielman,* Akerman stresses the banality of everyday activities by using long takes. The few events that interrupt Jeanne in her housewife duties are reduced to fragmentary glimpses: seeing her son, the reception of a client, or the rare visit of a neighbor. The potentially agonizing impact of a static framing becomes even more poignant when the long take is used to mimic the boredom of everyday routine.

At medium distance the quiescent camera observes the monotonous gesture of Jeanne peeling potatoes at the kitchen table. When the first potato is properly peeled Jeanne puts it in a bowl of water, and the scene does not end until she has finished the third potato. The extended framing makes us attentive to details and microevents of inscribed motion. For instance, it is possible to discover minor changes in Jeanne's face and maybe also changes in the actress Delphine Seyrig's face. The sound of potatoes being peeled emphasizes the repetitive rhythm of the scene.

With reference to *Jeanne Dielman,* François Jost has paid attention to the isochronal representation of a quotidian gesture and, in particular, its symbolic impact. To show somebody who is peeling potatoes is not to transmit the very duration of the act, Jost argues, but a means with which to accomplish a symbolic dimension: the monotony of everyday life.[29] The primary function of the long take is to complete a symbolic figuration, whose purpose is to represent Jeanne's iterative activities and distressful situation. In Jost's opinion the understanding of cinematic time depends on our immediate presumption that somebody wants to say something by means of this temporal manifestation. Aside from the agonizing impact of cramped space provoked by the static camera, the negative experience is provoked by the spectator's heightened awareness of her voyeurism, which makes us wonder "what am I doing here watching what this woman is doing?"[30]

In fiction film isochronal representation may result in a *punctum temporis,* with important implications for symbolic meaning and identification. *Jeanne Dielman* is an illuminating example of how the cinematic manipulation of space-time affects the unfolding of narrative time. *Jeanne Dielman* also shows how *lived time* materializes in the documentation of everyday gestures. Akerman's approach to cinematic duration demands a deepened account from a more explicitly documentary perspective. There are certainly documentary counterparts to the moment of temporal thickness in *Jeanne Dielman. In Vanda's Room* exemplifies a similar ambiguity of the extended take, although in documenting the shantytown the anxiety provoked by the staging of the gaze combines with the compelling referent to a social realm.

In the context of experimental documentary the problem of time measurement becomes more radically linked to a metacinematography of filmic representation and voyeurism, of the thrill of the real and the aesthetic pleasure of photographic abstraction. James Benning's California trilogy stresses the creative and critical potential of duration as a frame-breaking event. *El Valley Centro* (2000), *Los* (2001), and *Sogobi* (2002) are 16-mm films that exemplify the literal sense of time measurement in cinema—each shot is deliberately made to match the metric logic of thirty-five shots per film, each of two minutes and thirty seconds in length. Aside from the arithmetical principle of the takes, which could be compared with the musical and mathematical ideals that recurrently have marked the history of experimental cinema, duration in the qualitative sense of lived time is crucial to Benning's films. In this context lived time is not primarily a matter of recording the gestures of man but to document various traces of social life and capitalist society in a mode that posits the very act of looking at, and responding to, different physical and mental landscapes of contemporary America. Although narrative time is a subordinate issue, the poetic and symbolic potential of cinematic duration in Benning's work should not be overlooked. The filmed motifs have been organized thematically according to the ascribed landscape of each film: rural views from *El Valley Centro*, urban sites in Los Angeles, and images of the Californian wilderness. Each static shot extends into a slice of time demarcated by black frames, and the scenes rarely coincide with a filmed event. Rather, Benning's views posit the motif through a structural play with screen duration and the monocular view of the camera. The image composition is at once the result of mathematical precision and the effect of chance: an insect suddenly passes the camera or, for a moment, the unexpected formation of a cloud represents the major attraction of the image.

El Valley Centro shows images of a desert landscape and rural views in which the presence of the Corcoran State Prison and an industrialized cattle farm stands out as poignant indicators of modern society or grotesque indicators of civilization. Here, time brackets are employed in more than one sense, and the plasticity of a static outlook is counterbalanced by filmed events that have cautiously been chosen to match (or create an internal rhythm within the scope of) the individual shot. For example, one of the takes shows a field bordering a channel. A large ship enters from the right, seemingly making its way through the fields. A smaller boat appears from the other side, and they pass each other in the middle of the frame. The view is cut at the moment when the stern of the ship disappears off frame.

In *El Valley Centro* the long take offers a metacinematic gesture that critically conceptualizes the relation between the filmic recording of a landscape or an event and the mediating process through which reality is transformed. In this context the effect of real-time approximation is less bound to narrative and symbolic functions than to a mode of critical contemplation, where the viewer is invited to reflect upon the different meanings and associations that the filmed motif may invoke, and to engage in this perceptual play with camera optics and the time-based quality of the film image.

Despite the important differences and filmic contexts of *Sleep, In Vanda's Room, Jeanne Dielman,* and *El Valley Centro,* the play with real time and the long take in these examples results in a frame-breaking event that emphasizes the passing of time as well as film viewing. To understand the psychological implications of this ambiguity within the image, we need to examine a short essay by Jean-François Lyotard that is closely related to the phenomenology of lived time in classical film theory. Here, the existential aspect of time experience in moving images meets with a psychoanalytical account of how the static view may correspond with the voyeuristic attempt of cinema, and how it may move, please, disturb, or upset the viewer.

In "L'acinéma" Lyotard addresses the noncinematic aspects through the two extremes of the graphic art of movement: the immobilizing motion *(la motion immobilisante)* and the immobilized mobilization *(la mobilisation immobilisée)*.[31] In Lyotard's opinion the arts of representation generally provide two variants of these extremes: one of immobility, *tableau vivant,* and one of agitation, lyrical abstraction.[32] To discuss the implied voyeurism of *tableau vivant,* Lyotard turns to its most libidinal variant: the pornographic posing where a girl, framed in objectified distance, presents the pose demanded by a client. Because of the artificial pose the girl becomes part of a framed image whose static posture may trigger agitation. During the peep show the asymmetric relation between the girl and the customer is manifest in the fact that she has to perform the requested pose, to be exposed to his desire and gaze, whereas he is safely invisible in the dark or behind a screen.

Hence, the immobilizing motion evokes the voyeuristic gaze, which is immanent to photographic and filmic representation in the large. For Lyotard *tableau vivant* is the metaphor of representation as an erotic object, whereas *the abstraction* represents the possibility of critical reflection. He stresses the potentiality of the latter to immobilize the structural support instead of the referent/model of the image. The cinematic counterpart to abstraction would then reverse the relationship between the seer and the seen, making the viewer the object of the gaze.[33] The formal and ethical problem of the gaze and the time of the framing in documentary demand a closer consideration. Also, Lyotard's notion of *tableau vivant* applies to the difference indicated by the examples above between isochronal representation in the large and isochronal representation as an *ek-static* dimension of time that invokes a negative experience (Goffman) or an ambiguity within the image (Bazin).

Akerman's constant explorations and transgressions of the border between fiction film and documentary offer examples that are of special interest for reassessing image and time. Similar to James Benning's experimental landscapes, Akerman's metacinematography posits the problems of narrative reality and filmic representation and adds a recurrent conceptualization of film viewing and the voyeuristic pleasure of cinema. *Je, tu, il, elle* offers a poignant example that illuminates the stark impact of cinematic duration, while collapsing in an interesting way Lyotard's distinction between the *tableau vivant* and the critical potential of *abstraction*. Although the entire film is composed of long takes, the love scene at the end of the film provides a final, frame-breaking questioning of narrative reality. The sequence covers nine minutes and consists of only three shots. During the first five minutes the static camera is placed beside the bed, recording the two women making love. In the following one-minute shot they are filmed from another angle showing only their heads as they kiss. Another three-minute shot offers a full view of the lovers. The seemingly endless documentation of their lovemaking breaks with every convention of narrative film. Apart from the duration of the sequence and the lack of music or other additional sounds, the scene differs both from the disembodied close views of pornographic film and from the aesthetics of traditional love scenes. Concerning this unabashed view of lovemaking the taboo of lesbian love and the fact that "Julie" is played by Chantal Akerman also add to the frame-breaking event. Hence, the diegetic time of the narrative becomes subordinate to this ecstatic event in real time, which stresses the relation between the camera and the viewer's gaze: "the screen reveals the 'vulgarity of an attitude, ... awkwardness of a gesture, ... shame of a look.' "[34]

▶ ───

Duration and the Returned Gaze in *From the East*

If the staging of ecstatic moments in *Je, tu, il, elle* brings attention to the voyeuristic pleasure of cinema and the potential Peeping Tom of any film viewer, *D'est* (*From the East*, Belgium, 1993) reinvests in the minimalism of structural cinema to question the ethnographic gaze of documentary film.[35] Similar to *El Valley Centro*, *From the East* combines a metric structure of long takes with the themed documentation of people and places: James Benning offers a collection of views to represent a specific part of California, and Akerman explores the idea of the former East Europe by collecting views from various countries, landscapes, and cities that remain unidentified in the film.

  From the East consists of slow lateral pans and static long takes shot in Germany, Poland, and Russia, which results in a highly poetic and fragmentary representation of the Eastern European situation after the fall of Communism. The lack of interviews and voice-over adds to the

D'est/From the East. Courtesy of Paradise Films, Brussels.

impression of a poetic contemplation. Each shot represents a demarcated scene, many of which are characterized by a fixed camera recording the action of that particular location: people walk into and out of frame and react accidentally to the camera. The shot often tends to outlast the filmed event, and together with slow pans that cause unexpected sensations of spatiality, the staging of time passing supports a recurrent visual theme: lingering long takes of people waiting for the bus, for the train and maybe also for social change.

The camera observes anonymous people and places. From distant camera positions and through shots that posit the frame, the film shows fragments of a specific historical, socioeconomic, and cultural context. The structural aesthetic of *From the East* produces a mode of abstraction that questions the viewer's gaze and the meaning of the image. Two recurrent devices of the film may distinguish a critical approach to *tableau vivant:* (a) the fixed, yet moving frame, which represents public places in surprisingly lengthy shots; and (b) the framings of private rooms that are realized through frontal shots of people posing in their homes. These devices have been applied to create rhythmic juxtapositions, where the sudden beginning and the unpredictable ending of each scene are demarcated through a montage of discontinuous editing.[36]

The first lateral pan appears four minutes into the film, as the camera tracks the iterative path of an old lady assumingly on her daily stroll to the food store. The camera moves steadily beside her as she walks slowly along the street, holding to her red plastic bag. Containers and parked cars occasionally block the insistent camera gaze. There is no added music, and aside from the distant alarm of passing cars and people the cautious footsteps of the old lady dominate the soundscape. This one-minute framing draws attention to the camera and its insistent tracking of a person unaware of the fact that she is being filmed.

Another poignant figure of duration is realized by a steady pan, moving through 360 degrees, which circles twice from a point in the middle of a crowded train station. During these three minutes people almost brush past the camera, stop at seeing it, and look back. Opposing the transit and racket of the train station, the camera slowly tracks toward the hurrying passersby. During a brief moment at the start of the pan the camera lingers on a woman who looks at the camera with a disapproving air. Then, the camera moves off in perfect line with a disabled man, whose walking frame squeaks as he crosses the floor and angrily returns the camera gaze. The camera movement causes a significant transgression between the time of the image and the time of film viewing, transforming the image into a compelling event of seeing and being seen.

The second mode of *tableau vivant* in *From the East* could be described in terms of a mapping of private rooms: people are posing in their apartments, whose intimate and personal sphere simultaneously transcends socioeconomic, cultural, and historical aspects of society in the large. The mode of framing domestic space in filmic tableaus results in a highly stylized motif that partly refuses the implied voyeurism of the immobilizing motion: the frame is anticipated and, again, the extended shot returns the viewer's gaze. At first, the image of a woman sitting at a table in the living room looks like an establishing shot, although the scene is taken out of context and reduced to the documentation of a static gesture: the woman has obviously been instructed to hold her pose for half a minute. A remarkable tension is created between the fixed camera and the various street-sounds that enter through the open window. The woman keeps her static posture throughout the take, her left hand resting beside the coffee cup as she keeps looking at the camera. Another domestic one-minute view shows two teenage girls who sit turned away from each other, one close to a window and the other on a bed. The older girl applies lipstick and the other one, probably her sister, looks in the opposite direction out of frame.

None of the sisters looks at the camera, but their pose is staged nevertheless: one girl seems to be caught in an act of contemplation or daydreaming, while the other is fully occupied with her make-up. A baby's cry breaks into the scene to suggest other family members off screen.

From the East offers a collage of dissociated views and a symbolic depiction of life in the former East Europe. As in Benning's California trilogy, the experience of documentary time is propelled by the highly self-conscious mode of filming a social and historical realm and stressing the constructed space-time of the image. In both examples, the ecstatic event of stasis and change, which is crucial to the cinematic time-image, meets with the historical and existential signification of the trace. Hence, the *punctum temporis* is achieved by a figure of duration that is marked by the presence of somebody's home, family situation, and social class. The particular mode of framing anonymous locations and individuals in *From the East* completes the realization of a poetic whole—an imaginary realm with which to question the shared Western image of the East and of the contemporary situation in the former Eastern block. In this film the extended views stress the attraction of a camera on the street or inside a home, so that the coincidental inscription of gestures, facial expressions, and audiovisual rhythms intervenes and interacts with the symbolic.

As in other projects by Akerman, the time of the gaze is emphasized through the insistent pans and framings of private space. In Lyotard's terms this is a strategy that reverses the relation between the seer and the seen: the passive mode of viewing that is immanent to the classical *tableau vivant* turns into a moment of critical reflection. Aside from the meaning of the returned gaze in this film, it is important not to overlook the symbolic potential of time measurement in documentary. Fragmentary views are shown without explanation, which results in a poetic narrative where people are framed as to harmonize with an overall symbolic image of the East. One may claim that a staged enactment of the subject protects his integrity from exploration. At the same time it could be argued that the social actor becomes reduced to an enigma of pure otherness, because the action is staged and direct address is refused. In this context, however, the important contribution of *From the East* is found in the denial of voice-over and in the structural elaboration of the long take into abstraction and frame-breaking event.

[6] *Telling Signs of Loss: Beginnings of Possible Stories*

> Trace and aura. The trace is the appearance of a nearness,
> however far removed the thing that left it behind may be.
> The aura is the appearance of a distance, however close
> the thing that calls it forth. In the trace, we gain possession
> of the thing; in the aura, it takes possession of us.
> ::   Walter Benjamin, "The Flâneur"

For André Bazin, as for Jean-Paul Sartre, Maurice Merleau-Ponty, and
Roland Barthes, the trace is always a trace *of* something; the image cannot
automatically turn into a sign effect. With reference to *Camera Lucida*
I stressed the semiotic dimension of Barthes's photo-trace, that is, the
importance of extratextual knowledge, the animation through which the
image may turn into a trace of the past. Aside from the possibility of novels
and film narratives to thematically and symbolically explore the relations
between history, memory, and imagination, narration in moving pictures
has the means to explore the temporal and mnemonic contingency of
photographs, images, sounds, and other vestiges.

   In documentary the trace belongs to poetic enactment, but it also
belongs to the selection of source material, testimonies, and narrative
strategies of representing the past, of invoking the events and experiences
of historical events. Problems of image and memory are implied in the
use and reuse of photographs and film images and their implied aura
of the imprint, although in documentary film and video the recorded
image and sound are framed as mnemonic signs. In this context, cinema
stands out as a promising technology of memory, a possible tool with
which to represent historical time and to invoke the experience of past
events through recorded testimonies, compiled archival footage, and the
presentation of other vestiges and imprints of historical importance. Similar
to the historian the documentary filmmaker uses material vestiges of the

past to recreate and narrate the historical event. The implied ambivalence of the trace as passage and mark is related to the historiographic incentive of this documentary quest and the culture of recollection and forgetting that belongs to the image as archive.

Cultural preservation, collective memory, and oblivion are recurrent themes in films where the trace turns into a critical allegory. For example, Chris Marker has recurrently brought attention to the trace as a refracted sign of reframed sequences and image contexts. By stressing the interval between the time of recording and the later act of looking at the footage, Marker comments on the trace as temporal transition and static mark in *Le fond de l'air est rouge* (France, 1977). To a series of images from the Olympic Games held in Munich in 1972 the narrator laconically suggests that "you never know what you are filming." One sequence shows a successful rider dressed in military fashion, the horse making a beautiful leap, and the narrator explains:

> When I filmed the master of the Chilean team I thought that I filmed a horse-man, a rider, but in fact, I had filmed a "Putschist"—the lieutenant Mendoza who was to become the general Mendoza, one of the four leaders of Pinochet's junta … you never know what you actually are filming.[1]

The image remains a subjective framing and therefore is not more eternalized than it is innocent. We cannot foresee the split between the temporal context of inscription/recording and the space-time of our contemplation of it: *You never know what you actually are filming*.

The fact that the meaning of an image often changes over time adds to the possibility of documentary to provide an alternative approach to history and memory, or even to counterbalance the grand narrative of history provided by official records and representations of political events. The critical potential of the trace depends on the awareness of alternative film archives, tapes being erased, images destroyed, and the obvious incompleteness of any historical narrative.

In line with Paul Ricœur's reassessment of the phenomenology of memory, I have demarcated the following discussion into two interrelated aspects of the trace and the trope. The first concerns the existential impact of the trace as presence of absence and as an incentive for both imagination and historical representation. The second aspect deals with film as a historical object and archive. The poetic enactment of the trace brings attention to the social dimension of film as cultural memory, which may imply a critique of existential phenomenology. Hence, the following consideration of the *mise en scène* of the trace refers to the transformation of the image into a mnemonic sign and to Ricœur's notion of emplotment in the more general sense of narrative time and historical representation. In Ricœur's opinion the poetic figuration of historical experience may present the trace as an ethical possibility of narrating history alternatively. Although I share this belief in narrative time to link the experience of the past to the responsibility of the future, my attempt is less to reproduce this idealist position than to discuss its relevance in the theory and practice of documentary. The aura of the trace represents a recurrent theme in documentary film, where it is both affirmed and questioned, because archive memory may imply a reversal movement between the trace and historical time; that is, the trace may be less an imprint of what happened in the past than a constituting sign in the narrative reinvention of history.

▶
Historical Sites and Imaginary Vistas: *Récits d'Ellis Island*

The following reflection appears in the beginning of the film *Récits d'Ellis Island: Histoires d'errance et d'espoir* (Robert Bober and Georges Perec, France 1979), the first part of which is titled *Traces*.

> How to describe? How to tell? How to look?
> By the plain facts of official statistics, or the reassuring hum of anecdotes, endlessly repeated by guides in scout hats?
> Or by the official arrangement of everyday objects that have become museum specimen, rare vestiges, historical objects, and precious images? By the artificial composure of these frozen photographs, once and for all given through the apparent evidence of their black and white? How are we to know this site, to recreate what there was? How should we read these traces?...[2]

Readers familiar with Perec's novels, or other film projects in which he was involved, would easily recognize the formal metalevel of this film where a desire to document and to recollect meets with the insufficiency of language, mirrored by meticulously detailed lists of names, objects, and numbers.[3] In *Récits d'Ellis Island* the reflexive approach to the trace involves a remark on the image as uncanny presence of the past that requires a narrative context to materialize as a significant sign of historical time.

The major purpose of this film is to represent the history of Ellis Island, New York, where the federal bureau of immigration from 1892 strengthened the control of immigrants (the total number of which peaked at sixteen million in 1924).

The film inquires into various meanings of the historical site by zooming into the traces at display in the museum, by reproducing the photographic record of Ellis Island (constructed by the views of family albums and newsreels) and the narrative delivered by a local guide, and by recording the testimonies of immigrants who had once arrived at this transit station and border. Bober and Perec analyze the problem of representing the past and simultaneously interlink a tourist site, a photographic collection, a montage of archival images, and images of their visit to New York and the making of the film. The result mirrors the multiple features of historical time in cinema, as image, memory, archive, museum, and historiography.

On a personal level the filmmakers share an interest in this site and its history because Bober and Perec are both of Jewish descent and the destinies of their ancestors connect them to the problem of exile and Diaspora. The film narrative becomes a complex site of memory work, family history, and an imaginary reconstruction of events, impressions, and experiences at Ellis Island in the early twentieth century.

The material and existential aspects of the trace are illustrated on different levels in the film: through the materiality of collected and reframed photographs, but also through the discursive and symbolic attempt to reconstruct the past, or rather, to unpack the trace as a photographic object, a shared image-memory, as well as a sign of insufficiency and lack. Moreover, the reflexive enactment of historical time is realized through the interrelated levels between Bober's and Perec's travel experience, the poetic contemplation of a site, and the testimony offered by interviewees.

Cinema offers a gratifying medium with which to stress the existential impact of the photograph or film image as a trace of the past. Words may unveil what and who we see represented in the picture, music makes us emotionally attuned to the photographs, and the sound-image display of their grainy texture may offer a virtual feel for the represented site. In the process where the unfolding of moving images is most apparent, the image represents a historical object—a trace in the common sense of a material imprint.

Récits d'Ellis Island adds another level to the filmic *mise en scène* of the trace. Similar to the common practice of inserted photographs and film images in documentary, the visual record of the image is used to legitimize historical facts. There is also an ambition to stress the anonymity of found footage in order to provoke a critical reflection on the construction of history and public memory. The enigmatic trace status of the photograph is further suggested through the enlarged images that become part of the setting.[4] Photographs by Lewis W. Hine from the beginning of the twentieth century have been dramatically enlarged and placed at the actual site of their representation, which stresses the interval between the time in which the image was made and the present time of contemplation. Here, Susan Sontag's characterization of the photograph as "a neat slice of time" is mirrored in the filmic practice of *mise en scène*.[5]

The following example occurs in the beginning of the film when the ferry arrives at Ellis Island. A part of the shore, viewed from the seaside, is gradually revealed by a slow pan from left to right. The narrator tells us about the first immigrant who arrived January 1, 1892—Annie Moore, a fifteen-year-old Irish girl, who originated from the county of Cork and who received a gold coin worth ten dollars as a welcome gift. At this point the continuous camera movement shows the wreck of an old ferry, slowly unveiling it from stem to stern, as the narrator tells the story of this ferry. The camera suddenly reveals an enlarged photograph that poses on the rail of the ferry. The image from 1907, which is shown in a moment of silent contemplation, represents an Italian family of mother, father, and two children, who look out from the same rail and the same boat.

A long take shows the ferry, and Perec refers to the almost sixteen million men, women, and children who passed through Ellis Island, notably between 1892 and 1914. The camera tracks toward the left to reveal another photograph, placed upright on the quayside. It represents a group of immigrants at exactly the same Ellis Island harbor, loaded with belongings on their march from the ferry. Again, silence suggestively stresses the image-imprint, uncannily intensifying the presence of the past, as the camera zooms into the face of a man carrying two heavy bags, while holding his certificate of registration between his teeth. Silence persists as a fade-in presents us with a similar image, showing another group of newcomers. Suddenly, the photograph comes alive as film footage, and men and women walk, laugh, and wave at the camera.

Similar effects of stop-motion and animated views make the literal staging of the photograph an important device of this film. The slow pan or the extended shot matches the narrator's reflections and adds to the overall reflection on Ellis Island, the meaning of its history, and the traces at display in the museum. The alternation of sound and silence adds to the work on rhythm, which also stresses the pensive aura of the staged photographs. Consequently, the mute and often anonymous image appears in its eerie magnitude as an imprint of the past.

Aside from the photographs the vestiges of Ellis Island add to the enactment of the trace: the objects at the museum, things and marks left behind by visiting tourists, a scribbled name on a wall, the worn aspect of the buildings, and a room not yet ready to be exposed to the museum guide and his visitors. Bober's photographs from 1978 are subject to a reflection

Récits d'Ellis Island. Histoires d'errance et d'espoir (Robert Bober and Georges Perec, 1979). Courtesy of Institut National de l'Audiovisuel (INA), Paris.

on the pragmatic meaning of the image as document. The image of a huge, empty room in decay cannot automatically be associated with the history of Ellis Island. It "could have been some old hangar, forgotten factory, or any deserted stockroom whatever." As the representation of a guided tour indicates, this, however, is a museum, an official site of public memory.

The conducted tour is represented twice, which again stresses the symbolic impact and narrative function of time measurement in documentary. A handheld camera approaches the entrance to the museum. The following shot shows a guide who receives a group of tourists. He asks how many of them have relatives who passed through Ellis Island as immigrants. After a shot of the audience's positive response, there is a close-up of the guide as he offers the introductory discourse. The following sequences show a large part of the tour: when the group walks into another room the camera stays behind, slowly revealing the markings of the past along the floor and on the walls.

The narrator returns for an explicit reflection on the trace, part of which was quoted above. A pan shot scales the huge room, and then the focus is on the enlarged photographs that have been cautiously placed at the exact location of their representation. The sequence is juxtaposed to the representation of the conducted tour. A fixed framing shows the guide telling his anecdote. The group moves into another room, and a new sequence of silent, empty space and carefully positioned photographs follows. In the following shot of the guide and a new group of tourists, the anecdote reappears. It is the story about a Russian Jew who was proposed the name of "Rockefeller" ("funny" European names were changed to understandable American names in the bureaucratic practice of registration) and who, some hours later when an official asked for his name, mumbled in Yiddish that he has forgotten, *schon vergessen*, and the man behind the desk immediately confirmed his new name as "John Ferguson." On this occasion the camera is directed toward the visitors. The voice of the guide is partly overlapped by the narration of Georges Perec, who reflects upon the meaning and the lack of meaning that the tour produces in him.

Ellis Island appears as a shared space of memory-work but a site that nevertheless remains a site of loss and of incomplete stories. The narrator suggests that most of the visitors on this tour are not here to learn but to find indications of a shared history and to find a link to their ancestors and relatives. The theme reoccurs in a passage that appears later in the film:

> Today, I do not think that people visit Ellis Island by chance. Those who actually managed to pass this site would hardly feel like coming back, and their children or grandchildren come back for their sake, to seek for a trace: For the latter, a trying site of uncertainty, and, for the former, a site of memory where a relation is achieved between themselves and their history.[6]

In *Récits d'Ellis Island* a private archive of images adds to the emplotment of historical time, which is realized through the filmed testimonies of interviewees and their family photographs. Bober and Perec paid attention to the affective impact of history as lived experience, represented by the personal encounters with old immigrants. *Memoires* (memories) is consequently the title of the second part of the film, where Perec is talking to immigrants about their arrival on Ellis Island. To them, Ellis Island coincides with the significant moment when their dream of America for the first time met with new experiences of identity and the uncertain and hard everyday life as an immigrant.

Apart from the stories and fragmentary memories delivered by the interviewees, the photographic imprint stands out as the major *leit motif* of the film. A close-up sequence of hands turning the leaves of a photo album introduces Parts 1 and 2. The images belong to Bober's and Perec's collection of images from Ellis Island in 1978, including photographs documenting the making of the film. This photo-film outset already suggests the intimate sphere of the photo-album and the filmmakers' subjective enunciation accomplished through the interval between the time of inscription and the time of contemplation. Also, during the second part of the film, where personal memories add to the collection of traces, we are reminded of the alternative histories that found footage offers to any official version of history. For example, Nathan Solomon, who arrived in 1923, shows family albums, including pictures from his European hometown Sombor that used to be part of the Austrian emperor Francois-Joseph. These are the image-memories of Mr. Solomon

Mr. Nathan Solomon looks back at his childhood in Europe and remembers his arrival in New York in 1923 in *Récits d'Ellis Island*. Courtesy of Institut National de l'Audiovisuel (INA), Paris.

and, despite their incomplete record, the major support of his personal memory. Simultaneously, these photographs also perform as *found footage*, which, animated through the man's personal account and the documentation of his encounter with the filmmakers, adds to our film archive of shared images and stories. In the art of moving images this staged interrelation between images and memory may even be realized in contexts deprived of interviewees and their performed acts of testimony and recollection.

▶
Alternative Archives of Amateur Film

In the extensive project of Péter Forgács to evoke individual and shared histories of the Hungarian and European past, the trace materializes in the fragmentary and scratched feature of collected amateur films. In *The Bartos Family*—the first film in the series *Private Hungary* (*Privát Magyarország*, 1988)—*Az Orveny* (*Free Fall, Private Hungary 10*, 1996), and *The Maelstrom: A Family Chronicle* (1997), all of which offer family sagas in the shadow of the Holocaust, the existential relation between image and death finds stark illustration. From this perspective Forgács's videos relate to the phenomenology of the trace in its most classical sense because the aura of these old home movies offers the very core of drama and poetic enactment. Yet the reframing of these home movies suggests a possible microlevel historiography, an archeology accomplished by research and interviews to gradually unmask the anonymity of these pictures.

The film fragments are recomposed and layered in a way that emphasizes the materiality of the image-object as a trace of the past. Nevertheless, this manifest process of indexing and decontextualization defies any notion of transcendence. The amateur films are framed as insufficient indicators of the past, marked by missing information, unanswered questions, and the invisible conflicts and complex relations that always hide beneath the apparent coherence of domestic self-representation.

Similar to the literary work by Hungarian author Imre Kertész, these narratives appeal to our empathy with our historical others and simultaneously challenge any reduction of history into an enclosed drama. Where Kertész uses the novel and his experiences as a survivor of the Holocaust, Forgács uses the expressive possibilities of video montage and the affective power of Tibor Szemsö's music for other people's visual record of the past. The materiality and uncanny transcendence of these amateur films are subject to poetic articulation. The scratched texture of each frame and the use of silence, music, and added sound stress the image-imprint and the implied testimony of the footage.

Récits d'Ellis Islands exemplifies how the photograph and the film image become significant traces of the past in film. Forgács's work posits the potential archive-memory of amateur films. In his video compilations the trace is manifest on multiple levels, through the cultural and social signification of found footage in contrast to the official archival images, and through the devices of montage and *mise en scène*.

In terms of historical source material the amateur films represent an alternative film archive that is marked by the universal content of family pictures and home movies: smiling family members posing for the photographer at Christmas parties, marriages, birthdays, or successful examinations. The universal quality of domestic photography and film stems from the practice of ideal self-representation, a family constructing a unified image of the past.[7] Family pictures offer suggestive material to documentary filmmaking, precisely because of what is not shown: tensions in family relationships, forced smiles, rivalries, and secret passion. An autobiographic narrative may reinvent these invisible intrigues within recollection, contemplation, and imagination. On the other hand, cinema may preserve the enigmatic anonymity of photographs and footage, such as

György ("Gyuri") Petö, the amateur filmmaker whose films are presented in *Az Orveny/Free Fall*, part 9 in the series *Private Hungary* (Péter Forgács, 1996). Courtesy of Péter Forgács.

Éva and Gyuri (on left) with friends in *Az Orveny/Free Fall*. Courtesy of Péter Forgács.

in *Récits d'Ellis Island* where the photographic enlargements are staged as suggestive traces linked to the histories of a particular site.

Free Fall is based on the work of Hungarian and Jewish amateur filmmaker György Petö, called Gyuri, who documented his life with friends and family between 1937 and 1945. This film pictures the everyday life of a Jewish family at a point where the "Nazi Endlösung" still would have seemed a monstrous fantasy. Presenting a world that was soon to disappear, Forgács orchestrates Petö's films into an imaginary realm of historical experience. The historical context is well known, and facts regarding the political situation in Hungary during World War II contribute to the contextualization of the home movie material, but the narrative is a subjective outlook on the past as experienced from within the everyday life of a family. An added note, such as "Szeged ... where this story takes place," offers an indexing of particular sites, and another, "Life at Tisza 1938," indicates what the pictures show, whereas "Paula, Éva's mother, Lajos Lengyel's wife, who died in the camp of Neukirchen in 1944" identifies people in the footage, while indicating what eventually was going to happen to them. It is not the inserted captions per se that complete the enactment of the trace but the ways in which the text appears on the screen and the amateur films are reframed. The following example illustrates how the family circle is introduced, while also allowing individual portraits and life stories.

Forgács's reuse of the home movie from a birthday party in 1938 is characterized by the added music, and the transformation of the black-and-white footage into a video sequence that has been colored and rhythmically halted by stop-motion just before each cut. Short explanatory captions, which resemble those of family albums, have been inserted to identify the depicted persons, for example, "Gyuri's aunt Henrietta Krausz on her 78th birthday." The text is displayed vertically on one side of Henrietta, who is sitting at a table laughing. The image freezes and is cut into a scene of some men playing cards, and a thin white line encircles a man on the left, "Sándor Súgar, the son-in-law of Henrietta." The camera pans right, and another circle is drawn to emphasize "Laci, Gyuri's brother, who recently separated from his wife." The pan is completed when the face of the next man is shown in stop-motion, as a new line reads, "the brother-in-law, Laci Osváth, the lieutenant."

The next sequence presents Henrietta and two other women; the camera pauses for a while on one of them, presented as "his wife Rózsi, Guyri's sister...." The camera moves slightly to the right, "... and her cousin, married to Sándor Súgar," to frame the two women. Suddenly, the image freezes and a small frame of blue-tinted footage appears within the image, showing Sándor in a swimming suit: a small image box appears between the cousins, followed by a text explaining that "Rózsi was secretely in love with Sándor Súgar." As the music fades out, the pan continues rightward and freezes at the smile of Gyuri's mother, "the wife of Ernö Petö."

This sequence illustrates Forgács's compilation aesthetics, where the frame suddenly multiplies, and where textual indications are not limited to naming but also allude to details beyond the shown. Brief textual comments and the use of stop-motion contribute to the *mise en scène* of the amateur films, although the emplotment of historical time depends on other devices as well.[8]

▶

The Future of the Past in *Free Fall*

In *Free Fall* the pragmatic relation between image and meaning becomes a dramatic tool, an incentive for creating a shared image-memory: the destiny of the Petö family concerns us. The interval between the historical date of the amateur film and the present moment of contemplation and recollection is a crucial principle for the *mise en scène* of home movies. To recall Goffman's theory about the manufacture of negative experience in stage performance, this represents a stark counterpart in the poetics of video compilation. We watch an ordinary event such as a mother bathing her baby, and her ignorance of the future is violently contrasted to the threatening shadow of increased Nazi politics. The threat materializes through inserted fragments of official history that contaminate the intimate sphere of family pictures. A range of expressive elements help accomplish this frame-breaking event: inserted archival images, a radio broadcast of an historical speech, inserted text that indicates what is going to happen, Nazi laws transmitted as song, a symbolic use of sound effects and color, and the significant manipulation of speed. The music accomplishes the apocalyptic beat, beyond sentimentality or narrative enclosure.

Hence, the imprint is decontextualized and its referent is subject to reflection: Who is this? What is shown and what is not? Another important problem is the fact that the meaning of an image may alter depending on who is looking at it. This relates to Marker's point. What seemed insignificant during filmmaking may be very important to a contemporary viewer.

In *Free Fall* the interval between then and there and here and now is a prerequisite for the narrative and audiovisual structuring of Petö's films. Forgács plays with the banality of everyday life and at times reveals a secret relationship between two images by imposing one image upon another. The visualization of this gap between the future and the past coincides with a sinister foreboding of the Holocaust: a dark shadow invades the happy images of a birthday party, such as the *no longer now* of photographic inscription turns into the *not yet now* of a coming disaster.

The inserted text contributes to the structuring of the narrative and supports the presentation and identification of people and places depicted in the amateur films. A chronological ordering of Petö's films (some sequences are repeated with slight modification of speed and color) meets with the realization of the Hungarian Holocaust in late 1944. Hence, the official history and the life story of the Petö family are juxtaposed in a movement toward the end of the war, and the indications of what will *eventually* happen create a mode of apocalyptic foreboding. This is accomplished by the plastic elaboration of the screen and the sound track into multiple layers. Through sound, wipes, fade-ins, and inserted boxes, official history invades the happy pictures of family life, friendship, and love. For example, Guyri's record of his summer holiday at the riverside in Tisza in 1938 is accompanied by music and song and contrasted with a harsh line reading, "On May 25, 1939, both houses of the parliament accepted with great majority 'the first Jew law,' proposed by count Pál Teleki." The content of the law is chanted (and translated in voice-over) to the images of Gyuri and his friend Bandi Kardos on a boat trip. There is a cut in Gyuri's film, to other images of beach life and swimming. The sound track offers a recording of Samu Stern, the head of the Jewish community in Budapest, who protests against the maltreatment of farmers in the Bratislava province. His talk is matched with a shot in slow motion of Kardos diving into the water, and a synchronized splashing sound is heard at the moment when he hits the water.

A similar example of political events breaking into, or contaminating, the domestic sphere of the home movies appears in the sequence showing a birthday party in 1939. The sequence begins with a close-up of a menu, which is explained by inserted text: "The menu of Gyuri's 33rd birthday." A continuous take, tinted in a mauve color, reveals the guests presented as "Ica and Gábor Szantó ... Rószi Petö ... Ila ... the brother-in-law Laci Osváth ... and Gyuri Petö." A black-and-white sequence suddenly wipes in from the right, partly overlapping the home movie. Text: "Hungary's Head of state inaugurates the new parliament with pomp and splendor." The inserted footage is then narrowed to a small box in the upper right of the frame and then to a rectangle at the bottom. A new text reads, "Head of state, Horthy," whose speech is interpreted as voice-over. The contrast between a birthday party and a parliamentary meeting is further stressed by the flickering image quality, which results from the changing position of the inserted box as well as from the play with stop-motion in the reframing of Petö's home movie.

This process of juxtaposing different image contexts and sound contributes to the historical narrative of *Free Fall*. Together with the music, the gradual overlapping and interaction of these layers result in a poetic score that evokes the metaphoric signification suggested by the title: At the moment of celebrating a birthday, or enjoying their summer vacation, Gyuri's family as well as innumerable others was already doomed by the gradual and meticulous realization of the Holocaust. The textual indication of an irrevocable disaster—which is already confirmed as a historical fact but which appears even more striking from this microperspective—is emphasized by the montage effects and the manipulated speed. The score by Tibor Szemsö completes the staging of the mute film fragment and also directs the rhythm of overlapping image boxes within the frame.

On one occasion the sinister foreboding of death is stressed by the classic Baroque motif of a peeled apple, a symbol of death and perishableness. This example occurs when the voice-over recites the fourth Jew law established in 1939 and is accompanied by music. The still image of the apple is simultaneously accompanied by text: "March 15, 1939, as a result of the first Vienna resolution, Carpathia-Rutenia was incorporated with Hungary ... " Moving images appear in a box, partly covering the apple, and indicated as "Pictures from Carpathia-Rutenia shot by Dr. T.T, 1940 ... the number of people amounts to 665.000, of which 78.000 are Jews. A year later, the Hungarian authorities transfer 18.000 'stateless' Carpathian Jews to the SS, who execute them in Kamenec-Podolskij, Ukraine." In significant silence, and heart beat rhythm, the image of the apple becomes a palimpsest through which peacetime street scenes from a Jewish community in Carpathian Ruthenia are shown. Moreover, the inserted film sequence is halted by stop-motion, which further interlinks the omniscient narrative, the symbolic power of a baroque motif, and the resulting *punctum effect* of a vivid street scene, uncannily restrained in the shadow of death.

Aside from the figure of restrained motion there is another device that is even more symbolically tied to Barthes's "un pur ça a été" and Bazin's notion of the photograph and death—the inverted image. The use of negative is a rare event in itself, but in this narrative context of foreshadowed disaster it strongly contributes to the formal and symbolic intersection of found footage and official record.[9] The use of repetition and color completes the powerful appearance of the inverted image. For example, the second time we see the inverted slow-motion sequence of Éva (Gyuri's fiancée) diving into the river, it is colored red and the added sound of splashing water breaks into the recitation of another law. Regarding the content of the Jew law it is impossible not to associate the sequence with the Hungarian Holocaust a few years later that forever would change the life of this and other doomed families.

Gyuri's films are unusually well accomplished and ambitiously produced with painted intertitles. The testimony of everyday life provided by the film is perhaps most apparent in movies shot during the filmmaker's stay at Kiszombor, Hungary, between 1940 and 1941. Similar to most Hungarian Jews, Gyuri was ordered to work at a camp. Titles such as "Souvenirs from the Work Company," "Formation," "March," and "The Washing Department" structure the footage from this period, but the symbolic indications of concentration camps radically disturbed the images of smiling and joking friends. One of the sequences showing men marching to their work is suddenly inverted and decelerated into slow motion. A melancholic song dominates the sound track, and the verse is subtitled, "I cannot get a wink of sleep tonight, silent, silent night ... without any comfort ...." Again, the negative image and the altered speed emphasize the photographic trace and reinforce the narrative foreshadowing of Nazi genocide.

Phenomenology holds that vision is the most noble of senses and that, consequently, the trace is grounded upon a visual a priori, a notion characteristic of a tradition of Western philosophy. In the diversity of media culture, however, the recording of a testimonial act or sound recording may evoke the trace. For example, in *The Bartos Family*, Forgács uses the auditory record of Mr. Zoltan's popular songs (his first record appeared in 1928). Mr. Zoltan's voice adds to the haunting presence of the past and to the overall rhythm of the film. In Forgács's video compilations sound effects are commonly used to animate and dramatize the silent home movies. As further exemplified in *Free Fall* these auditory inserts may not be traces of the past in any material sense, but together with the music they add to the animation of the visual record and accomplish a poetic staging of historical experience. Forgács's orchestration of the silent images illuminates the fact that in documentary, fiction film, and video art alike, our emotional response to the screen is dependent on, or at least directed by, the use of music, sound, and moments of silence.

In film narration the trace goes beyond the material support of the imprint, making the image a contemplative site of intersubjective memory and imagination. Throughout the *Private Hungary* series, music and sound effects increase our emotional response to the narrative. The compiled images are not only being colored and contrasted; their quality as imprints of the past is stressed by the musical drama of Tibor Szemsö's score and by added sounds that reinforce an uncanny indication of the future of the past: a splash of water as György's girlfriend dives into the river, the disciplined steps of a military boot march, or the aggressive sound of gunfire added to images of autumn hunting.

The minimalist yet highly dramatic music is a prerequisite for the film's engulfing of the viewer, as we engage in the privacy of domestic scenes and moments that already were threatened by Nazi politics. Music completes the unfolding of drama, distancing the viewer from the calm routines of everyday life. In *Free Fall* music is involved in the project to upset viewing by means of disquieting chock effects. Accordingly, the anti-Semitic Jew laws are chanted in alarming contrast to the peaceful and happy images of Petö's home movies. Aside from the function of music and sound as discursive markers, the soundscape in *Free Fall* reminds us of the fact that the trace may be enacted beyond the parameters of the visual. The inserted fragments of political history in wartime Hungary involve not only archival images but also recorded speech. Voices of political leaders, representing both Nazis and the Jewish community in Budapest, offer an auditory record that provides to the material aspect of cinema as a technology of memory.

Sound operates on yet another level in *Private Hungary*. The intimacy achieved by the added sound of water, heartbeats, or the lighting of a cigarette may be said to increase the impression of an imaginary realm of historical experience. These inserted sound effects may be compared to the similarly intimate, although reflexive, sounds of representation and inscription. Occasionally, the sound track offers but the rattling sound of the home movie projector. These are important moments when we are invited to share Forgács's fascination with the found footage, this adventure of peeping into the private archive of home movies. Hence, in significant ways sound is important in stressing the ghostlike appearance of a vanished world.[10] An ambiguous present tense (in Christian Metz's sense of presence being the appropriate tense of identification) is created by the use of sound effects. Sound reduces the distance between then and there and here and now. It brings the viewer closer to the lived time suggested by the recorded view, for example, the heavy, disciplined sound of coordinated marching that is added to a sequence from the forced labor camp or the peaceful sounds of birds and the lighting of a cigarette that have been added to the sequence showing Gyuri in Szeged during one of his rare leaves from the camp. As these examples indicate sound is crucial to the compelling staging of the trace in *Free Fall*, highlighting its existential and material signification in a narrative that constantly transgresses the past, the present, and the future of the reframed amateur films.

A poetics of the trace has been suggested in film examples where issues of image, history, and memory are allegorically brought to the fore. These metadiscourses on historical representation call for a reassessment of the phenomenology of the trace, but their self-referential design simultaneously provokes a reflection on the important social and cultural aspects of historical representation as well as on the film viewer's preconception of different genres of pastness. Despite the critical metalevel of these films the photographic trace is evoked as a haunting enigma, whose aura offers the ideal means to bridge the gap between the present and the past.

[7]   *The Trace in Contemporary Media*

This chapter considers some examples that radically question the phenomenology of the trace. I will acknowledge representations and media contexts beyond photography and film or narratives that involve a critical reflection on the production and reproduction of public memory in moving images. I stress the thematic persistence of the trace in documentary, while at the same time reflecting on the limitations of the phenomenological discourse in relation to contemporary media. At this point it is also relevant to acknowledge an important theme in Ricœur's reassessment of the philosophy of memory: the possibility of the erroneous memory and the fact that memory and recollection are inevitably bound up with forgetting.

In documentary the emplotment of historical time may involve a reflection on the pragmatic relation between image and meaning, the therapeutic use of images where memory is blocked, and the potential of audiovisual narration to visualize the interval between the present and the past. In these cases the staging of the trace coincides with a critical discourse concerned with the sociocultural and psychological aspects of image and memory. For example, Marita Sturken accounts for cultural aspects of forgetting, of voids and blanks where there are no images and no testimonies collected. In representing the past, photographs and films may "screen out" historical experience. With reference to Freud's notion of *screen memory* Sturken asserts that images tend to "screen out other often unphotographed memories and offer itself as the 'real memory,' becoming our memory."[1] In *Tangled Memories: The Vietnam War, the AIDS Epidemic, and the Politics of Remembering,* she gives various examples of how media representations of historical events depend on specific aspects of technology and politics and how they align with historical continuities of cultural memory.[2] From Vietnam to the AIDS crisis of the 1980s, to the Gulf War in 1991, Sturken emphasizes the complex interrelations between, on the one hand, the intersubjective perception of historical time as television production and public memorial and, on the other hand, the politics of representation that is achieved according to ideological aims and commercial calculations.

The September 11 attacks, and the wars against Afghanistan and Iraq, in retrospect seem to add uncannily to the examples of *Tangled Memories*. I will turn my attention back to the Gulf War and the intersection of military optics and war coverage, which is also the subject of Harun Farocki's video *Erkennen und Verfolgen* (*War at a Distance*, Germany, 2003).

As illuminated by the following examples, a contemporary discourse of the trace has to consider technologies and modes of narration beyond film and video. In digital media, for example, the classical discourse of the photo-trace is challenged by nonanalog images deprived of any referent, and accordingly, digital filmmaking and video editing demand new conceptual tools to conceive of cinematic realism as expectation and perception in contemporary media culture. Narratives on the Web provoke an overwhelming suspicion that things are not what they seem to be. If an image is presented as a record of the real, we tend to believe that it is probably manipulated; if a narrative is presented as a first-person testimony of an historical event, we automatically presume that it is a hoax. The existential signification of the trace, however, is not ruled out by this paranoid reading of the digital.

▶

Memories of a Ghost Town: Elena's Roadmap to Chernobyl

The Web site *Ghost Town* provides a first-person narrative about the 1986 nuclear disaster in Chernobyl.[3] This Web site offers an outlook on the recent history of Ukraine—a digital emplotment of historical time. Different from a copy of a film or a video, this archive memory is of uncertain continuance. But as long as the Web site is accessible, it represents an example that supports the utopian idea that we are all potential contributors to the representation of the past.

Ghost Town consists of twenty-seven Web pages, or "chapters," with photographs, maps, and text. Above a photograph of a female biker the opening line reads, "My name is Elena. I run this website and I don't have anything to sell. What I do have is my motorbike and the absolute freedom to ride it wherever curiosity and the speed demon take me." She lives 130 kilometers from "the dead zone" of Chernobyl, an ideal place for endless cruises on the motorbike, "without ever having to fear the police or to risk running into living beings." Elena takes the reader for a virtual ride through the deserted landscape of a place that was devastated in one of the worst nuclear catastrophes the world has known. The collage of images and text offers a narrative that is marked by the personal address of an essay. The first chapter provides some general information about how nuclear radiation is measured:

> 1,000 microroentgens equal one milliroentgen and 1,000 milliroentgens equal 1 roentgen. So one roentgen is 100,000 times the average radiation of a typical city. A dose of 500 roentgens within 5 hours is fatal to humans. Interestingly, it takes about 2 1/2 times that dosage to kill a chicken and over 100 times that to kill a cockroach.
>
> This sort of radiation level can not be found in Chernobyl now. In the first days after explosion, some places around the reactor were emitting 3,000–30,000 roentgens per hour. The firemen who were sent to put out the reactor fire were fried on the spot by gamma radiation. The remains of the reactor were entombed within an enormous steel and concrete sarcophagus, so it is now relatively safe to travel to the area—as long as we do not step off of the roadway…

Chapter 4 shows images of deserted farms in a part of Belarus, the neighboring country of Ukraine, where, the narrator emphasizes, the wind brought 70 percent of the Chernobyl radiation. Another image depicts one of twenty-four checkpoints that lead into the dead zone. A succession of photographs and notes take the reader closer to Chernobyl. Traces of innumerable losses are evident in the huge number of radioactive vehicles that are abandoned on a field: trucks and fire engines that were driven by firefighters who all died of radiation in days and weeks after the accident. In another photograph, a group of wild horses pose. So far, the horses have survived on a diet of radioactive grass, but, as the narrator recalls with irony, they are of a hardy Russian strain. A former election house of a village is presented as a ruin. Scraps of posters and notices in the center of the image indicate that this used to be a place of meetings and social events. Entering the ghost town of Chernobyl, we see a series of photographs that represent a cityscape deprived of life:

> At first glance, Ghost Town seems like a normal town. There is a taxi stop, a grocery store, someone's wash hangs from the balcony and the windows are open.
>
> But then I see a slogan on a building that says—"The Party of Lenin Will Lead Us To The Triumph Of Communism" … and I realize that those windows were opened to the sp[r]ing air of April of 1986.

Photographs taken inside a hotel and some private homes testify to the desperate moment of evacuation, when, finally, information about the lethal radiation reached the inhabitants. Among these images there are also snapshots of Elena (apparently taken by her father) measuring the level of radiation. There are flashbacks too, family snapshots of the town from the early 1980s. An image of a May 1 parade in 1985 is contrasted to the ruins of Chernobyl today: "May 1st never came in this town."

"Elena" might be a fictive character, or maybe there is an activist group behind this historical mapping of Chernobyl and the nuclear disaster. This uncertainty adds to the enactment of the trace in *Ghost Town*. The collage of images and text offers a digital approach to the pristine signification of the image-imprint as a presence of absence and as a sign of loss. In *Ghost Town* the critical account of the official version of the disaster, promoted by the government in 1986 and preserved ever since, is contrasted to the fragmentary picture of a Soviet childhood and personal memories of the catastrophe in 1986, when the invisible, nonscented gamma death spread in wide circles, splitting Chernobyl in the "before" and "after" of the accident. Elena's survival is claimed to depend on the professional insights of her father. A nuclear physiologist well aware of the risks, he managed to send the children to their grandmother, who lived eight hundred kilometers from Chernobyl. A week after the event, foreign radio stations cracked the news to the inhabitants of Chernobyl. The communist regime had concealed the proportions and consequences of the meltdown.

Ghost Town brings attention to the untold stories of a historical trauma—memories that were oppressed by the Soviet regime and that which still beg for acknowledgment in contemporary Ukraine. Moreover, the framing and contextualization of the about one hundred photographs at display on the Web site exemplify the possibility of historical time in a documentary context beyond cinema. As in *Récits d'Ellis Island,* the material and existential signification of the photo-trace stands out as a recurrent narrative and symbolic theme. For example, one image depicts a wall covered with worn paper, on which is pinned a calendar from 1986. The text elaborates on the meaning of this vestige, by providing an imaginary picture of the owner of the calendar and the plans he had for the particular day of the catastrophe:

> This man never got his paper. The news in it suddenly became unimportant. The calendar shows that Saturday, April 26 was a special day. Judging by things he left at the door, he liked to fish. The Sundays and Year on this calendar were in red ink and has now faded. He probably left for a fishing trip and never came back. I wonder how he felt. It's like you[r] life has been cut into two pieces. In one is your slippers still under you[r] bed, photos of a first love that are left on the piano … in the other is you yourself, you[r] memories and a fishing rod.

The interval between the time of the image and the later process of recollection and interpretation may be staged in various media, including this digital collage of photographs and text. The narrator's affective response to these desolate views aligns with the highly personal outlook in recent documentary cinema. Historical time materializes in a microcosm of imagined life stories, where the structural mechanisms of history as a grand narrative are replaced by a personal inquiry into the irrevocable experiences of the past. As Ricœur argues, this is, and has always been, an important incentive of narrative time and the poetic enactment of historical time as lived experience. The narrative of *Ghost Town* ends at the site of a former kindergarten:

> The last photos are of the town kindergar[t]en.
> There are hundreds of little gas masks, a teacher[']s diary and a last note saying that their walk on Saturday has been canceled due to some unforeseen contingency.
> The remaining photos don't need any comments—they tell the Ghost Town's story in a way that no words can.

The final image shows an iron sculpture and the narrator concludes, "This sculpture was in the center of the town, it was moved to the nuclear power plant after the accident. It is Prometheus stealing fire from Gods and giving it to the humans …"

A plain collage of stills and text, Elena's roadmap to Chernobyl lacks the critical self-analysis that characterizes the staging of the trace in an essay film such as *Récits d'Ellis Island*. In both examples, however, the aura of the image-imprint propels narration into an open-ended process of memory work. *Ghost Town* brings attention to a disaster whose consequences were aggravated by a politics of amnesia intended by the Soviet regime. The frightening meaning of Chernobyl is found in the literal danger of this contaminated landscape. It is not an historical site in the sense of a monument where the past may rest in peace, because, as suggested by the photographs, Chernobyl is a town marked by the terror that caused its citizens to run away. Abandoned and almost forgotten by the world, it is the opposite of a place of mourning.

Ghost Town may be acknowledged as a narrative beyond the borders of fiction and nonfiction, pushing the boundaries of documentary representation. It appears to have been accomplished without any other ambition than to offer a personal account of the past and an *open* archive memory in the utopian sense of a site accessible to everybody and a narrative in the continuous act of becoming.

Ghost Town. Image from www.kiddofspeed.com/default.htm (accessed 28 July 2006).

Visual Technology and History in the Making

The art by Sigmar Polke has often been characterized as European Pop art, because Polke reuses the icons of media culture for picturing the politics and ironies of commodity worship and for questioning the idea of specific subject matters appropriate for the gallery room. For the recent *machine paintings* (2002) Polke used images from posters, magazines, or newspapers that have been tinted and altered on the computer and then photographically transferred onto large sheets of fabric. One example, *Die Jagd auf die Taliban und Al Qaeda* (*The Hunt for the Taliban and Al Qaeda*, 2002), is based on a German newspaper diagram that explains satellite technology used in the U.S.-led hunt for the Taliban in Afghanistan. It offers a disturbingly apt reflection on perception, satellite technology, and contemporary warfare.

Polke brings attention to the common use of graphics in contemporary news media to explain the tactics of warfare. The image stresses the unequal battle between the optical and clinic realization of Western warfare, where the target is dealt with at a safe distance, and the physical defeat of the archaic horseman warrior of the Third World. Within the scope of 1.5 seconds the camera shot and the extermination of the enemy coincide. A small group of Afghan soldiers on horseback is photographed from a bomber at 7,600 meters, and the image is transmitted to a satellite that, in turn, sends the information back to the U.S. army through a commando station in Kuwait and back to the drone plane for a granted attack.

Polke's appropriation of the diagram highlights three general problems of visual technology and warfare: (a) the empowered vision of surveillance, (b) the immediacy of real-time representation, and (c) the reduced perception of simulated realities. His fascination with machine perception and the construction of media events involves contemporary meanings of representation and the historical kinship of visual technologies and military aims.

In the context of documentary film and video Harun Farocki has addressed these problems of war and visual technology. The connection between Polke's machine paintings and Farocki's films and videos illuminates different uses of media as inscription and archive and ways in which our everyday perception of the present and the past is defined by truth-claiming images in real time, principles of surveillance, and preservation.

In the film essays and video installations of Farocki, the image as inscription is never more innocent or automatic than the process of recombining and juxtaposing sequences at the editing table. The moving image is less a mystery than the policy according to which a certain visual technology is used. In the context of experimental documentary, there is, I believe, no filmmaker or video artist to match Farocki's approach to media technology and perception. His films and videos explore the interface between image and meaning, machine perception and natural perception, and the making and remaking of images.

We have seen how film as a technology of memory may be reflected through documentary modes of montage and narration. A common assertion of these examples deals with the fact that the meaning of images changes over time, and to paraphrase Chris Marker, "you never know what you are actually filming." For good and bad, film and video represent ideal means with which to anticipate historical moments, to suggest interrelations between the future and the past, and to construct analogies between the present and the past. Afterward, when critically questioned and reframed, recent events are often more immediate and significant than they did as current affairs in live broadcast. The parallel to more recent

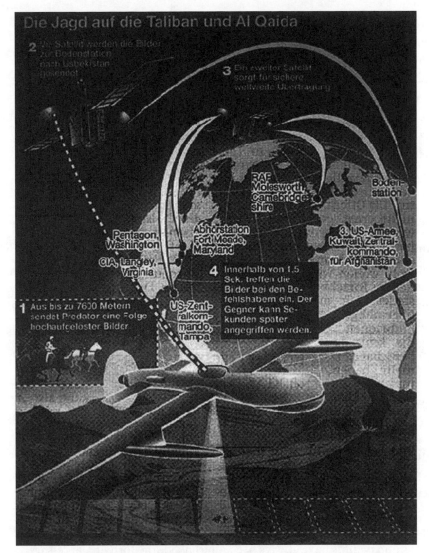

Die Jagd auf die Taliban und Al Qaida

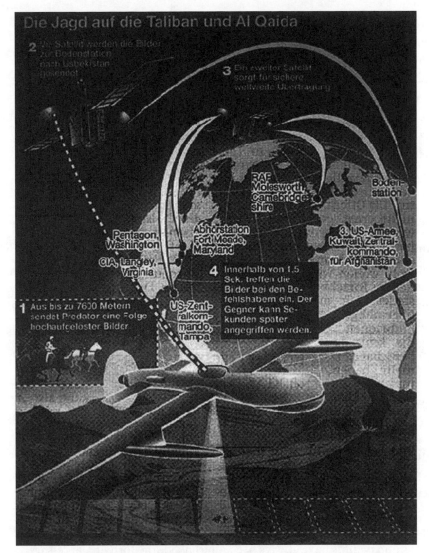

Die Jagd auf die Taliban und Al Qaida/The Hunt for the Taliban and Al Qaeda (Sigmar Polke, 2002). After a picture in the German newspaper *Die Welt*. Copyright Sigmar Polke.

events is striking in *Erkennen und Verfolgen,* which deals with electronic warfare, guided missiles, and war reporting during the Gulf War of 1991. In this film a recent example of war technology and the optics of modern warfare are discussed in dialog with the problems of perception and aerial footage, which Farocki approached in *Bilder der Welt und Inschrift des Krieges (Images of the World and the Inscription of War,* Germany, 1988).[4]

In the scholarly discourse on contemporary media, the Gulf War is to war reporting what the Rodney King's beating is to video surveillance: a case in point of representation policy and a paradigmatic event that brought attention to the mediating processes through which reality is represented and transformed. During the spring of 2003 the news coverage of the U.S. attack on Iraq was realized in conscious response to the critique of the CNN docudrama, which became synonymous with the war reporting of 1991.[5] This time, and weeks before the war officially began, American journalists and photographers were trained to report from the battleground. If the Desert Storm offered the illusion of a war pedagogically explained by sophisticated images of missiles reaching endless *uninhabited* targets, the new Iraqi Freedom story involved the promise of a continuous coverage from the ground. Masquerading as spectacular news reporting, Fox News replaced CNN as the dominant provider of efficient war propaganda and patriotic optimism to American audiences. Al Jazeera and Al Arabiya represented a significant change in the global media arena. As to the experience of war as a televised docudrama, there was not a big change from the previous war. The visual spectacle of night-sensor images of Baghdad from 1991 was uncannily repeated and found a less spectacular counterpart in the distanced shots of U.S. tanks fighting sandstorms.

The visual attraction of activated weapons, hit buildings, and micronarratives of war heroes represented a spectacular time-image of history in the making, which drew attention from the lived hell of war victims. This restricted and strategically measured optics of war crystallizes in Farocki's film *War at a Distance,* where the civil uses of military technology are subject to reflection. With reference to the media representation of the 1991 Gulf War, *War at a Distance* deals with the sensory perception of robots and guided missiles. This is a new vision of the world, Farocki argues, which in our electronic age interrelates warfare, war reporting, and industrial reproduction. Visual technology and military aims have always been interlinked, the former a necessary incentive for developing the latter.[6] The most disturbing motif of *War at a Distance* is the perverted attraction of rushing views seen through the guidance head of missiles.

The video begins with a series of images shot from missiles hurtling toward their target. At the moment of their blast the image goes blank. These views are repeated throughout the film to illustrate the strange connection between production and destruction, associated with the sophisticated optics of warfare and machine perception in the electronic era. Looking at these images today, it is particularly striking how this meticulous inscription of an attack is achieved as to hide its result. To see a distant building explode through a crosshair, or to follow a bomb toward its target, reduces the world to the virtual space-time of a computer game.

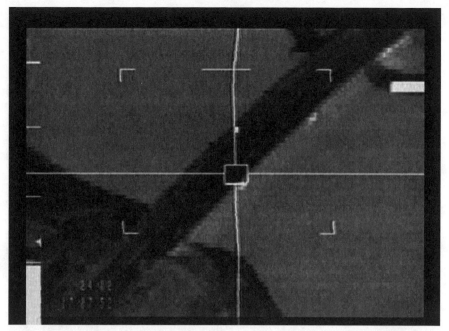

A view seen through the guidance head of a missile. *Erkennen und Verfolgen/War at a Distance* (Harun Farocki, 2003). Courtesy of Harun Farocki Filmproduktion, Berlin.

During the Gulf War the narrator emphasized that "warfare and war reporting coincided." Farocki compares these images to a punch machine of the mechanical era and then to the publicity footage for Taurus Systems, where a guided missile is shown to the beat of dance music. The following sequence, shot in Germany 1943, shows a demonstration of a simulator for practicing bombing. Throughout the video, image technologies from military and civilian contexts are mirrored, contrasted, and compared, which results in a web of reflections where new meanings appear in the interstice between sequences that are plucked out of context and reframed.

In the collection of military views represented in *War at a Distance,* a tracking device recognizes moving objects and bodies and puts them in frames. This cognition–recognition–tracking program mirrors an even worse reduction of people to bodies and material targets. A virtual image, this simulation offers a kind of embodied crosshair that repeatedly tries to find and match the precise form of its target. In a striking way the machine's act of vision, recognition, and action is made visible: "the silhouette operates as a preconceived notion seeking to be matched with reality." The scary result is an image deprived of humanity but in which a man can be literally contained and exterminated in real time.

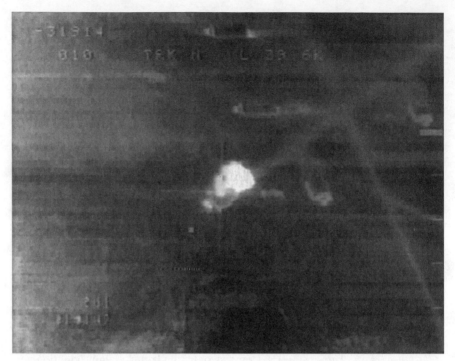

Erkennen und Verfolgen/War at a Distance. Courtesy of Harun Farocki Filmproduktion, Berlin.

At the Control Desk of the Filmmaker/Historian

The seemingly spontaneous and haphazard act of association characterizes Farocki's films and video installations. He metaphorically compares this act to an arithmetic grid (*As You See* and *Interface*).[7] The editing table represents the actual disposition of this metric device, "the workstation for the reworking of images and sound; the control desk; the player, the recorder" (*Interface*). Editing provides the *Schnittstelle* (*Interface*) where both the point of intersection between two images—the interval between one image and another, celebrated by Vertov as the very epicenter of cinematic expression—and the interval between the time of inscription and the moment of recollection are indicated. In *Interface* the napalm sequence from *Inextinguishable Fire* (Germany, 1969) is reproduced and inserted next to the contemporary image of Farocki, who looks back at his symbolic demonstration of napalm while repeating the commentary of the scene.

Hence, the interface is also that between man and machine, between individual and community, culture and capital, production and reproduction, text and intertext, as well as between subjective recollection

Erkennen und Verfolgen/War at a Distance. Courtesy of Harun Farocki Filmproduktion, Berlin.

and intersubjective memory. The editing table ultimately appears as the metaphoric control desk of the editor/filmmaker/storyteller/historian. As Thomas Elsaesser suggests, Farocki is "first and foremost an archivist" who collects and reorganizes the found images and texts, although an archivist well aware of the fact that the fragments "in their necessary arbitrariness and ultimate incoherence ... demarcate their own landscape and demand their own territory."[8]

Sequences are being decontextualized and contrasted, their meaning constantly being disclosed by opposed discourses. As Farocki explains in *Interface,* "I write into the images and then read something out of them." The cultural signification of intertextuality becomes highlighted through a strategy of cutting and pasting, of keying and contrasting, which in turn results in new intertexts. Similar to *War at a Distance, Wie man sieht* (*As You See,* Germany, 1986), *Arbeiter verlassen die Fabrik* (*Workers Leaving the Factory,* Germany, 1995), *Schnittstelle* (*Interface,* Germany, 1995), and *Ich glaubte Gefangene zu sehen* (*I Thought I Was Seeing Convicts,* Germany, 2000) are less about the image as a trace of the past, than about images as signs, coded by the sociohistorical realm of media culture. In this context, recollection is perhaps less connected to a mnemonic process than to the material activity of inverting and recombining sequences and of making images comment on themselves.

Interface mirrors the display of the apparatus in a mode reminiscent of *Man with the Movie Camera*. It also offers a personal reflection on the intellectual and tactile relation between the maker and making of film, between man and machine, and explicitly frames the practice of film editing versus video editing. Many sequences from his earlier films are quoted, reframed, and contrasted, as Farocki chooses motifs to interlink the associations evoked by *Schnittstelle*. For example, the metaphor between filmmaking and the encoding and decoding of messages materializes in an image of the German encoding machine Enigma. On another occasion the workstation of the filmmaker is compared to an artificial pool that simulates the production of waves, the movements of which may be associated with the function of image reproduction in his work, "The sea unfurling on the shore, irregular but not haphazard, binds one's view with its movement, without capturing it, thus setting thoughts free."

Interface is characterized by the vertical montage of video editing, of the frame splitting and partly overlapping in two images. One offers a compiled sequence, and the other shows Farocki at the editing table, where he shows and comments on sequences from his earlier films. The aesthetics of *Interface* is literally grounded in the idea of two frames in continuous communication, conflict, or in an ambiguous sound-image concert. As a prelude the upper left box shows a hand writing in a notebook, a flickering blue screen in the background, whereas the sequence down at the right side presents a television showing images of the Romanian dictator Ceausescu. In voice-over, Farocki says, "I can hardly write a word these days if there isn't an image on the screen at the same time. Actually, on both screens." At this point the first screen turns into a medium shot of Farocki at the work panel in front of two video screens, and the other shows a part of a room and a window; the camera closes into the window, to reveal a street scene: "This is a workstation, an editing station for the reworking of images and sounds. The control desk; the player; the recorder."

This contrasting of two frames, touching and overlapping at the center of a black screen, may be compared to the juxtaposed image boxes in *Free Fall*. If Forgács's video offered a plastic event of image contexts contaminating each other, the focus of *Interface* stringently remains on the space separating the compiled sequences. In this video the movement of juxtaposition and decontextualization maintains an analytical distance to the image-object, whereas, for example, the palimpsest of layered image-memories in *Free Fall* rather engages the viewer in the unfolding of a historical narrative.

Owing to his outspoken concern with the social disposition of media culture and the technological support of any image trace produced by photography, film, or video, Farocki adds a critical perspective to the present reassessment of the trace. In chapter 6, I referred to a sequence in *Le fond de l'air est rouge,* where the interval is stressed between the image's date of recording and the subsequent moment of its reframing. The same idea echoes at the beginning of *Interface,* where in addition the ascribed immediacy of television images is combined with the production of a media event and the intersubjective signification of the moving image as archive memory.

On the left screen a television shows footage from Romania in 1989, and on the right screen Farocki's hands frame the same image displayed on another television. The narrator informs us that "Paul Cozighian shot this footage in Bucharest on December 21, 1989, shortly before the revolution began. With his camera he established a connection between the TV set and the street." The two frames show Ceaucescu at a political rally, followed by a street scene from Bucharest. Hence, Farocki compiles Cozighian's framing of a Romanian television broadcast of the speech that preceded the dictator's forced resignation.

When revising this footage in 1995 Farocki is struck by the moment of hesitation in the middle of Ceaucescu's speech when the excited outburst of the people increases off-screen and an assistant breaks in to inform him that "they have entered the building." Farocki's two screens turn into red boxes, marked only by "Transmisiune Directa," and the speaker recalls the recording of a historical moment:

> For over a minute, viewers saw only this "live transmission" notice before Ceaucescu continued. This disturbance, this interruption, was it a sign of revolt? Cozighian moved his camera from the TV screen to the window. He juxtaposed the official image with the street image: image with counter-image. It was now time to abandon the TV-set and go into the streets. The camera-eye trained itself on the street in the hope that something might happen there. With this gesture the street was called in to turn into a productive location. An incantation.

As Farocki speaks, the left frame shows Cozighian's camera turning away from the television screen to the street. At this point the trace is invoked through the extratextual knowledge of the public uprising that eventually happened during that transmission and that which propelled the revolution. In Farocki's remodeling of Cozighian's footage, there are two important indications of the image as a mnemonic sign.

First, Cozighian's camera movement from the television to the street scene may be read as to incarnate the ideological implication of news media, which is not necessarily limited to the television coverage of a nondemocratic state television but which generally points to political and economical interests behind the news coverage of current affairs. Hence, in the broader perspective of media culture, the photographic trace cannot be dissociated from the processes of an institutionalized framing device. Second, through the symbolic contrasting of official television images to Cozighian's street view, Farocki reproduces a common trope in political documentary: the shaky street scene representing a *true* image of the past, the trace turning into a revolutionary sign.

▶

The Tactile of the Real/Reel

The word *interface* automatically connotes to computer culture and the devices with which to master computer programs or to navigate the Internet. The relation between man and machine offers the thematic outset of *Interface*. Yet the German word *Schnittstelle* gives a much more tactile sense to "interface" and implies the material trace of the cut in the image or sound. A tactile dimension of editing is suggestively evoked in the beginning of this work, where Farocki refers to the difference between film and video editing. As the two opposed screens contrast film editing with video editing, Farocki accounts for the actual cut in the filmstrip versus the imaginary cut of video editing, where sequences are copied from one tape to the next:

> While working at the film editing table, I keep the tip of my finger on the running image or sound reel to feel the cut or the glue before I see it or hear it. This is a gesture indicating fine perception or sensitivity [*Fingerspitzengefühl*]. The hand had almost no contact with the object, but perceived it nonetheless. When working with video, I don't touch the tape, I only push buttons.

The word *Fingerspitzengefühl,* which in this context is too witty to be translated, signifies the professional skill of editing and the sensitivity of the editor's fingertips, as he feels the cut or the glue before seeing or hearing it. The suggested difference between film and video indicates that the quality of the specific medium is, first of all, a matter of practice and experience. Although the feel of a strip differs from the pushing of buttons, the timing of the cut in both film and video demands the same sensitivity and skills for the conceptual reframing of sound-image and meaning.

The example of *Interface* offers an interesting response to the enclosed discussion of image ontology in classical discourses on image and time. Earlier in this chapter the ways in which the poetics of documentary modifies and impacts the idea of the photographic trace have been discussed. The significant use of sound and the inevitable social context of the film archive forced us to remember that the trace of the past has less to do with essence than with a complex production of historical time, where narration and the reframing of media events rule out any preconception of the photograph as a window on the past.

"Interface" refers to both the tactile of the reel and the tactile of *the real,* signifying the narrative matrix of history as an organized reinvention of the past. In *Interface,* modes of repetition and reframing question the constructed linearity of historical time, which results in an associative process that critically calls attention to the narrative function of the filmmaker/historian. At the editing table, fragments of the past may be discerned in sequences and then shattered and recomposed, new meanings appearing at new points of intersection. While celebrating the filmmaker's creative practice of compilation and reorganization, the tactile of the real would simultaneously indicate the controlling power of the workstation.

A material aspect of this is, of course, looking at and collecting images and sequences from various contexts. The real, however, may not be located on the scale between fictitious and nonfictitious representation. Farocki suggests that reality may be glimpsed through the haphazard fractures between images, so that the arithmetic logic of his sound-image puzzle suddenly displays a motif that is repeated and modified throughout history. To clarify this allegory of media memory, I will look closer at another sequence of *Interface.*

Farocki asks whether the work at an editing station may be compared to a scientific study. The answer he suggests is that, according to modern science, the scientist's hand is not allowed to interfere in a procedure: "During the procedure, the scientist is purely intellect." But just as an experimental pool for exploring ocean waves offers a simulation of real ocean waves, Farocki argues that his film offers the model of an editing station. Moreover, the process of browsing through collected images in search of hidden meanings is related to the work of the historian. This passage coincides with a series of compiled and rearranged sequences from *Workers Leaving the Factory*—a video entirely composed by inserted sequences from fiction film and actualities, showing variations of the same motif.

On the left screen we see *La sortie des usines* (Workers Leaving The Factory, Louis and Auguste Lumière, France, 1895), and on the other screen we see a sequence from *Metropolis* (Fritz Lang, Germany, 1927), which is quickly replaced by "images from the following 100 years that repeat, adapt and further develop the first motif," and Farocki continues:

> For over a year I collected and studied film sequences with the motif "workers leaving the factory." What could be the aim of this visual study? Must there be an aim at all? Think about the view of the historian, the art historian. His eye roams over thousands of statues and discovers something new in this figure, in this boy by Critios—For the first time, the legs and feet are not equally weighted: the body weight rests on the left leg—consequently, the right hip is a bit sunken, the right shoulder too: the head turns slightly to the side.

The comparison between the repeated film motif of workers leaving the factory and the image of the Critios boy reminds us of the selective and recontextualizing process of filmic compilation, which marks the narrative construction of history and the constructed demarcation and perspective of interpretation in the large. More generally, Farocki's visual study poses questions about media culture and the production and reproduction of archive memory. The use of a repeated and altered motif evokes the material aspect of preservation—image-memories from both fictive and documentary contexts disclosed by cinema as a technology of memory. In this sense the filmic compilation is comparable to an historical narrative, where the archive represents an interface between the historian and the past.

▶
When Surveillance of Life Turns into Inscription of Death

In his essay, "Subjunctive Documentary: Computer Imaging and Simulation," Mark J. P. Wolf raises some crucial questions that digital culture in general and computer simulation in particular pose to the debate about documentary representation.[9] In comparison with photographic representation, computer imaging technologies, Wolf argues, have changed the relation between observation and documentation. On a technical/material level, computer imaging "is often indexically less direct than film-based photography, due to the active mediation of hardware and software, as well as the storage of the image as a signal instead of a fixed record."[10] From an aesthetic point of view the monitoring of a graphic computer simulation appears as a simplified model of space, albeit as a three-dimensional time-space that, despite its lack of photographic realism, is related to the two-dimensional architecture of film images.

Moreover, *documentation* and *observation* are suddenly dislocated from *index*, in the sense of a photographic trace of the real. By suggesting the term *conceptual indices*, Wolf indicates a shift "from the perceptual to the conceptual" and emphasizes the close bond in computer simulation between reconstruction, visualization, and interpretation:

> [C]omputer simulations are often made from data taken from the outside world, but not always. Just as the digital image does not always have a real-world referent, computer simulation can be used to image real or imaginary constructs, or some combination of the two.... As a simulation is constructed, and the data set becomes larger and more comprehensive, its indexical link to the physical world grows stronger, until the simulation is thought to be sufficiently representative of some portion or aspect of the physical world.[11]

Computer simulation offers an illustration of how contemporary media technology may question the indexical trace. Alternatively, the surveillance video may similarly force us to complicate the above-outlined relation between archive and media memory. In media studies the surveillance camera is continuously related to the signification that Foucault ascribed to Jeremy Bentham's prison system, called "the Panopticon."[12] The surveillance camera, therefore, has already become a critical trope of social control, and the increased use of surveillance footage as legal evidence continuously confirms the truth claim and objectivity associated with this disembodied device of observation.[13]

Ghost Town and *War at a Distance* exemplified the trace in media contexts beyond cinema. The screen cultures of computer simulation and video surveillance provide for the media critique of another piece by Farocki: *I Thought I Was Seeing Convicts* (2000). This time, the compiled material included images produced by computer simulation and surveillance video. The reference to these technologies added to Farocki's reflection on interface, index, intertext, and historical time.[14] Indeed, what is more illustrative for an account of social control mechanisms versus visual technologies, than the example of a modern prison? Farocki offers a video essay in the heritage of Foucault.[15] The range of prison technology—a mix of surveillance camera, electronic body search, simulation, and electronic ankle bracelets—echoes the latter's discussion on both literal and metaphoric levels. Images show the ground plan of an American prison, which Farocki characterizes as "a control booth like in a factory," where the staff, using monitors connected to the video surveillance system, observe activities in the whole building.

The model of the workplace from *Interface* extends into this video, where the frame is similarly divided into two rectangles that show a double view and the interval between inserted sequences. In addition, *I Thought I Was Seeing Convicts* deepens the conceptual charting of overlapping media contexts, in order to posit the computer screen and the surveillance camera. This is a video compilation where images of computer graphics meet with surveillance footage of an American prison and sequences from silent movies that feature prison life. The feature of the split-screen is emphasized by the punctuation of a black screen, which simultaneously offers textual clarifications of what we see. Different from the intertitles in silent cinema, however, the commentary often appears in double on both the screens. This device functions as a black screen, a denial of vision, which offers a vertical spacing of the screens, rather than a visualized cut between two sequences. Hence, the text appears as marginal notes in the black field outside the compiled footage. On some occasions we also see how the black screen is used to slice the real-life footage of a surveillance camera into significant traces of the past.

The introductory doubled view of *I Thought I Was Seeing Convicts* offers silently and without commentary two computer screens that display a graphic outline of sixteen bars, symmetrically arranged in parallel rows of eight. Dots move irregularly along these mysterious bars, the number and movement of which differ between the left and the right frame. The image on the right is then replaced by the following text on a black background: "These dots represent customers moving through the aisles of a supermarket." Then, a modified reconstruction appears, as the black frame switches to the opposite side, "The objective is to determine which route the customers take and how it can be extended."

Let us return for a moment to Wolf's discussion of conceptual indices. In this case the link to the real is suggested by a reconstruction based on statistics about customer behavior, "The longer the route, the more likely it is that the customer will make a spontaneous purchase." In terms of documentation this is a reconstruction that graphically mimics both real and ideal movement in space and where the customers are reduced to dots moving through the model of an existing space. In terms of observation the simulation visualizes the probability of a customer's "walk-through" in a sufficiently precise way, so that a remodeling of the architecture would further stimulate customer's purchase.

Apart from visualizing "what could be, would be, or might have been,"[16] the graphic simulation reproduced in Farocki's film suggests the process of an interactive documentation of a social phenomenon, because in order to obtain some information about the mapped customers and their purchased items, one has to click on the moving dot. This is even more striking when Farocki juxtaposes the simulation of the shopping space to that of a prison: the left frame offers a light blue field demarcated by darker blue lines into sections with moving green dots, the text in the right corner

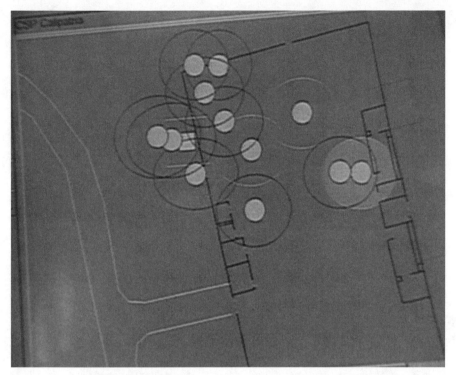

"These dots represent prison inmates who have been outfitted with electronic ankle bracelets." *Ich glaubte Gefangene zu sehen/I Thought I Was Seeing Convicts* (Harun Farocki, 2000). Courtesy of Harun Farocki Filmproduktion, Berlin.

indicating that "[t]hese dots represent prison inmates who have been outfitted with electronic ankle bracelets.... Click on any inmate and learn his or her identity"; a list of names appears in the right frame. Different from the customer simulation, the representation of inmates in the prison yard offers a real-time display, because the information is directly transmitted from the electronic ankle bracelet to the graphic display of the computer. Consequently, a more complex set of data strengthens the link between the referent and the representation.

Farocki decontextualizes the imagery of computer simulation and compares the reconstruction of a food store with that of a prison, so that the control of the customer's movement along the shelves mirrors the inmate's controlled movement inside the prison. Realized through a video compilation of computer imagery, the discursive impact of this critical preface is symbolically completed in the related function between the computer simulation and the surveillance video, which is the dominant motif in the remainder of the film. The spatial logic of the food store, where prolonged aisles equal additional purchase, inverts the prison yard,

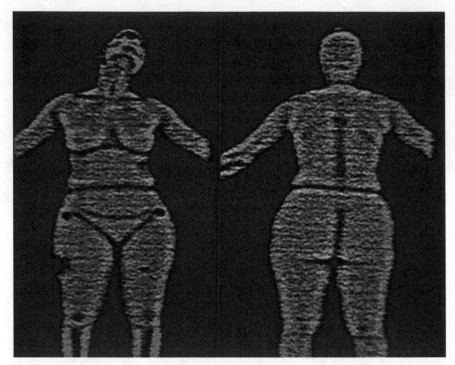

The X-ray of a female prisoner at body search. *Ich glaubte Gefangene zu sehen/I Thought I Was Seeing Convicts*. Courtesy of Harun Farocki Filmproduktion, Berlin.

where restricted space equals restrained action. Still, their architectures coincide in computer simulation where it mirrors the disciplinary and controlling principle of Panopticon.

Through its merely functional reason for being the imagery of a surveillance, camera offers an example to the present account of the aesthetics and experience of documentary time. With its flickering, unfocused, fragmentary sound, and a poor, bluish color representation, the tape of the surveillance video stands out as an automatic recording, a mechanic observer of real life. The blurred images result from an automatic recording, a framing of what occurs within the limited view of the camera eye, and this is, of course, the legitimizing factor of its objective inscription of real life. *I Thought I Was Seeing Convicts* critically posits the material feel of surveillance tape and the functions and effects of the surveillance camera as a symbol of regulation and control.

One part of the video shows images and sounds registered by the prison surveillance system. Farocki notes that "surveillance cameras show the norm and anticipate deviations from it." In the following frame the bluish videotape is contrasted to the black-and-white sequence of an old prison movie set where a girl greets her lover through the bars. The prisoner manages to bribe the guard so that he can step outside to embrace her. Another split-screen offers a surveillance overview and a closer view of a long table where inmates receive their visitors. The left frame zooms into a couple holding hands and is then replaced by a black frame that reads, "Visitors in prison; surveillance from the ceiling."

A close-up of the same couple's hands appears on both frames, and we hear fragments of speech and sound from the staff at the control board; the screen turns black, and the double-spaced text reads, "A visitor opens a transparent purse." The action is shown in the next few frames, which is then replaced by a new text, "and extracts two coins, an old quarter and the new one—The new coin speaks of life beyond the prison walls." A close-up of the two coins is juxtaposed to a pan shot of the surroundings outside the prison gates.

At this point the juxtaposed images result in a symbolic staging of surveillance technology, a trope of controlled real time. In the reframed episode with the transparent purse the excessive and continuous control of the inmate's gestures offers the ultimate contrast to everyday life in freedom. Yet a trace of historical time—the new coin—slides into the regulated present tense of prison life.

Apart from the technology of power represented by the surveillance camera, Farocki also conceptualizes a media context whose temporal status is that of real time but which nevertheless may provide evidence of what actually happened. For this discussion of the trace, the example draws attention to current cases in media culture where the preservation of moving images is dependent on the spectacular of the recorded event. From this point of view the discourse of *I Thought I Was Seeing Convicts* refers to wider media phenomena such as reality television or the increasing use of surveillance footage as legal evidence in trials.[17]

An important part of the film recycles surveillance footage from Corcoran State Prison in California. It is a high-security prison with an advanced system of armed guards and cameras that are supposed to guarantee the safety of both inmates and staff. Since its construction, however, guards have opened fire two thousand times, hundreds of inmates have been wounded, twelve of them seriously, and five have been killed. Farocki reuses material provided by a Californian activist project Prison Focus to critically stress the mechanized brutality of prison surveillance and punishment—"Behind the window, armed guards; above them, the camera. Field of vision and field of fire coincide."[18] The reference to surveillance technology adds a new dimension to the material and existential signification of the trace. The Shooting Review Board is the

A fight at Corcoran State Prison. *Ich glaubte Gefangene zu sehen/I Thought I Was Seeing Convicts*. Courtesy of Harun Farocki Filmproduktion, Berlin.

workstation at Corcoran State Prison, where each provocation of firearm is recorded and preserved. Among the fragments of surveillance footage the compilation in *I Thought I Was Seeing Convicts* reproduces the recorded death of a convict, fatally shot on April 7, 1989.

An image of a prison yard is shown in the upper left corner, under which it is indicated "Pictures from surveillance cameras." The next frame shows two prisoners in the same yard, appearing in the right corner; another text indicates "They are only worthy of attention in exceptional cases." With the ensuing sequence taken by another camera, Farocki emphasizes that "[o]nly in exceptional cases are the tapes not erased and reused." The following series of images shows an illustrative example, beginning with the same framing of a prison yard and Farocki's marginal note, "An exceptional case: death."

The same slow-motion sequence of blurred black-and-white footage unfolds on both frames: a man moves toward the left corner of the frame, kicking somebody off screen. A text enters from the left, to explain what we see, "A fight in the yard at Corcoran State Prison in California." One can barely discern what is happening, as the violent action partly disappears off frame, beyond the left corner of the image, but there is soon

William Martinez, age 30, shot by a prison guard. *Ich glaubte Gefangene zu sehen/I Thought I Was Seeing Convicts*. Courtesy of Harun Farocki Filmproduktion, Berlin.

another marginal note in the upper left to explain that "Bystanders run for cover." For a second, the fighting men move into view of the camera, which is doubled on Farocki's split-screen. Then, another black frame covers the left with the inscription, "White gun smoke moves across the image: A guard has opened fire." The smoke dissolves in the slow-motion reproduction of the video, and then another intertitle explains that "William Martinez is hit." The following sequence shows one of the men stumble and fall, "William Martinez, aged 30, convicted of armed robbery, lies there for nine more minutes." At this point the silence is broken by a voice-over, explaining that, because of security restrictions it takes staff nine minutes and fourteen seconds to move over the yard to take care of Martinez, "a process we have condensed with this video."

Although the procedure of extracting Martinez's body from the yard has been compressed to a little more than one minute, the doubled sequence in Farocki's video results in a contemplative moment where, in particular, two things are brought to the fore: the insufficient record of the surveillance tape and the principle according to which it has been preserved—the deviance and fatal outcome of the inscribed event. Ever since the Rodney King case in 1991 the visual evidence of amateur footage and surveillance devices is continuously subject to televised narratives and legal processes. *I Thought I Was Seeing Convicts* highlights a crucial aspect of the trace status that these real-life documentations occasionally achieve in the mainstream culture of spectacular media events and fragmented narratives of repetition. The truth claim of such optics of surveillance is always propelled by the raw, seemingly nonmanipulated footage of automatic inscription. Yet the usual poor quality of vision and sound makes the signification of the shown even more dependent on extratextual knowledge.

In Farocki's video this insufficient mimesis or pragmatic meaning of camera inscription is stressed through the prioritized space of written commentary, such as "White gun smoke moves across the image: A guard has opened fire." Context is needed in order to understand what the image represents, and yet there is no doubt that one of the men is hit and falls to the ground. Writing about related issues of indexicality in another context of media technology, Wolf gives another turn to this idea of the limits of representation:

> In one sense, a blurred image is an indication that the technology has reached its limits; sharp images with dubious indexical linkages may be more harmful in that their shortcomings are less noticeable. The instrument does not indicate what it does not see, and so one must take this into account when studying objects viewed with it.[19]

Accordingly, the reframing of a fatal shooting in this film turns into "the death of Martinez" through the correspondence between the recorded footage and the knowledge of an incident in the history of the Corcoran State Prison. So far, with respect to the cultural signification of the image-imprint, the surveillance tape does not differ from other visual media. The function and use of camcorders, however, offer a context where preservation is only the destiny of exceptional recordings. Videos showing the disciplined time-space of everyday routine, of normality, await nothing but erasure and reuse.[20]

And so, paradoxically, we find ourselves back at Bazin's formula of the representation of an irrevocable moment, which in the realm of moving images may be repeated again, in order to revitalize the ghostlike gesture of a body collapsing in the past.

The aim of this chapter was to illustrate how the trace may be critically reassessed as a figure of documentary time within and beyond the context of cinema in contemporary media. The phenomenological themes of inscription and recollection were here combined with critical insights into the media production of historical time. I used Sigmar Polke's painting *The Hunt for the Taliban and Al Qaeda* as a point of departure, because it offers a current metaphor of how our vision of the world has become inseparable from the image world of media culture and how our perception, knowledge, and beliefs therefore are linked to the time-images of visual technology. In line with Paul Virilio and others, I turned to the paradigmatic example of machine perception provided by video surveillance, military optics, and war reporting. This choice was motivated by the apparent nonphenomenological context of a perspective driven by a critical ambition to display relations of power and the politics of representation and how this affects our relation to images and media memory.

Examples illustrated how the phenomenology of the trace is both affirmed and questioned in contemporary media. These examples brought attention to the limitations of philosophy, as we divert our attention from the aesthetics of moving images to the policies of representation and other sociocultural mechanisms involved in the framing of social and historical realms. Still, in Ghost Town and *I Thought I Was Seeing Convicts* the aura of the trace remains a crucial incentive for narrative imagination.

Documentary Time: An Afterword

Image and time represent a pristine problem of classical film theory and film aesthetics, which has primarily been associated with assertions regarding the physical medium of cinema and qualities of film as a visual art. The purpose of this book was to reconsider these issues from the perspective of documentary cinema and account for the inheritance of existential phenomenology in classical film theory. Consequently, a reassessment of cinematic temporality in early film criticism and in experimental filmmaking brought attention to the historical persistence of phenomenological themes in film theory and visual culture. Moreover, the aim of this metatheoretical outline was to stress the important continuities and common interests of classical film theory and contemporary film studies—a theoretical continuity that today risks being omitted as classical texts tend to be overlooked in a discipline highly dominated by critical studies and postmodern theory. The discussions of the previous chapters have illustrated that a rereading of film and phenomenology not necessarily has to be at odds with the critical perspectives of contemporary theory. A return to, and discussion of, classical film theory is especially rewarding for studying image and time in documentary because documentary cinema has only rarely been addressed in discourses on film aesthetics.

My ambition also was to offer a reflection on cinema and phenomenology and to address the promises and shortcomings of a phenomenological perspective on documentary film and video. I have addressed some recurrent issues of documentary theory where the problems of existential phenomenology are especially salient, such as the visceral impact of documentary images, aspects of image-affect, the index argument, and aspects of representing past events and enacting historical experience. Despite many implied references to phenomenology in contemporary approaches to time and memory, there have been few attempts at a more explicit reflection on the position of phenomenology in contemporary theory.

Although we have to question the murky side of introspection that inevitably clings to phenomenology as a method and research attitude, there is reason to acknowledge the persistence of certain phenomenological themes in film theory, which apply to the aesthetic experience of moving images in film and media. There are still things to learn from the achievements of early film theory and the sensitivity with which André Bazin and other critics acknowledged the creative and existential aspects of film as image-object and screen event. In this regard, this book adds to recent rereadings of, for example, André Bazin, who deserves recognition beyond the label of naïve realism that has commonly been ascribed to his work.

In the crossover between the phenomenology of cinema and the phenomenology of time consciousness, the moving image has propelled a parallel concern with the ontology of the film image and the experience of time-bound images. This is true for the reflection on photography, the musical analogy in film theories and experimentations in the 1920s, as well as for the alleged antiphenomenology of Gilles Deleuze's *Cinema*. A major assertion of the previous discussions was that the overlapping discourses of the time-image and the trace fundamentally define temporalization as a phenomenological issue in film theory, which deserves both critical attention and modification in line with the varied status of the moving image in contemporary film culture. Examples have shown that cinema and temporality is a problem that welcomes and rewards phenomenology. The esoteric and yet tactile quality of time in moving images requires a perspective that is sensitive to film as screen event. Different from a conception of film as a static image-object, this perspective has to grant the spectacular event of unfolding sound-images. Throughout film history some poignant phenomenological themes crystallize within the reflection on image and time and the filmic experimentation with time and space. In attempts to define the temporal status of cinema, assumptions of immanent qualities meet with ideas of the affective impact of temporalization in film. My ambition was to clarify interesting intersections between the phenomenology of cinema and the phenomenology of time experience, which is far from any exhaustive and verified affirmation regarding the direct influence of Husserl and his followers on theories and filmmakers. The purpose was to display a unifying tendency in this varied discourse on image and time, in order to contextualize the problem in the history of ideas and, finally, to attempt a modification of its themes in relation to documentary film and contemporary theory.

A parallel concern with phenomenology and film theory represented the other level of the discussion, where a phenomenological direction was charted from the work of Bazin to the phenomenology of film experience promoted by Vivian Sobchack. During the process of writing this book my skepticism toward phenomenology as a method gradually increased. At its worst, the wider sociocultural and historical aspects of both film and film experience are subordinate to an exclusively personal *hic et nunc* sensation of cinema. In this sense the *subject* and *subjectivity*—terms excluded in semiotics, psychoanalysis, and poststructuralism—can be hidden in an existential theory of the sensuous body. The question remains whether this excessively personal perspective really increases our knowledge of the sociopsychological mechanisms and shared desires and expectations that direct our reception of filmic representation.

As an inspiring set of thoughts, semiotic phenomenology may, however, increase our sensitivity toward the affective side of moving images. It may provide conceptual tools for an approach that aims simultaneously at the complex expression and attraction of moving images. Historically, we cannot overlook the influence of existential phenomenology on aesthetic theory. The problems of phenomenology are not only part of our cultural history but existential concerns that will always be subject to the theory and practice of cinema.

Rather than a new phenomenology of film experience, this book suggested a case-oriented approach to the phenomenology of documentary time. The discussion focused on the expressive possibilities of temporalization in documentary representation, including thematic approaches to historical time and the film archive. In looking at some alternative references to semiotic phenomenology, my ambition has been to provide a constructive reflection on the analysis of documentary film and video. The discussion was biased toward the space-time malleability of moving images and the creative work of documentary filmmakers to use the formal and expressive potential of their medium to orchestrate the recorded sound-images into compelling representations of social and historical experience. Aspects of veracity and the documentary incentive to reveal and explain social problems were here subordinated to meanings of aesthetic experience and imagination, which also add to the attraction of documentary cinema.

Time measurement refers to the material and creative dimension of framing and transforming space-time relations in moving images. Applied to cinema, it offers a theme that stresses film as a temporal art and an art of record. In line with Dominique Janicaud's notion, time measurement suggests a notion of time experience that goes beyond metaphysics because it combines the sensory judgment of a temporal dimension with quantitative strategies to measure time. On a metaphoric level this notion applies to the chronofiction of film because the production of duration and tempo is achieved through an elaboration of measured interval, the length of each shot, and the manipulation of speed. In turn, our experience of duration, flux, and rupture in moving images is often related to the structuring of a narrative and to existential meanings of time, although experimental cinema continuously reminds us that temporalization may offer an attraction in itself. The formal possibilities of extending, accelerating, decelerating, stopping, and fragmentizing the filmed event motivated a consideration of examples where the cinematic figuration of time and space causes a frame-breaking event. Erving Goffman's notion opens up to a sociopsychological consideration of how the viewer responds both individually and intersubjectively to a stage performance or film. In this context *frame* denotes the socioculturally constructed preconception that governs our definition of, and reaction to, a given situation. Although a thorough reflection and analysis of spectator psychology go beyond the demarcations of this book, the reference to Goffman's phenomenology of everyday life suggested a promising path in that direction. For the present consideration of documentary time, the discussion of the frame-breaking event has the merit of recognizing the important interrelation between the creative achievement of representation and the social realm of spectatorship.

Regarding the possibility of space-time manipulation as a *negative experience* in documentary, I turned to a recurrent figure of time that is at the core of both existential phenomenology and film theory: the disquieting image of death. The image of death aligns perfectly with the classical conception of film and photography: death signifies both the transformation from being to nonbeing and the immobile body, a sign of an irrevocable ending. André Bazin accounted for *the thrill of the real* and stressed the perverse pleasure of repeatedly looking at the filmed bullfight, with the defeated bull collapsing in the past. Vivian Sobchack convincingly argues that the framing of actual violence and death reminds us of the documentary moment as *ethically charged*. The frame-breaking event of the recorded death represents a radical example where the phenomenology of the time-image coincides with the phenomenology of the trace.

Aside from the literal meaning of the historical vestige or the image-imprint as a trace of the past, I acknowledged the trace as a phenomenological discourse and a salient theme in documentary filmmaking. A contextualization of the trace may be helpful in bringing attention to the complex material and existential meaning of, respectively, the sound-image as a mnemonic sign and the materiality of the photograph or film image. For the present account of documentary time, I suggested a rereading of the trace as a salient theme in visual culture and a documentary trope achieved through strategies of *mise en scène* and narrative imagination.

The existential impact of the trace as a presence of absence closely relates to Charles Sanders Peirce's description of the index as a "hollowed-out sign" (Mary Ann Doane), a sign function beyond description, or a "disarrangement expressing itself" (Emmanuel Lévinas). Aside from the pristine meaning of the trace as the uncanny appearance of a sign that denotes the presence of a static imprint, as well as the dynamic transition between the present, the future, and the past, my aim was to acknowledge the trace as an important theme in documentary. Paul Ricœur represents an important reference in this context, and his approach to the interrelation between the trace and the trope in *Time and Narrative* and *Memory, History, Forgetting* welcomes and encourages a related discussion in documentary studies. There are some obvious clashes between Ricœur's argument and the complex documentary realm of history and memory. By suggesting a perfect symmetry between narrative and temporality, he excluded other processes of temporalization. Hence, Ricœur overlooked the production and reception of chronofictions beyond the novel and the historian's narrative representation of the past. In relating Ricœur's reflection on narrative time and memory to cinema, we have to grapple with a poetic enactment of the trace, which depends both on the construction of a narrative and on the formal elaboration of time and space in moving images. Documentary film complicates the discussion even further because this is a culture of representation where narrative imagination and a poetics of time blend with the objective of a social and historical quest. Hence, in important ways, documentary film would collapse the implied difference between the time of fictive and historical narratives. Yet the suggested reading of Ricœur indicated the pertinence of the trace as a visual motif and a recurrent existential theme in contemporary media culture.

Special attention was paid to Ricœur's discussion about the creative emplotment of historical time and the dual meaning of the trace in classical philosophy where it relates to imagination and the appearance of image-memories (Plato) and to the conscious act of recollection and of representing a thing "formerly perceived, acquired, or learned" (Aristotle). Related to cinema and documentary film in particular, the discussion may provide new insights into the poetic staging of the trace as an uncanny presence of the past. To appear as a compelling sign of the past, however, the trace has to be *animated*. The imprint does not automatically become an affective sign of the past because it is dependent on extratextual knowledge. The important transformation of the image from static imprint to mnemonic sign represents a crucial theme in existential phenomenology, where it echoes in the writings of Maurice Merleau-Ponty, Jean-Paul Sartre, Emmanuel Lévinas, Roland Barthes, and Paul Ricœur.

In documentary filmmaking there are many ways to enact or animate the trace, some of which were exemplified in Part II. A series of close readings suggested that a consideration of the trace may contribute to a critical discourse on documentary and archive memory, which expands beyond cinema to stress-related media contexts, problems of film and historiography, and the production and reproduction of image-memories that, for good and for bad, contribute to the reinvention of historical time in visual culture.

In line with Ricœur, I also wanted to stress the creative potential of documentary to portray the features of historical experience and shared memories, including processes of forgetting and oblivion. Experimental approaches to the trace in film and video may provide for an alternative telling of history, which involves a reflection on the mediating process and narrative imagination without which *historical experience* would remain a meaningless abstraction. Cinematic strategies to reframe and double the trace make it a refracted sign, which may question ideas of presence and appearance in classical phenomenology. Moreover, the use of sound recordings, digital media, and alternative approaches to documentary narratives is an important reminder of the existential impact of the trace that cannot be reduced to the pristine signification of the visual imprint, or even to the context of film and photographic representation.

Finally, aside from the narrative possibility of creating a microperspective on time and memory, Ricœur brought attention to the ethical problem that is propelled by the encounter between the creative process of constructing an intrigue and the responsibility that awaits any attempt to represent the past. Documentary film represents a visual culture that has always been haunted by this problem, but it is also a creative context where the possibilities of the moving image as archive memory can be further explored. From a documentary perspective the phenomenology of the trace opens up to a variety of compelling subjects, where a consideration of film aesthetics and narrative imagination may result in a deepened consideration of film as a temporal art and a technology of memory.

Notes

Introduction

1. Jacques Aumont distinguishes between *l'image dans le temps* and *le temps de l'image*. Jacques Aumont, *L'image* (Paris: Éditions Nathan, 1990), 121–23.
2. Jacques Aumont, *L'oeil interminable. Cinéma et peinture* (Paris: Librairie Séguier, 1989), 80.
3. I borrow the expression of film as a *technology of memory* from Bernard Stiegler, "The Time of Cinema. On the 'New World' and 'Cultural Exception,'" *Technema: Journal of Philosophy and Technology* 4 (1998): 62–113.
4. Gilles Deleuze, *Cinema 1: The Movement-Image*, trans. Hugh Tomlinson and Barbara Habberjam (London: Continuum, 2005); Gilles Deleuze, *Cinema 2. The Time-Image*, trans. Hugh Tomlinson and Robert Galeta (London: Continuum, 2005).
5. Pierre Bourdieu, *Photography: A Middle-Brow Art*, trans. Shaun Whiteside (Stanford, Calif.: Stanford University Press, 1990), 9.
6. Semiotic phenomenology is not a field restricted to the French context but an ongoing project on both sides of the Atlantic. For example, Jeffrey A. Bell, Hugh J. Silverman, and Shaun Gallagher are scholars whose philosophical expertise I rely on for general references to the philosophy of time consciousness. Jeffrey A. Bell, *The Problem of Difference. Phenomenology and Poststructuralism* (Toronto, Ontario: University of Toronto Press, 1998); Shaun Gallagher, *The Inordinance of Time* (Evanston, Ill.: Northwestern University Press, 1998); Hugh J. Silverman, *Inscriptions: After Phenomenology and Structuralism* (Evanston, Ill.: Northwestern University Press, 1997). For obvious reasons of demarcation—my study is primarily designed as a contribution to film studies and documentary theory—this corpus of secondary literature offers important guidelines for readers who require a more thorough discussion of issues that are only briefly accounted for in this book.
7. Edmund Husserl, *Idées directrices pour une phenomenology*, trans. Paul Ricœur (Paris: Éditions Gallimard, 1950).
8. With the 1960s structuralist movement in France, existential phenomenology was the primary subject of rejection. Claude Lévi-Strauss, Michael Foucault, Jacques Lacan, Louis Althusser, and Roland Barthes represented the radical vanguard of structuralism. On an institutional level this paradigmatic shift is most clearly demarcated in 1969 when Foucault—and not Ricœur—inherited Jean Hyppolite's chair at Collège de France. Bengt Kristensson Uggla, *Kommunikation på bristningsgränsen* (Stockholm: Brutus Östlings Bokförlag, 1999), 20.
9. In this context there will also be reason to consider some of the enthusiastic opponents to phenomenology. Jean-François Lyotard, for example, argues that "we have better to stop phenomenologizing" (*Discours, figures*. Paris: Éditions Klinckseick, 1985: 56), and Gilles Deleuze criticizes the unnecessary either–or of phenomenology, as either "an abyss without differences and without properties; or a supremely individuated Being and an intensely personalized Form" (*Logic of Sense*. Trans. Mark Lester. New York: Columbia University Press, 1990: 105–6). Despite this critique these authors obtain an important position in the contemporary post–Merleau-Pontean context of thought. Silverman, *Inscriptions*, 124.
10. Mary Ann Doane, *The Emergence of Cinematic Time: Modernity, Contingency, The Archive* (Cambridge, Mass.: Harvard University Press, 2002). Sean Cubitt's account of the time-image suggests another film history, which has been outlined from the perspective of digital media. The suggested categories of *the pixel*, *the cut*, and *the vector* imply strong concern with the

materiality and experience of the moving image, although Cubitt's reading of classical film theory is of less interest for considering film and phenomenology in this book. Sean Cubitt, *The Cinema Effect* (Cambridge, Mass.: The MIT Press, 2004).

11. Gilles Deleuze's notion of the time-image represents an important reference in this context, although I will refer to *time-images* in a broader, more general sense. Gilles Deleuze, *Cinema 2. The Time-Image*, trans. Hugh Tomlinson and Robert Galeta (London: Continuum, 2005).

12. Thomas Elsaesser and Kay Hoffmann, eds., *Cinema Futures: Cain, Abel, or Cable? The Screen Arts in the Digital Age* (Amsterdam: Amsterdam University Press, 1998), 206.

13. Monique Sicard, "De la trace à la traque," *Les cahiers de médiologie* 9 (2000): 106.

14. Vivian Sobchack, *The Address of the Eye: A Phenomenology of Film Experience* (Princeton, N.J.: Princeton University Press, 1992).

15. Erving Goffman, *Frame Analysis: An Essay on the Organization of Experience* (Boston: Northeastern University Press, 1986).

16. Roger Odin, *Cinéma et production de sens* (Paris: Armand Colin, 1990), 50.

17. Ibid., 50. My translation of the following: "qui nous obligent à nous interroger sur la définition de l'objet cinéma tel qu'il fonctionne dans l'espace sociale ...."

1. The Phenomenology of Image and Time

1. Edmund Husserl, *On the Phenomenology of the Consciousness of Internal Time (1893–1917)*, trans. John Barnett Brough (Dordrecht: Kluwer Academic Publishers, 1991), 24.

2. Bernard Stiegler, "The Time of Cinema. On the 'New World' and 'Cultural Exception,'" *Technema: Journal of Philosophy and Technology* 4 (1998): 62–113.

3. André Bazin, "The Ontology of the Photographic Image," in *What Is Cinema? Volume 2*, trans. and ed. Hugh Gray (Berkeley and Los Angeles: University of California Press, 1967), 15.

4. "Lympha figuras/datque capitue novas." Quote from Ovid's *Metamorphoses XV*, reprinted in Erich Auerbach, *Figura*, trans. Marc André Bernier (Paris: Éditions Belin, 1993), 22.

5. Rudolf Arnheim, *Film as Art* (London: Faber & Faber Ltd., 1958), 31.

6. Christian Metz, *Film Language: A Semiotics of the Cinema*, trans. Michael Taylor (Chicago, Ill.: University of Chicago Press, 1974), 8.

7. Gilles Deleuze, *Cinema 2: The Time-Image*, trans. Hugh Tomlinson and Robert Galeta (London: Continuum, 2005), 24–26.

8. See, for example, Philip Rosen, *Change Mummified: Cinema, Historicity, Theory* (Minneapolis: University of Minnesota Press, 2001); Daniel Morgan, "Rethinking Bazin: Ontology and Realist Aesthetics," *Critical Inquiry* 32, no. 3 (Spring 2006): 443–81; Ivone Margulies, ed., *Rites of Realism: Essays on Corporeal Cinema* (Durham, N.C.: Duke University Press, 2002).

9. Bazin, *What Is Cinema? Volume 2*, 30.

10. Jean-Marie Schaeffer, *L'image précaire: Du dispositif photographique* (Paris: Éditions du Seuil, 1987), 64; my translation.

11. Ibid., 65–66; my translation.

12. Ibid., 65; my translation.

13. Bazin refers to this aspect of cinematic temporality in his bullfight essay, which I will discuss more thoroughly in chapter 2. André Bazin, "Death Every Afternoon," trans. Mark A. Cohern, in Margulies, *Rites of Realism*.

14. Roger Hallas, "Bearing Witness and the Queer Moving Image" (PhD diss., New York University, 2002), 261.

15. Michael Renov, *The Subject of Documentary* (Minneapolis: University of Minnesota Press, 2004). Elisabeth Cowie is another important scholar in this context. From the perspective of psychoanalysis she argues that the experience of documentary film depends both on the expectations of scientific truths and on the desire to understand the world and ourselves. Elisabeth Cowie, "The Spectacle of Actuality," in *Collecting Visible Evidence*, ed. Jane M. Gaines and Michael Renov (Minneapolis: University of Minnesota Press, 1999).

16. Laura U. Marks, *The Skin of the Film: Intercultural Cinema, Embodiment, and the Senses* (Durham, N.C.: Duke University Press, 2000), 2.

17. A less consistent example is *Atlas of Emotion: Journeys in Art, Architecture, and Film*, which addresses film aesthetics and haptic space more broadly from a feminist perspective that is biased toward embodied experience. Giuliana Bruno, *Atlas of Emotion: Journeys in Art, Architecture, and Film* (New York: Verso, 2002).

18. David MacDougall, *The Corporeal Image: Film, Ethnography, and the Senses* (Princeton, N.J.: Princeton University Press, 2006), 3.

19. Among other important references in this context of the documentary and image-affect, and that which also contribute to MacDougall's argument, are the following: Linda Williams, "Corporealized Observers: Visual Pornographies and the 'Carnal Density of Vision,'" in

Fugitive Images: From Photography to Video, ed. Patrice Petro (Bloomington, Ind.: Indiana University Press, 1995); Bill Nichols, *Representing Reality: Issues and Concepts in Documentary* (Bloomington, Ind.: Indiana University Press, 1991).

20. François Brunet, *La naissance de l'idée de photographie* (Paris: Presses Universitaires de France, 2000), 31.
21. Louis Delluc, *Photogénie* (Paris: Maurice de Brunoff, 1920), 5; my translation.
22. Jean Epstein, *Écrits sur le cinéma, 1921–1953* (Paris: Éditions Seghers, 1974), 94; my translation.
23. Mary Ann Doane, "The Object of Theory," in *Rites of Realism: Essays on Corporeal Cinema*, ed. Ivone Margulies (Durham, N.C.: Duke University Press, 2002), 82.
24. MacDougall, *The Corporeal Image*, 17.
25. Mary Ann Doane, *The Emergence of Cinematic Time: Modernity, Contingency, the Archive* (Cambridge, Mass.: Harvard University Press, 2002), 226.
26. Mary Ann Doane refers to Paul Willemen and Miriam Hansen, in whose work on the historical role of indexicality in the cinema "the indexical trace as filmic inscription of contingency is indissociable from affect." Doane, *The Emergence of Cinematic Time*, 225.
27. Dudley Andrew, "The Neglected Tradition of Phenomenology in Film Theory," in *Movies and Methods, Volume 2*, ed. Bill Nichols (Berkeley and Los Angeles: University of California Press, 1985), 625. See also Dudley Andrew, *Major Film Theories: An Introduction* (New York: Oxford University Press, 1976), 242–53.
28. *Quarterly Review of Film and Video* 12, no. 3 (1990).
29. Frank P. Tomasulo, "Phenomenology: Philosophy and Media Theory—An Introduction," *Quarterly Review of Film and Television* 12, no. 3 (1990): 2.
30. Bill Nichols, "Film Theory and the Revolt Against Master Narratives," in *Reinventing Film Studies*, ed. Christine Gledhill and Linda Williams (London: Arnold, 2000). Phenomenology is still a marginalized field in film studies, in the sense of theories that explicitly refer to the work of Edmund Husserl or existential phenomenology. However, as I argue elsewhere in this book, problems of classical phenomenology seem to reappear in predominant discussions about film aesthetics, spectatorship, or film experience and the body.
31. Allan Casebier, *Film and Phenomenology. Toward a Realist Theory of Cinematic Representation* (Cambridge, Mass.: Cambridge University Press, 1991).
32. A reading of Husserl's philosophy as a realist theory is grounded in the philosopher's early work, most notably *Ideas* and *Logical Investigations*, where a realist position indeed can be found in his account of "what we see." In this context Husserl approaches the objects of our perception as already given: things "which stand before us in propria persona." See, for example, Edmund Husserl, *Logical Investigations V §11, §14*, trans. J. N. Findlay (London: Routledge and Kegan Paul, 1973). Paul Ricœur, however, claims the opposite: "The phenomenology which is elaborated in the Ideas is incontestably an idealism and even a transcendental idealism." Paul Ricœur, *A Key to Edmund Husserl's Ideas I* (Milwaukee, Wis.: Marquette University Press, 1996), 47. See also Herman Philipse, "Transcendental Idealism," in *The Cambridge Companion to Husserl*, ed. Barry Smith and David Woodruff Smith (Cambridge, Mass.: Cambridge University Press, 1995); and David Woodruff Smith, "Mind and Body," in *The Cambridge Companion to Husserl*, ed. Barry Smith and David Woodruff Smith (Cambridge, Mass.: Cambridge University Press, 1995).
33. This was equally the purpose of Casebier's earlier work *Film Appreciation* (New York: Harcourt Brace Jovanovich, 1976).
34. Casebier, *Film and Phenomenology*, 13.
35. "Spectators are discoverers of the objects represented by the motion pictures...." Ibid., 155.
36. Ibid., 137.
37. Ibid., 138.
38. Ibid., 145.
39. Ibid., 144.
40. A more renowned and cited work is Stanley Cavell's *The World Viewed*. I position Cavell on the side of transcendental realism, because in opposition to Sobchack, he focuses on the ontological content of filmic perception and not on the embodied encounter between the viewer and the sensory aspect of audiovisual representation. Cavell writes, "The world of a moving picture is screened. The screen is not a support, not like the canvas; there is nothing to support, that way.... That the projected world does not exist (now) is its only difference from reality" (24).
41. Vivian Sobchack, *The Address of the Eye: A Phenomenology of Film Experience* (Princeton, N.J.: Princeton University Press, 1991), 55.
42. Vivian Sobchack, "Toward a Phenomenology of Nonfictional Film Experience," in *Collecting Visible Evidence*, ed. Jane M. Gaines and Michael Renov (Minneapolis: University of Minnesota Press, 1999).
43. Ibid., 250.

44. Ibid., 247.
45. Ibid., 252.
46. "Noetic act" is the Husserlian term for the mental process of intending an object. This category also involves "hyletic data," specific qualities that we may apperceive when consciously "taking in" the object. "Noema" finally designates the apperceived thing; the thing in itself, which Husserl argues has an existence in the material world, beyond consciousness. This core concept in Husserl's philosophy has been a long-standing debate. The complexity of the term is addressed in the following way by Pol Vandevelde: "The noema is supposed to be a mediation, but a mediation that does not account for its own possibility, hence the various interpretations of it as: an abstract sense belonging to a third realm—besides subject and object (Føllesdahl 1982), as a linguistic meaning (McIntyre and Smith 1982), or just as what the phenomenological analysis produces (Sokolowski 1984)." Pol Vandevelde, "Paul Ricœur: Narrative and Phenomenon," in *A Key to Edmund Husserl's Ideas I*, ed. Paul Ricœur (Milwaukee, Wis.: Marquette University Press, 1996), For Husserl's discussion of "noema," see *Ideas*, trans. W. R. Boyce (London: Collier Books, 1962), chaps 9 and 10.
47. Sobchack, *The Address of the Eye*, 133.
48. In her discussion about cinematic technologies and film viewing, Sobchack draws primarily on Don Ihde, *Experimental Phenomenology: An Introduction* (New York: Paragon Books, 1979). In Ihde's opinion, a film is a perceptual activity transmitted through a technological apparatus. It is an activity whose indirect presence is constantly incorporated in our shared experience of the world. Sobchack, *The Address of the Eye*, 169.
49. Sobchack, *The Address of the Eye*, 131.
50. Ibid., 133.
51. Ibid. The philosophy of Merleau-Ponty seeks to reformulate Husserl's notion of essence through a strategy to define the essences. Accordingly, Sobchack rejects the idea of a film as a thing in itself (or rather a perception in itself). She argues that a film is inseparable from a spectator subject's experience of it, and the film's mediated expression is inseparable from the perceptual modalities of cinema. Also, this more relativist position implies a critique of the solipsism inherent in Husserl's theory. Merleau-Ponty opposes the transcendental ego through an explicit account of meaning and language, the subject being conceived of as an expressive and perceptive agent in a speech act: "There is in particular one cultural object that plays a primordial role for the perception of the other, that is language" ("Il y a, en particulier, un objet culturel qui va jouer un rôle essentiel dans la perception d'autrui: c'est le langage"). Maurice Merleau-Ponty, *Phénoménologie de la perception* (Paris: Librairie Gallimard, 1945), 407. *The Address of the Eye* offers a reading of Merleau-Ponty where his existential concern of perception is a major issue. Here, vision is not equivalent to seeing with one's eyes. Rather, vision depends on a bodily experience and the act of being seen, which stresses intersubjectivity as a predominant factor in our understanding of perception. Hence, the individual is both subject and object at the same time; see, for example, Merleau-Ponty, *Le visible et l'invisible* (Paris: Éditions Gallimard, 1964), 100–104. This idea motivates Sobchack's concept of the lived body, which relates to both the film and the viewer: "Perception is the bodily access or agency for being-in-the-world, for having both a world and a being" (*The Address of the Eye*, 40).
52. Sobchack, *The Address of the Eye*, 71.
53. Ibid., 61.
54. Ibid., 60.
55. Ibid., XVI.
56. *Lady in the Lake* (Robert Montgomery, USA, 1947) represents one of the rare film examples upon which Sobchack dwells at length. In the context of Merleau-Ponty's existential reversal of subject and object, this film functions as a mere object of exemplification: the camera's replacement of the hero's field of vision (the only glimpses of his persona that we get are hands and feet as the camera eye/I is supposed to see them) stages the problem of "the seer and the seen" (Sobchack, *The Address of the Eye*, 230–32). The question remains, however, whether *Lady in the Lake* is not a too literal and, at the same time, reductive example of perceiving the camera eye/I.
57. Vivian Sobchack, *Carnal Thoughts: Embodiment and Moving Image Culture* (Berkeley and Los Angeles: University of California Press, 2004).
58. Ibid., 3.
59. Ibid., 7.
60. Marks, *The Skin of the Film*.
61. Sobchack, *Carnal Thoughts*, 5.
62. Ibid., 53.
63. Ibid., 61.

64. Giuliana Bruno, *Atlas of Emotion. Journeys in Art, Architecture, and Film* (New york: Verso, 2002)

65. Vivian Sobchack, "Inscribing Ethical Space: Ten Propositions on Death, Representation and Documentary," *Quarterly Review of Film Studies* 9, no. 4 (1984): 283–300; "Toward a Phenomenology of Nonfictional Film Experience," in *Collecting Visible Evidence*, ed. Jane M. Gaines and Michael Renov (Minneapolis: University of Minnesota Press, 1999).

2. The Time-Image and the Trace

1. "The original cause of all such phenomena is the circle. It is quite natural that this should be so; for there is nothing strange in a lesser marvel being caused by a greater marvel, and it is a very great marvel that contraries should be present together, and the circle is made up of contraries. For to begin with, it is formed by motion and rest, things which are by nature opposed to one another." Aristotle, "Mechanics," in *The Complete Works of Aristotle II*, ed., Jonathan Barnes (Princeton, N.J.: Princeton University Press, 1981), 1299, 847b, 15–21.

2. Shaun Gallagher, *The Inordinance of Time* (Evanston, Ill.: Northwestern University Press, 1998), 17.

3. Quote from *Physics*, Jonathan Barnes, ed., *The Complete Works of Aristotle, Volume 1* (Princeton, N.J.: Princeton University Press, 1984), 377, 223a, 22.

4. This paradox not only is a fundamental issue for classical phenomenology but also appears in terms of the cognitive paradox within the logical and empiricist tradition, represented by Hume, Locke, James, and others. For a thorough account on the problem of time consciousness within the field of phenomenology and cognitive theory, see Gallagher, *The Inordinance of Time*.

5. *Chronos* and *Aion* are stoic notions, introduced by Zeno of Citium (c.335 B.C.–262 B.C.), who defined time as "the extension of movement and the measure of swiftness and slowness." According to the stoics the experience of the flux is the experience of a dynamic present that continuously divides into the past/future time of *Aion*. We recognize this idea both in Heidegger's account of ecstatic-horizontal temporality and in Henri Bergson's (as well as Gilles Deleuze's) approach to the paradoxical instant. Philip Turetzky, *Time* (London: Routledge, 1998), 38. See also the discussion about Zeno, Bergson, and Epstein in Mary Ann Doane, *The Emergence of Cinematic Time: Modernity, Contingency, the Archive* (Cambridge, Mass.: Harvard University Press, 2002), 172–76.

6. A famous quote by Whitehead in Gallagher, *The Inordinance of Time*, 87.

7. Edmund Husserl, *On the Phenomenology of the Consciousness of Internal Time (1893–1917)*, trans. John Barnett Brough (Dordrecht: Kluwer Academic Publishers, 1991).

8. Gallagher discusses the differences and similarities between Lotz, James, and Broad, versus Husserl, the latter who "not only explain how the specious present is possible given an enduring act of consciousness, [he] also explain how consciousness unites itself (qua *Präsenzzeit*) through time." Gallagher, *The Inordinance of Time*, 49; see also Figure 3.1–3.4, 38–50.

9. Gallagher, *The Inordinance of Time*, 64.

10. Ibid., 101.

11. Dominique Janicaud, *Chronos* (Paris: Bernard Grasset, 1997), 106; my translation.

12. Ibid., 109.

13. The problems of intersubjectivity, language, and historical time were never explicitly integrated within Husserl's thought, although they frequently haunt his later work. It is primarily the problem of solipsism and the transcendental ego that inform modification and criticism of Husserl's phenomenology (Martin Heidegger: historical time and intersubjectivity; Maurice Merleau-Ponty: intersubjectivity, language, and embodied perception). This limitation of Husserl's philosophy also inspired the debate of Jacques Derrida, Jean-François Lyotard, and Gilles Deleuze. For an introductory account on the relation between Husserl and Merleau-Ponty, see Hugh J. Silverman, *Inscriptions: After Phenomenology and Structuralism* (Evanston, Ill.: Northwestern University Press, 1997). For a thorough account on the presence of Husserl in Deleuze's work, see Francisco José Martinez, "Échos husserliens dans l'oeuvre de G. Deleuze," in *Gilles Deleuze*, ed. Pierre Verstraeten and Isabelle Stengers (Paris: Librairie Philosophique J. Vrin, 1998). Gallagher not only comments on the critique of intentionality within the post-Husserlian context of continental thought but equally shows how the problem of solipsism and subjectivity haunts the discourse on temporality in the empiricist tradition of Hume and Locke and in the contemporary context of cognitive psychology. Gallagher, *The Inordinance of Time*, 108.

14. Deleuze's critique of classical phenomenology is not only a disagreement with, for example, "the subject," but rather a more general critique of transcendental philosophy and metaphysics. In *Logic of Sense* Deleuze rejects this tradition, which to his mind is trapped in

a dilemma, an unnecessary either/or: "What is common to metaphysics and transcendental philosophy is, above all, this alternative which they both impose on us: either an undifferentiated ground, a groundlessness, formless nonbeing, or an abyss without differences and without properties; or a supremely individuated Being and an intensely personalized Form." Gilles Deleuze, *Logic of Sense*, trans. Mark Lester (New York: Colombia University Press, 1990), 105–106.

15. Doane, *The Emergence of Cinematic Time*, 17.

16. Gilles Deleuze, *Cinema 2: The Time-Image*, trans. Hugh Tomlinson and Robert Galeta (London: Continuum, 2005), 111.

17. Ibid.

18. Ibid., 17.

19. Raymond Bellour, *L'Entre-Images 2. Mots, Images* (Paris: P.O.L. éditeur, 1999), 141. "[U]ne pure image-temps dans le temps même de l'image-mouvement."

20. Doane, *The Emergence of Cinematic Time*, 176–177.

21. Jeffrey A. Bell, *The Problem of Difference: Phenomenology and Poststructuralism* (Toronto, Ontario: University of Toronto Press, 1998), 187.

22. Gilles Deleuze, *Cinema 1: The Movement-Image* (Minneapolis: University of Minnesota Press, 1991), 1–2.

23. Ibid., 217. According to Tom Conley, Deleuze's notion of interval also relates to the signification of *event* in *Cinema*, which further indicates an implied concern for the experience of the moving image. Tom Conley, "The Film Event: From Interval to Interstice," in *The Brain is the Screen: Deleuze and the Philosophy of Cinema*, ed. Gregory Flaxman (Minneapolis: University of Minnesota Press, 2000), 316.

24. Dudley Andrew, "Tracing Ricœur," *Diacritics* 30, no. 2 (Summer 2000): 44. See also Dudley Andrew, "Foreword to the 2004 Edition," in *What Is Cinema? Volume 1*, trans. Hugh Gray (Berkeley and Los Angeles: University of California Press, 2005), xi–xv.

25. Edmund Husserl, *Ideas: General Introduction to Pure Phenomenology*, trans. W. R. Boyce Gibson (New York: Collier Books, 1962), 226. For an introduction on *sensa, sensile,* and *hyle,* see Laurent Cournarie and Pascal Dupont, *La sensibilité* (Paris: Éllipses, 1998), 5.

26. Raymond Court, "Temps et musique. Esquisse phénoménologique," in *Phénoménologie et Esthétique*, ed. Éliane Escoubas (La Vérsanne: Encre Marine, 1998), 213.

27. Mikel Dufrenne, *Phénoménologie de l'expérience esthétique* (Paris: Presses Universitaires de France, 1953); Mikel Dufrenne, *The Phenomenology of Aesthetic Experience*, trans. Edward S. Casey (Evanston, Ill.: Northwestern University Press, 1973). Aside from the innovative phenomenological investigation of this book Dufrenne also offered a critique of the prevalent aesthetics. He primarily enlarged the aesthetic account by including literary, theater, dance, and cinema to a discourse, which, up to then, uniquely celebrated fine art painting.

28. António Pedro Pita, "Le cinéma et la peinture: Mikel Dufrenne et les problèmes du voir," in *Mikel Dufrenne et les arts*, ed. Maryvonne Saison (Nanterre: Le temps philosophique, Université Paris X-Nanterre, 1998), 60.

29. Dufrenne, *The Phenomenology of Aesthetic Experience*, 91.

30. Ibid., 139.

31. Ibid., 59.

32. *Esthétique et psychologie du cinéma* was published in two volumes: *Esthétique et psychologie du cinéma 1. Les structures* (Paris: Éditions universitaires, 1963) and *Esthétique et psychologie du cinéma 2. Les formes* (Paris: Éditions universitaires, 1965). This work, which amounts to approximately 860 pages, was in 1990 reedited into an abridged and shortened volume in French (510 pages) that Christopher King translated to English in 1997, Jean Mitry, *The Aesthetics and Psychology of the Cinema* (Bloomington, Ind.: Indiana University Press, 1997). The 1990 version is questionable in its dismissal of whole sections where Mitry discusses problems of cinema and film experience that are closely related to the aesthetic phenomenology of Mikel Dufrenne (chapters 1, 7, and 9 in volume 1 and chapter 13 in Volume 2). Chapters 9 and 13 in the original edition deal with, respectively, musical rhythm ("Rythme musical et rhythme prosodique") and the phenomenology of cinema ("La conscience du réel"). The editor, Benoît Patar (doctor in philosophy), obviously had a problem with these archaic reflections on film art and film experience. Revising the strong phenomenological influence on early French film theory, I find Mitry's fragmented references to Husserl, Dufrenne, and Merleau-Ponty to be significant.

33. Mitry, *The Aesthetics and Psychology of the Cinema*, 29.

34. "To consider the film image as a 'statement of the real world,' by virtue of its objectivity considered as absolute, to say that it is 'cosmophanic in its essence,' is to posit the world as 'in-itself' and to posit this 'in-itself' as necessarily identical (and yet 'purer') with the object as we know it, without realizing that the object is the way it is only by virtue of our perception.

This is to dabble in 'transcendental realism' ...." Mitry, *The Aesthetics and Psychology of the Cinema*, 45. See also Dudley Andrew, "The Film Theory of Jean Mitry," *Cinema Journal* 14, no. 3 (1975): 4.

35. Jean Mitry, *Esthétique et psychologie du cinéma 1. Les structures*, 90. "L'oeil mesure donc le temps grâce à des modifications spatiales"; my translation.

36. For a thorough account of this critique, see Philip Rosen, *Change Mummified: Cinema, Historicity, Theory* (Minneapolis: University of Minnesota Press, 2001).

37. André Bazin, "The Evolution of the Language of Cinema," in *What Is Cinema? Volume 1*, trans. Hugh Grant (Berkeley and Los Angeles: University of California Press, 1967), 27.

38. Vivian Sobchack, *The Address of the Eye: A Phenomenology of Film Experience* (Princeton, N.J.: Princeton University Press, 1992), 16.

39. Rosen, *Change Mummified*, 11. See also Philip Rosen, "History of Image, Image of History: Subject and Ontology in Bazin," *Wide Angle* 9, no. 4 (1987): 7–34.

40. André Bazin, "The Ontology of the Photographic Image," in *What Is Cinema? Volume 2*, trans. Hugh Gray (Berkeley and Los Angeles: University of California Press, 1971), 12.

41. Andrew, "Foreword to the 2004 Edition," xvi.

42. Ibid., xv.

43. Daniel Morgan, "Rethinking Bazin: Ontology and Realist Aesthetics," *Critical Inquiry* 32, no. 3 (Spring 2006): 445.

44. Ibid., 448.

45. Bazin, "The Ontology of the Photographic Image," 13–14; cf. Morgan, "Rethinking Bazin," 7.

46. André Bazin, "The Evolution of the Language of Cinema," 27.

47. About the use of depth of focus, Bazin talked about the ambiguity reintroduced into the structure of the image. Ibid., 35–37.

48. Ivone Margulies, ed., *Rites of Realism: Essays on Corporeal Cinema* (Durham, N.C.: Duke University Press, 2002).

49. Ibid., 3. André Bazin, "Death Every Afternoon," in *Rites of Realism: Essays on Corporeal Cinema*, ed. Ivone Margulies (Durham, N.C.: Duke University Press, 2002), 27–31.

50. Ibid., 28–29.

51. For a critical overview of the index argument, see Morgan, "Rethinking Bazin," 443–454.

52. Doane, *The Emergence of Cinematic Time*, 230–31.

53. Paul Ricœur, *Time and Narrative, Volume 3*, trans. Kathleen Blamey and David Pellauer (Chicago, Ill.: University of Chicago Press, 1988), 125. In Lévinas's work the trace is transformed into an ethical metaphor, designating a potential intersubjective encounter that bridges the experience of past and present time. Emmanuel Lévinas, *Humanisme de l'autre homme* (Paris: Fata Morgana, 1972), 69.

54. André Bazin, "A la recherche du temps perdu: 'Paris 1900,' " in *Qu'est-ce que le cinéma? 1* (Paris: Les Éditions du Cerf, 1958), 42–43. "Ici au contraire, la joie esthétique naît d'un déchirement, car ces 'souvenirs' ne nous appartiennent pas. Ils réalisent le paradoxe d'un passé objectif, d'une mémoire extérieure à notre conscience. *Le cinema est une machine à retrouver le temps pour mieux le perdre*" (my emphasis).

55. Rosen, "History of Image, Image of History"; Margulies, *Rites of Realism*, 58.

56. Ibid., 49.

57. André Bazin, "Cinema and Exploration," in *What Is Cinema? Volume 1*, trans. Hugh Grant (Berkeley and Los Angeles: University of California Press, 1967), 161.

58. Ibid., 161.

59. Bernard Stiegler, "The Time of Cinema. On the 'New World' and 'Cultural Exception,' " *Technema: Journal of Philosophy and Technology* 4 (1998): 62–113.

60. Bernard Stiegler, *La technique et le temps. Tome 2. La désorientation* (Paris: Éditions Galilée, 1996), 141. "The photographic experience of past time is that of a layer of the proof, which is given in the intuition of a past that we have not lived ourselves—but a past to which we nevertheless have access despite our lack of inductive knowledge" (my translation).

61. Paul Ricœur, *Memory, History, Forgetting*, trans. Kathleen Blamey and David Pellauer (Chicago, Ill.: University of Chicago Press, 2004).

62. Ibid., 9.

63. Ibid.

64. Ibid.

65. Paul Ricœur, *Temps et récit. I. L'intrigue et le récit historique* (Paris: Éditions du Seuil, 1983); Paul Ricœur, *Temps et récit. II. La configuration dans le récit de fiction* (Paris: Éditions du Seuil, 1984); Paul Ricœur, *Temps et récit. III. Le temps raconté* (Éditions du Seuil, Paris, 1985). See also Paul Ricœur, *Time and Narrative*. 3 vols. Trans. Kathleen McLaughlin and David Pellauer (Chicago, Ill.: University of Chicago Press, 1984–1985).

66. Paul Ricœur, *Time and Narrative, Volume 1*, trans. Kathleen Blamey and David Pellauer (Chicago, Ill.: University of Chicago Press, 1984), 3.

67. *Mimesis 1* represents the level of a prenarrative world and the diverse conceptions that are primordial to a Western epistemology of time and time experience. For example, the material position of Aristotle is compared with the experiential counterpart of Augustine. *Mimesis 2: Poesis* represents an important dimension because Ricœur stresses the expressive as well as ethical possibilities of narratives to suggest modes of revising the taken for granted, to articulate enigmas, and to imagine worlds that possibly could come true. *Mimesis 3* represents the result of this process, the impact that narratives have on practical life.

68. Ricœur, *Temps et récit. III.*

69. Paul Ricœur, "Memory and forgetting," in *Questioning Ethics: Contemporary Debates in Philosophy*, ed. Richard Kearney and Mark Dooley (London: Routledge, 1999), 9.

70. Janicaud, *Chronos*, 185.

71. Don DeLillo, *Underworld* (New York: Scribner Paperback Fiction, Simon & Schuster Inc., 1998), 82.

72. Ricœur, *Time and Narrative, Volume 3*, 156.

73. Ibid., 120.

74. Catherine Russell, *Experimental Ethnography: The Work of Film in the Age of Video* (Durham, N.C.: Duke University Press, 1999), 240.

3. Frame-Breaking Events and Motifs beyond Representation

1. "Le cinéma et la nouvelle psychologie" was originally a lecture held at the l'Institut des hautes études cinématographiques, March 13, 1945. It is reprinted in Maurice Merleau-Ponty, *Sens et non-sens* (Paris: Gallimard, 1996).

2. Roland Barthes, *La chambre claire: Note sur la photographie* (Paris: Éditions de l'Étoile, Le Seuil), 148–49.

3. Amos Vogel in the foreword of Jean-Pol Ferbus, Dominique Garny, and Thierry Zeno, *Des Morts (Of the Dead): The Subtitles and Dialogues of the Film* (Brussels: Zeno Films, 1981), 4.

4. Vivian Sobchack, "Inscribing Ethical Space: Ten Propositions on Death, Representation and Documentary," *Quarterly Review of Film Studies* 9, no. 4 (1984): 283–300.

5. Akira Mizuta Lippit, "The Death of an Animal," *Film Quarterly* 56, no. 1 (Fall 2002): 9–22.

6. André Bazin, "Death Every Afternoon," in *Rites of Realism: Essays on Corporeal Cinema*, ed. Ivone Margulies, trans. Mark A. Cohen (Durham, N.C.: Duke University Press, 2002), 27–32.

7. Emmanuel Lévinas, *La mort et le temps* (Paris: Éditions de l'Herne, 1991), 10.

8. Sobchack, "Inscribing Ethical Space."

9. Ibid., 287.

10. Ibid.

11. Ibid., 292.

12. Ibid. See also Susan Sontag, *Regarding the Pain of Others* (New York: Farrar, Straus and Giroux, 2003).

13. Erving Goffman, *Frame Analysis: An Essay on the Organization of Experience* (Boston: Northeastern University Press, 1986).

14. Alfred Schutz could be another reference of relevance for current semiotic phenomenology. Alfred Schutz, "Philosophy and Phenomenological Research, V" [1945], in *Collected Papers. I. The Problem of Social Reality*, ed. and trans. Maurice Natanson (The Hague: Martinus Nijhoff, 1962). Cf. Goffman, *Frame Analysis*, 3.

15. Goffman, *Frame Analysis*, 346.

16. Ibid., 345.

17. Ibid., 388.

18. Ibid., 367.

19. Ibid.

20. The other two, the character-audience line, and the role-character formula fall outside the present discussion. Goffman, *Frame Analysis*, 395.

21. Andrea Liss, *Trespassing through Shadows: Memory, Photography, and the Holocaust* (Minneapolis: University of Minnesota Press, 1998), xiii.

22. For example, see Gérard Wajcman, "De la croyance photographique," *Les Temps Modernes* LVI, no. 613 (2001): 47–83; Élisabeth Pagnoux, "Reporter photographe à Auschwitz," *Les Temps Modernes* LVI, no. 613 (2001): 84–108.

23. Georges Didi-Huberman, *Images malgré tout* (Paris: les Éditions de Minuit, 2003).

24. Quote by Wajcman in Didi-Huberman, *Images malgré tout*, 167; my translation.

25. Ibid., 157; my translation.

26. Ibid., 22; my translation.

27. Ibid., 50–53.

28. Ibid., 11.

29. Maurice Merleau-Ponty, *Phenomenology of Perception*, trans. Colin Smith (London: Routledge, 1962), 413.

30. Roland Barthes, *Camera Lucida: Reflections on Photography*, trans. Richard Howard (New York: Hill and Wary, 1981), 20.

31. Jean-Paul Sartre, *L'imaginaire* (Paris: Éditions Gallimard, 1986), 44.

32. Paul Ricœur, *Memory, History, Forgetting*, trans. Kathleen Blamey and David Pellauer (Chicago, Ill.: University of Chicago Press, 2004), 7–8.

33. For example, see Vincente Sánchez-Biosca, "Shoah: le lieu, le personage, la mémoire," in *La mise en scène*, ed. Jacques Aumont (Bruxelles: Éditions de Boeck Université, 2000).

34. Laura U. Marks, *The Skin of the Film: Intercultural Cinema, Embodiment, and the Senses* (Durham, N.C.: Duke University Press, 2000), 31.

35. Michael Renov, "Toward a Poetics of Documentary," in *Theorizing Documentary*, ed. Michael Renov (New York: Routledge, 1993), 30.

4. The Interval and Pulse Beat of Rhythm

1. Hogenkamp, "De Witte jas of 'oneindige variaties op hetzelfde thema': J.C. Mol als mentor van wetenschappelijke, amateur en avant-garde film in Nederland 1924–32," *GBG-Nieuws* 32 (Spring 1995): 7.

2. Between 1925 and 1929 Mol published eighty-seven articles in various Dutch photograph and film journals, some of which I refer to in this article. Bert Hogenkamp, *J.C. Mol: Een fimografisch en bibliografisch overzicht van zijn Nederlandse werk* (Hilversum: Nederlands Audiovisueel Archief, 2000).

3. Jan-Christopher Horak, "The First American Film Avant-Garde, 1919–1945," in *Lovers of Cinema: The First American Film Avant-Garde, 1919–1945*, ed. Jan-Christopher Horak (Madison: University of Wisconsin Press, 1995), 3.

4. The essays in Horak's anthology *Lovers of Cinema* address social, cultural, and economic aspects of experimental cinema beyond a mere history of film *auteurs*, thus assisting in understanding the variety of experimental film beyond the canonized field of avant-garde cinema. See, for example, Patricia Zimmerman, "Startling Angles: Amateur Film and the Early Avant-Garde" in *Lovers of Cinema: The First American Film Avant-Garde, 1919–1945*, ed. Jan-Christopher Horak (Madison: University of Wisconsin Press, 1995), 137–55.

5. Walter Benjamin, "The Work of Art in the Age of Mechanical Reproduction," in *Illuminations: Essays and Reflections*, ed. Hannah Arendt, trans. Harry Zohn (New York: Schocken Books, 1988), 238.

6. Rosalind E. Krauss, *The Originality of the Avant-Garde and Other Modernist Myths* (Cambridge, Mass.: MIT Press), 116.

7. Horak, "The First American Film Avant-Garde, 1919–1945," 35.

8. Émile Vuillermoz, "La musique des images," in *L'art cinématographique III* (Paris: Librairie Félix Alcan, 1927), 60; my translation of the following: "Il [le cineaste] devra calculer l'équilibre de ses dévelopements, savoir quelle longueur il peut donner à son arabesque sans risquer de faire perdre aux spectateurs ce que l'on pourrait appeler le sentiment tonal de sa composition."

9. Émile Vuillermoz, "La musique des images"; my translation of the following: "Le nerf optique et le nerf auditif ont, malgré tout, les mêmes facultés de vibration."

10. Germaine Dulac, "Les esthétiques. Les entraves. La cinégraphie intégrale," in *L'art cinématographique II*, ed. Germaine Dulac (Paris: Librairie Félix Alcan, 1927), 44; my translation of the following: "Le mouvement cinématographique, les rythmes visuels correspondant aux rythmes musicaux, qui donnent au mouvement général sa signification et sa force, faits de valeurs analogues aux valeurs de durée harmoniques devaient se parfaire, si j'ose dire, des sonorités constituées par l'émotion contenue dans l'image elle-même."

11. Louis Delluc, also from 1919, was eager to stress *mathematical precision* as a common trait of film and music. Moreover, montage in Delluc's texts often related to algebra, the mathematical aspect of music and film being evoked in terms of logical measurement, the precision of counting, and enigma. Noureddine Ghali, *L'avant-garde cinématographique en France dans les années vingt* (Paris: Éditions Paris Expérimental, 1995), 146.

12. Ghali, *L'avant-garde cinématographique en France dans les années vingt*, 144; my translation of the following: "Le réalisateur est un monsieur qui compte. Quand il ne compte pas, il mesure. La précision mathématique est à la base du cinéma comme elle est à la base de la musique."

13. The *Manifest Filmliga Amsterdam* was written in 1927 by Henrik Scholte, Menno Ter Braak, Cees Laseur, L. J. Jordaan, Joris Ivens, Charley Toorop, H. J. G. Ivens, and Ed Pelster. The manifesto, together with the first issue of *Orgaan der Nederlandsche Filmliga*, was reprinted

in *Skrien* 100 (October 1980): 1–14, 28. Quote at page 1; my translation of the following: "Eens op de honderd keer zien wij: de film. Voor de rest zien wij: bioscoop. De kudde, het commercieele regime, Amerika, Kitsch."

14. *Manifest Filmliga Amsterdam*, 1; my translation of the following: "In het seizoen 1927–1928 zullen wij te Amsterdam geven een 12-tal matinées op Zaterdagen waarop wij telkens, als première voor Nederland, zullen vertoonen één groote, niewe film, die op belangstelling van een werkelijk kunstzinnig publiek recht heeft."

15. El. D. De Roos, "Film en Publiek," in *Manifest Filmliga Amsterdam*, 4.

16. Joris Ivens, "Filmtechniek. Eenige Notities over de Opvolging van de Beeldenin de film," in *Manifest Filmliga Amsterdam*, 5.

17. Ibid.

18. "In Tzara's *Vaseline symphonique* … twenty people sing ascending scales first on the syllable *cra*, followed by ascending scales one third higher on the syllable *cri* … etcetera, ad infinitum." Christopher Schiff, "Banging on the Windowpane," in *Wireless Imagination: Sound, Radio, and the Avant-Garde*, ed. Douglas Kahn and Gregory Whitehead (Cambridge, Mass.: MIT Press, 1992), 151.

19. See, for example, Sergei Eisenstein, "The Fourth Dimension in Cinema," in *Eisenstein Writings 1922–1934*, ed. Richard Taylor (Bloomington, Ind.: Indiana University Press, 1988), 186–87.

20. Dziga Vertov, "From Kino-Eye to Radio-Eye," in *Kino-Eye: The Writings of Dziga Vertov*, ed. Annette Michelson (Berkeley and Los Angeles: University of California Press, 1984), 90.

21. To this should be added that Vertov's approach to rhythm and the sensory pulse beat of film involves important experiments with sound, silence, and music, such as in *Entuziazm: Simfonija Donbassa* (USSR, 1930). For a thorough analysis of the auditory aspects of Vertov's theory and practice, see John MacKay, "Disorganized Noise: *Enthusiasm* and the Ear of the Collective," *KinoKultura* 7 (January 2005).

22. Marta Braun, *Picturing Time: The Work of Etienne-Jules Marey (1830–1904)* (Chicago, Ill.: University of Chicago Press, 1992), 24, 27, 61.

23. Lisa Cartwright, *Screening the Body: Tracing Medicine's Visual Culture* (Minneapolis, Minn.: University of Minnesota Press), 91.

24. Ibid.

25. In 1923 Mol wrote a series of eight articles on soft-focus photography in *Focus*.

26. J. C. Mol, "Het fotografeeren van ijsbloemen," *De Camera* 18, no. 7 (1926): 90–92.

27. See, for example, J. C. Mol, "Een nieuwe Fotometer," *De Camera* 19, no. 8 (1926): 129–30; J. C. Mol, "Filmknipsels IX. Filmtrucs," *De Camera* 19, no. 11 (1926): 129, 175–77; J. C. Mol, "Filmknipsels XI. Filmtrucs II (De vertraagde film)," *De Camera* 19, no. 14 (1927): 224–25.

28. J .C. Mol, "Een Filmpraatje," *Focus* 10, no. 6 (1923): 115; my translation of the following: "[M]aar ook op bijna ieder gebied van wetenschap en techniek heeft de film toepassing gevonden en diensten bewezen."

29. Mol, "Een Filmpraatje," 117; my translation of the following: "Het is nog niet te voorzien, welke diensten de tijdloupe de wetenschap nog zal bewijzen."

30. Mol, "Een Filmpraatje," 8.

31. The filmography of Jean Painlevé consists of thirty-eight films, of which, according to their context of screening, eleven have been dubbed *popular films* and twenty-seven *research films*. Brigitte Berg, "Contradictory Forces: Jean Painlevé, 1902–1989," in *Science Is Fiction: The Films of Jean Painlevé*, ed. Andy Masaki Bellows and Marina McDougall (Cambridge, Mass.: MIT Press, 2000), 25. Brigitte Berg, "Filmography," in *Science Is Fiction: The Films of Jean Painlevé*, ed. Andy Masaki Bellows and Marina McDougall (Cambridge, Mass.: MIT Press, 2000), 180–87. See also Alexis Martinet, *Le cinéma et la science* (Paris: CNRS, 1994).

32. In 1947, however, Mol contributed to the making of *Metamorphose* (The Netherlands), a poetic contemplation on the short life of butterflies by Herman van der Horst. This film, which was also produced by Mol's company, Multifilm in Haarlem, comes very close to the work by Painlevé. The voiceover by J. van der Vlugt is in French, and the jazzy guitar music adds to the personal and humorous narration. *Metamorphose* is in the collection of Mol films at the Amsterdam Film Museum.

33. A written account of the filmic devices of *De tijd en de film* is found in an article with the same title by J. C. Mol, "De tijd en de film," *Het Lichtbeel* 6, no. 1 (January 1928): 5–9. Another film made in 1928, *Wetenschap en Film* (Science and Film) provided similar illustrations of slow motion and high speed, while also demonstrating the principles of microcinematography.

34. Intertitles from *De tijd en de film*, quoted from the English version at the Amsterdam Film Museum.

35. Hogenkamp, "De Witte jas of 'oneindige variaties op hetzelfde thema'," 9.

36. With reference to Freud, Jean-François Lyotard argues that *the figural (le figurale)* is ultimately realized through the imagination and desire of the reader or spectator: "This

energy is transmitted in a negative, threatening, and agonizing fashion: disorder. Unmasking the good form, the good object, and the lucid discourse, it refuses order, to announce another order" (my translation). Jean-François Lyotard, *Discours, Figure* (Paris: Éditions Klinckseick, 1985), 323.

37. Bert Hogenkamp and Paul Kusters, *J.C. Mol. Een filmografisch en bibliografisch overzicht van zijn Nederlandse werk* (Hilversum: Nederlands Audiovisueel Archief, 2000), 8–9.

38. Quote from the *Filmliga* program at the Amsterdam Film Museum Web site: http://www.polderdocumentaries.nl/eng/text/kristallen-eng.htm. A tinted version of *From the Domain of Crystals* was probably used for the avant-garde screenings in Paris and Amsterdam, which would have intensified the already psychedelic experience of this microcosmic metamorphosis.

5. Screen Events of Velocity and Duration

1. Roger Leenhardt quoted in Maurice Merleau-Ponty, "Le cinéma et la nouvelle psychologie," in *Sens et non-sens*, ed. Maurice Merleau-Ponty (Paris: Éditions Gallimard, 1996), 74; my translation of the following: "une courte durée convient au sourire amusé, une durée moyenne au visage indifférent, une longue durée à l'expression douloureuse."

2. For a thorough account of the city film, see Helmut Weihsmann, "The City in Twilight: Charting the Genre of the 'City Film' 1900–1930," in *Cinema & Architecture: Méliès, Mallet-Stevens, Multimedia*, ed. François Penz and Maureen Thomas (London: British Film Institute, 1997); Anthony Vidler, "The Explosion of Space: Architecture and the Filmic Imaginary," in *Film Architecture: Set Designs from Metropolis to Blade Runner*, ed. Dietrich Neumann (Munich: Prestel, 1996), 13–25; Anton Kaes, "Sites of Desire: The Weimar Street Film," in *Film Architecture: Set Designs from Metropolis to Blade Runner*, ed. Dietrich Neumann (Munich: Prestel, 1996), 26–32. For later, New York-based, city films, see, for example, Scott MacDonald, "The City as the Country: The New York City Symphony from Rudy Burckhardt to Spike Lee," *Film Quarterly* 51, no. 2 (Winter 1997–1998): 2–20.

3. For a discussion on *the haptic* in spatial arts (motion pictures included), see Giuliana Bruno, "Thing as Feeling: Emotion Pictures," in *Anything*, ed. Cynthia C. Davidson (Cambridge, Mass.: MIT Press, 2001), 140–48.

4. Tom Gunning, "From the Kaleidoscope to the X-Ray: Urban Spectatorship, Poe, Benjamin, and Traffic in Souls (1913)," *Wide Angle* 19, no. 4 (1997): 35.

5. Ibid., 33.

6. Ibid., 35.

7. Paul Spehr, "The Demolition of the Star Theatre," *Picturing a Metropolis: New York City Unveiled*, DVD, in Anthology Film Archives collection *Unseen Cinema: Early American Avant-Garde Film 1894–1941*, 2005.

8. The poem "From Noon to Starry Night: Mannahatta" and other extracts of Whitman's work were collected, sometimes altered, and arranged for the eleven intertitles in *Manhatta* by Strand and Sheeler. See Jan-Christopher Horak, "Paul Strand and Charles Sheeler's *Manhatta*," in *Lovers of Cinema: The First American Film Avant-Garde, 1919–1945*, ed. Jan-Christopher Horak (Madison, Wis.: University of Wisconsin Press, 1995).

9. Ibid., 276.

10. Weihsmann, "The City in Twilight," 20.

11. Thomas Elsaesser, "Dada/Cinema?" in *Dada and Surrealist Film*, ed. Rudolf E. Kuenzli (Cambridge, Mass.: MIT Press, 1996), 23.

12. Noel Burch, *To the Distant Observer: Form and Meaning in the Japanese Cinema* (Berkeley: University of California Press, 1979), 61–63.

13. William Uricchio, "The City Viewed: The Films of Leyda, Browning, and Weinberg," in *Lovers of Cinema: The First American Film Avant-Garde, 1919–1945*, ed. Jan-Christopher Horak (Madison: University of Wisconsin Press, 1995), 289.

14. Michael Renov, "Lost, Lost, Lost: Mekas as Essayist," in *To Free the Cinema: Jonas Mekas & The New York Underground*, ed. David E. James (Princeton, N.J.: Princeton University Press, 1992), 222.

15. Quotations by Yo Ota in this section are from correspondence with the filmmaker, between 1999 and 2000. For a presentation of Ota's film (from the 1980s to the present) and for a preview of clips, visit the following Web site: http://www.tokyo100.com/ota. See also Malin Wahlberg, "A Relative Timetable: Picturing Time in the Era of New Media," in *Allegories of Communication: Intermedial Concerns from Cinema to the Digital*, ed. John Fullerton and Jan Olsson (Rome: John Libbey, 2004).

16. "Real time" to Henri Bergson equals the time as "perceived and lived" ("le temps perçu et vécu"). Henri Bergson, *Durée et Simultanéité* (Paris: Presses Universitaires de France, 1968), 47.

17. Quote from *Gesamtausgabe* in Dominique Janicaud, *Chronos* (Paris: Bernard Grasset, 1997), 95.
18. Ibid.
19. Sergei Eisenstein, "Beyond the Shot," in *Eisenstein Writings 1922–1934*, ed. Richard Taylor (Bloomington, Ind.: Indiana University Press, 1988), 145.
20. P. Adams Sitney, *Visionary Film: The American Avant-Garde 1943–1978* (Oxford: Oxford University Press, 1979), 372–73.
21. Ibid., 374.
22. David James, *Allegories of Cinema: American Film in the Sixties* (Princeton, N.J.: Princeton University Press, 1989), 68.
23. Sitney, *Visionary Film*, 372.
24. André Bazin, "The Evolution of the Language of Cinema," in *What Is Cinema? Volume 1*, trans. Hugh Grant (Berkeley and Los Angeles: University of California Press, 1967), 27.
25. Ibid., 36.
26. Ingmar Bergman offers a less humoristic counterpart in *Vargtimmen* ("The Hour of the Wolf," 1968) where the event of timekeeping and the passing of a minute result in the agonizing sign of madness and death.
27. Béla Balázs, *Theory of the Film: Character and Growth of a New Art*, trans. Edith Bone (New York: Dover Publications, 1970), 143.
28. Merleau-Ponty, "Le cinéma et la nouvelle psychologie," 69.
29. François Jost, *Le temps d'un regard* (Paris: Méridens Klincksieck, 1998), 103.
30. Ivone Margulies, *Nothing Happens: Chantal Akerman's Hyperrealist Everyday* (Durham, N.C.: Duke University Press, 1996), 68. Related reflections on viewing appear in other films by Akerman, such as *Je, tu, il, elle* (*I, You, He, She*, Belgium, 1974), *Les rendez-vous d'Anna* (Belgium, 1978), and *Toute une nuit* (*All Night Long*, Belgium, 1982).
31. Jean-François Lyotard, "L'acinéma," in *Cinéma: théorie, lectures*, ed. Dominique Noguez (Paris: Klincksieck, 1978), 365.
32. Ibid., 365–66.
33. Ibid., 367–68.
34. Jean Epstein quoted in Edgar Morin, *The Cinema or the Imaginary Man*, trans. Lorraine Mortimer (Minneapolis, Minn.: University of Minnesota Press, 2005), 39.
35. In 1995 *From the East* was part of a multimedia installation entitled *Bordering on Fiction: Chantal Akerman's D'est*, which was dedicated to the European unification and programmed for exhibition in the United States, France, Belgium, Germany, and Spain. The museum installation consisted of three integrated parts: a darkened room where *From the East* runs continuously; a room with twenty-four video monitors arranged in eight triptychs, showing different fragments of the film; and a room with speakers placed on the floor, through which the visitor could listen to Akerman reciting passages from the Hebrew Bible and sections from her work journal. Kristine Butler, "Bordering on Fiction: Chantal Akerman's *From the East*," in *Identity and Memory: The Films of Chantal Akerman*, ed. Gwendolyn Audrey Foster (Wiltshire, UK: Flicks Books, 1999).
36. The stylistic emphasis on long static takes and extended camera movements is further elaborated in the other two parts of Akerman's trilogy: *Sud* (1999) and *De l'autre côté* (2003). Different from *D'est*, the two later films combine the personal framing of a specific geography with an outspoken focus on social problems: racial crimes in Jasper, Texas (*Sud*) and the maltreatment and hostility that await Mexicans who try to cross the American border (*De l'autre côté*). Also, in these two films Akerman chose to insert sequences of a more conventional, documentary mode, such as interviews and testimonies, which stresses the symbolic and narrative potential of space-time abstraction.

6. Telling Signs of Loss: Beginnings of Possible Stories

1. This sequence is from the second part of the film *Les mains coupées* (*The Cut Off Hands*) (*Le fond de l'air est rouge*, Chris Marker, France, 1977).
2. Quote from *Récits d'Ellis Island: Histoires d'errance et d'espoir* (Robert Bober and Georges Perec, France, 1979). Perec's text is reprinted in Georges Perec and Robert Bober, *Récits d'Ellis Island: Histoires d'errance et d'espoir* (Paris: P.O.L éditeur, 1994), 36–37.
3. See novels such as Georges Perec, *W ou le souvenir d'enfance* (Paris: Éditions Denoël, 1975); Georges Perec, *La disparition* (Paris: Éditions Denoël, 1969); Georges Perec, *La vie mode d'emploi* (Paris: Hachette, 1978); or the films *Un homme qui dort* (Bernard Queysanne, France, 1973) and *Les lieux d'une fugue* (Georges Perec, France, 1978).
4. Although Bober's and Perec's films offer a self-referential account of the construction of a historical narrative, this material enactment of the photograph rather evokes traditional ideas of the photo-trace as a presence of the past, emphasizing the phenomenology of the

photo-object per se. A postmodern variation of this practice of *mise en scène* is accomplished in *Art of Memory* (Woody Vasulka, U.S.A., 1987). Marita Sturken accounts for this piece and its elaborate video transformation of newsreel, documentary footage, and photographs "into image objects that appear to sit on a southwestern desert landscape." Marita Sturken, "The Politics of Video Memory: Electronic Erasures and Inscriptions," in *Resolutions: Contemporary Video Practices*, ed. Michael Renov and Erika Suderburg (Minneapolis: University of Minnesota Press, 1996), 4. See also Raymond Bellour, "Images of the World," in *Resolutions: Contemporary Video Practices*, ed. Michael Renov and Erika Suderburg (Minneapolis, Minn.: University of Minnesota Press, 1996). The reason why I chose *Récits d'Ellis Island* with its reframing of the photograph as a fetish object in our conception of history and memory is its more outspoken reference to the phenomenological discourse of the trace, which is both affirmed and critically elaborated in this film. Similar to Vasulka's video this film achieves a deconstruction of different kinds of image-memories.

5. Susan Sontag, *On Photography* (New York: Penguin Books), 17.

6. Perec and Bober, *Récits d'Ellis Island*, 36.

7. Marianne Hirsch, *Family Frames: Photography, Narrative, and Postmemory* (Cambridge, Mass.: Harvard University Press, 1997). See also Patricia R. Zimmermann, *Reel Families: A Social History of Amateur Film* (Bloomington: Indiana University Press, 1995) and Michelle Citron, *Home Movies and Other Necessary Fictions* (Minneapolis: University of Minnesota Press, 1999).

8. *Free Fall Oratorium*, the performance version (which is the originally intended version of *Free Fall*), was shown in Stockholm on February 2, 2004, as part of a Forgács retrospective organized by Paideia, The Dramatic Insitute (DI), The Swedish Film Institute (SFI), and the Department of Cinema Studies at Stockholm University. As a performance *Free Fall* is shown without the inserted text and voice-over. Conducted by Szemsö, who also plays the synthesizer, a three-person choir sings the Nazi laws, while Forgács reads the text and performs certain sound effects, such as the lighting of a cigarette. On a phenomenological level the experience of this version differs in important ways from the video I refer to in this chapter: the screen event turns into stage performance. Although sound effects and song are separated from the image, the compiled films that now are freed from inserted text even more stand out as eerie signs of the past.

9. The device of the inverted image, or whole sequences in negative, is occasionally used in experimental film. For example, in the context of American structural cinema, Bruce Baillie in his short film *Tung* (U.S.A., 1966) offers a portrait of a walking girl, screened entirely in negative. Sitney P. Adams, "Le film structurel," in *Cinéma: théorie, lectures*, ed. Dominique Noguez (Paris: Klincksieck, 1978), 341. In the documentary outset of Forgács's film, however, the unexpected appearance of an inverted image displays a powerful symbolism.

10. In *Bibó Brevariá* ("A Bibó Reader," *Private Hungary* 13, 2001) these two sound functions meet in the auditory theme of typing. The intellectual passion and social concern of politician and author István Bibó (1911–1979) come through symbolically in the clatter of typewriting, which simultaneously seems to mirror the narrative drive and poetic passion of Forgács's work.

7. The Trace in Contemporary Media

1. Marita Sturken, "The Politics of Video Memory: Electronic Erasures and Inscriptions," in *Resolutions: Contemporary Video Practices*, ed. Michael Renov and Erika Suderburg (Minneapolis, Minn.: University of Minnesota Press, 1996), 1.

2. Marita Sturken, *Tangled Memories: The Vietnam War, the AIDS Epidemic, and the Politics of Remembering* (Berkeley and Los Angeles: University of California Press, 1997).

3. http://www.elenafilatova.com. This Web site is updated regularly with added photographs, and since I visited the website in 2004, Elena Filatova has also included "chernoby/videos." (2007.09.17). Ghost Town has been subject to speculations as to the authenticity of the photographs and the narrative. I would argue that whether or not Elena Filatova is the author of this Web site is less important than the existence of the Web site and the fact that in 1986 a nuclear disaster occurred in Ukraine, whose health and environmental consequences are still tangible in Chernobyl and environs. Elena has accomplished similar Web sites; see, e.g., The Serpent's Wall (http://www.theserpentswall.com/), on the history of Kiev (2004), and Gulag Tales (http://www.gulagtales.com/), about prison life during the times of the former Soviet Union (2006).

4. For an extensive discussion of *Images of the World and the Inscription of War*, see Christa Blümlinger, "Slowly Forming a Thought While Working on Images," in *Harun Farocki: Working on the Sight-Lines*, ed. Thomas Elsaesser (Amsterdam: Amsterdam University Press, 2004).

5. See, for example, Marita Sturken, "Spectacles of Memory and Amnesia: Remembering the Persian Gulf War," in *Tangled Memories: The Vietnam War, the AIDS Epidemic, and the Politics of Remembering*, ed. Marita Sturken (Berkeley and Los Angeles: University of California Press, 1997), 122–44.

6. See Paul Virilio, *War and Cinema: The Logistics of Perception*, trans. Patrick Camiller (London: Verso, 1989).

7. For a monograph on the work by Farocki, see Rolf Aurich and Ulrich Kriest, eds., *Der Ärger mit den Bildern; Die Filme von Harun Farocki* (Konstanz: UVK Medien, 1998).

8. Thomas Elsaesser, ed., *Harun Farocki: Working on the Sight-Lines* (Amsterdam: Amsterdam University Press, 2004), 27.

9. Mark J. P. Wolf, "Subjunctive Documentary: Computer Imaging and Simulation," in *Collecting Visible Evidence*, ed. Jane M. Gaines and Michael Renov (Minneapolis, Minn.: University of Minnesota Press, 1999).

10. Ibid., 276.

11. Ibid., 280–81.

12. Michel Foucault, *Discipline and Punish. The Birth of the Prison*, trans. Alan Sheridan London: (Penguin Books, 1991), 200–208, 233–43.

13. The common reuse of this Foucault-inspired metaphor in culture studies could be questioned because today the social and political implications of surveillance exceed the notion of vision. Consider, for example, computer programs of control and regulation that may block illegal activities of copying, or the fact that somebody may track down my executed route on the Internet.

14. I discuss the film version of *I Thought I Was Seeing Convicts*, which also has been shown as video installation. In the film version the dialog of contrasted sequences is shown in split vision. On a phenomenological level there are, of course, significant differences between the video installation and the film version. In the gallery room, the visitor is placed between two large screens, which makes film viewing a combined act of contemplation and editing. The installation is intended and performed by the artist, although ultimately accomplished by the gallery visitor, and according to a spatial design that radically differs from the experience of the VHS version. Phenomenological aspects of moving images and their current appropriation as audiovisual installation are pressing issues of contemporary media, which demand the attention of a separate book. In this context I am content to notice that Farocki's recent production policy involves a cooperation with Berlin galleries and the German and French television.

15. *Gefängnisbilder* (Farocki, Germany) is another, longer piece from 2000. In this video the issues of surveillance and control, which are also discussed in *I Thought I Was Seeing Convicts*, are treated in a larger context of prison life and the optical and physical architectures that are constructed to contain, frame, hide, and visualize the convict.

16. Wolf, "Subjunctive Documentary," 281.

17. For an introductory discussion on amateur videos and surveillance footage, vis-à-vis the grammar of television composition, see Peter Humm, "Real TV: Camcorders, Access and Authenticity," in *The Television Studies Book*, ed. Christine Geraghty and David Lusted (London: Arnold, 1998); Bill Nichols, "At The Limits of Reality (TV)," *Blurred Boundaries: Questions of Meaning in Contemporary Culture*, ed. Bill Nichols (Bloomington, Ind.: Indiana University Press, 1994).

18. The activist group Prison Focus fights against the death penalty in general and, more specifically, against the unsatisfactory state of things at Corcoran State Prison in California. For more information about their work and present projects, visit http://www.prisons.org.

19. Wolf, "Subjunctive Documentary," 275.

20. The Web cam offers a radical counterexample. In this case we find a reversed relation between video recording and preservation because it is all about a nonstop screening of real time, and the registered events are mainly nonsignificant, banal everyday activities, or an empty room. Also, in contrast to the technology of power displayed by the surveillance system of a prison, this tracing of the real may practically be produced and viewed by anyone equipped with a camcorder and a Web site.

Index

Malin Wahlberg is a research fellow in cinema studies at Stockholm University. She has written on experimental cinema, documentary, and film theory, and she is working on a book on documentary filmmaking in early Swedish television.